DEAD STRAIGHT GUIDE TO

M O D

PAUL 'SMILER' ANDERSON

A catalogue record for this book is available from the British Library

This edition © Red Planet Books Ltd 2018. Text © Paul Anderson 2018

ISBN: 978 1 9113 4666 1

Printed in the UK

Page design/layout/cover: Harry Gregory
Publisher: Mark Neeter

Red Planet Music Books
Tremough Innovation Centre,
Penryn, Cornwall TR10 9TA

www.redplanetzone.com
Email: info@redplanetzone.com

AUTHOR'S NOTE

I t's bloody hard to imagine being a young teenager, high on life, all those years – no, decades ago! It was a life without adult responsibilities. When all that mattered was new clobber, new records, watching bands and having a laugh with your mates. Back then getting a scooter took you to another level and suddenly there were not so many boundaries – your world became bigger.

I never thought for one minute I'd end up writing about it. I was way too busy living it. Back then, in the mists of time, it was just a simple matter of choosing a path. Britain was full of youth cults. The whole land was brim full of angst-ridden uniformed armies: Punks, Skinheads, New Romantics, Rockabillies, Teds, Heavy Rock Merchants, Soul Boys, Goths, Two Tone Kids – the choice was amazing. I was too young for Punk when it first happened. I liked it, but in 1976 I was 11 years old. Besides, I remember my uncle laughing about these two blokes, Johnny Rotten and Sid Vicious, and suddenly I was interested – it just wasn't my time.

My time came later, and then it was obvious to me. There was only one path that I ever wanted to tread – and that was Mod. Little did I know where that path would take me. A journey that would take years. A journey that, in fact, I'm still travelling now with friends I have known for more than half a lifetime – friends that understand whilst outsiders mock or simply don't get it.

I certainly never imagined that I would go from donning a US fishtail parka, dogtooth trousers, a Fred Perry top and burgundy loafers to having my own tailor-made suits that I'd designed, and a shirt maker turning my ideas into a sartorial reality. And I never thought that I'd go from there to a fixation with designer labels: Lacoste, Paul Smith, Armani, Duffer St George and with my feet shod in Patrick Cox loafers or Adidas Gazelles.

That I'd go from wandering to my local record shop to purchase the latest offerings of Mod Revival bands to attending record fairs and specialist vinyl shops to hunt down obscure, long-forgotten, Soul, British Beat, Jazz, Ska and Blues records. Then later still searching for Reggae, Hip Hop, Funk, Brazilian music, Acid Jazz, House, Drum and bass and more – joining up the dots. Making sense to me – even if not so to others.

This limitless odyssey changed my life – giving it depth and meaning. It introduced me to like-minded people all over the world and to sharing with them my music as a DJ and my thoughts as a writer.

It's only when you look back that you realise you are part of a long legacy, one of a group of people who have walked the same path – part of a proud heritage stretching from the late Fifties right up to the very second you finish reading this. I don't expect everybody to agree with my views in this book – that would be very presumptuous of me. But I hope that everybody can maybe learn something new from it. It certainly should not be treated as a blueprint of how to live the Mod life. The thing about Mod is that each path is different and every journey is unique. It is, as it says on the cover, a guide. If it leaves you yearning to discover more then I consider my work is done.

I have no regrets about how I navigated any of my journey. I still love the whole Mod Revival – I still feel a kind of passion whilst listening to the lyrics of many of those songs. I'm also proud about my 'purist' retro phase in which I totally detached myself from normal modern life to wear tailor-made and vintage clothes and seek out obscure record labels to play on the club nights I presented at the time. But I am equally as joyful that I could see beyond that and learned to love the present and look to the future. There are always cool things going on, but they may not be visible at street level. You just have to go out and find them.

So, get ready to set sail, for there is a voyage of discovery ahead.

Keep your eyes open – along with your mind. And, don't let anybody tell you how to do it – tread your own path always.

Paul 'Smiler' Anderson
November 2018

84

CHAPTER

ONE

RULE NUMBER ONE:
DON'T ASK ME WHAT A MOD IS!

"Knowledge is a crucial factor and seen as most important in the scheme of things. To know about music, Mod history and details about clothing are essential when surrounded by others of the Mod persuasion. Therefore, the aim of this book is to spread such knowledge."

PAUL 'SMILER' ANDERSON

For many people, if they were confronted with the task of describing a 'Mod', the answer would seem very simple.

'Surely a Mod is somebody who wears one of those green anorak type coats? Is it called a parka? They're covered in badges and patches. They listen to bands like The Who and Oasis, and they ride mopeds with lots of lights and mirrors on them. Oh, and they have a fixation for targets.... lots and lots of targets."

In some ways the person would be right, but in many more ways completely wrong.

The Oxford English Dictionary describes it as follows:
adjective, informal, modern, 'boldly mix mod with trad for eye-catching results'
noun, British (especially in the early Sixties) a young person of a subculture characterized by a smart stylish appearance, the riding of motor scooters, and a liking for soul music.
origin, Abbreviation of modern or modernist.

So, then you look up 'Modernist' and you get:
noun, a believer in or supporter of modernism, especially in the arts. 'James Joyce and other 20th-century modernists'.

Once again, the definition is correct, but in many ways, completely wrong.

The point is that, nobody can give a precise answer because it is such a personal experience that many adopt the culture to suit themselves. Whilst for some, it may be a case of buying a Fred Perry jumper, buying a parka, covering it in badges and riding off to Brighton or the Isle of Wight every August Bank Holiday. For others, it may mean tailored suits with precise details such as an opening cuff, cloth-covered buttons and stepped-bottom trousers. They are eternally in search of their next holy grail of Fifties or Sixties R&B vinyl 45. If, and it is a big if, they decide to own a motor scooter, it would be a vintage Lambretta or Vespa, preferably dated sometime between 1962 to 1967. To these types of people, the thought of sharing their bank holiday with the aforementioned type drives them insane. They use derisory labels such as 'Comedy Mod' or 'Clowns' to express their hatred to people who they perceive to have missed the 'Golden Rule of Mod': Attention to detail.

Attention to detail is at the heart of Mod purity. Once again this can take on many forms. It may be somebody who takes the time to make sure that their watch strap matches their socks. It may be somebody that just recognises the soulful poetry of a song such as Curtis Mayfield's 'The Makings Of

You' or the sheer beauty of The Small Faces' I'm Only Dreaming'. It may be somebody who knows all the right dances to Russell Byrd's 'Hitchhike', on the UK Sue label of course.

The problem is there again! US label 45's or UK label 45's? Record collecting is often seen as a major part of the Mod experience. Often UK pressings of US recordings are more limited in number, so for instance a UK Tamla Motown pressing of 'Heatwave' by Martha Reeves and the Vandellas is more exclusive than the US pressing. But there are some than turn their noses up at the British pressing labelling them 'bootlegs', in other words not the very first format that the record was available on. Confusing isn't it?

Knowledge is another crucial factor and seen as most important in the scheme of things. To know about music, Mod history and details about clothing are essential when surrounded by others of the Mod persuasion.

Therefore, the aim of this book is to spread such knowledge. Others, who may have been given the opportunity to write such a book may have blagged it, cut corners and told the same old stories. My aim, however, is to try to get it down in the pages here, keeping in mind, the Mod golden rule. I chose people involved in the Mod scene from various phases, and who had different perspectives on it. It is therefore necessary to take you on several journeys throughout time to show you how this wonderful culture developed.

If I am guilty of anything in this book, it is that most of the stories relate to in and around London. Even though the cult spread nationwide, I intentionally tried to keep most of the sources of stories in one place.

Let us begin....

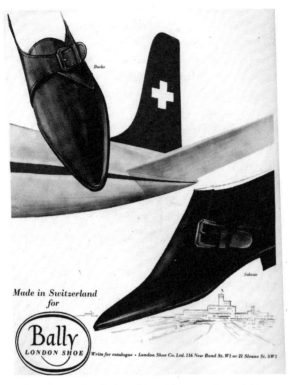

Made in Switzerland
for

Bally
LONDON SHOE

Write for catalogue • London Shoe Co. Ltd. 116 New Bond St. W1 or 21 Sloane St. SW1

October 1958: It's a dark, cold and foggy night and Wayne Kirvan, a young boy just celebrating his thirteenth birthday, is walking along the streets of London for a meeting. At the precise moment, he thinks it is little more than just to meet a kindly relative, but before the night is over, it will prove to be far more important than that. As he turns the corner he sees the familiar face of Uncle Albert stood outside Paul's record Shop in Whitechapel.

Albert is not alone, he is standing next to a boy aged about seventeen. As young Wayne approaches, he finds himself mesmerized with how the stranger is dressed.

Navy blue blazer with club badge on breast pocket.

Over his arm hangs a dark coat.

Prince of Wales checked trousers with stepped bottoms.

Sharp pointed toe shoes with buttons on the side.

"This is David" says Uncle Albert introducing the stranger." He works at Billingsgate Market, but he can't get up in the mornings, so he wants to be a hairdresser. David is a friend of Pam. He calls himself a Modernist."

Young Wayne is entranced and can barely hear his Uncle talking to him.

"Have you got any idea which records you would like me to buy you for your birthday?"

The young boy breaks his stare to look at his Uncle.

"Er…yeh. I have a list in my pocket."

Feeling inside his jacket pocket, Wayne produces a crumpled piece of paper. It contains a list.

MOVE IT – CLIFF RICHARD
BORN TOO LATE – THE PONI – TAILS
POOR LITTLE FOOL – RICKY NELSON
IT'S ONLY MAKE BELIEVE – CONWAY TWITTY

Wayne then looks up at David and enquires if he too is record buying.

"Yeah, Nothin' Shakin' by Eddie Fontaine." replies the smartly dressed youth.

As they enter the shop the assistant enquires what they'd like. David gestures to Wayne to go first.

"Have you got Nothin' Shakin' by Eddie Fontaine please?"

Wayne has taken the first step on a path that will last a lifetime.

At the time the place Modernists, who didn't live South of the river, wanted to be seen was Barry's dance Hall in the Narrow Way, Hackney. Italian scooters parked outside, whilst inside boys danced in short jackets with half belts and girls lived in a world of Juliette Greco film sets.

The paper-round savings are put to good use and by the Summer of '59, Wayne has invested in the clobber to enter this elite world. The shirt by 'Flash' Harry of Petticoat Lane has long pointed collars and will pass muster but sadly those Denson Pointers he is sporting on his feet may be the kiss of death. They are way too yesterday.

On the night in question, the scene outside Barry's doesn't look good, only four scooters parked up. Anyway, onwards and upwards literally. Up the staircase leading to the club. Greeted by the camp owner, Barry, whose bleach blonde locks contain so much peroxide that it can be smelt from Mayer Street. Stood next to Barry is his sister, only half his size but built like a truck.

She eyes young Wayne from head to toe. She's not impressed, but maybe because it's a quiet night, he gets the green light.

"Any trouble and I'll hang you from the fan." she sneers as he strides past.

Inside, the club is practically a ghost town but the youngster manages to gas with a smartly dressed blade with high cheekbones who introduces himself as Peter Sugar.

"It's not a good night" says Sugar "All the guys are going to the West End."

Wayne decides that this is the path he must now tread. In the coming weeks he is invited to a trip to Southend. The meeting point being The Fountain coffee shop in Kingsland Road. There's a light rain so blue pac-a-macs are de rigueur. A young face named Harvey kindly offers a place on the back of his scooter, and they're off.

It's another world away from the dreary grey streets of London. The lights and noise of the Kursaal Amusement Park and chatting to girls at Percy Dalton's peanut stall by the pier. Wayne smiles to himself, he is now on the path of the Modernist way of life.

As for Peter Sugar, he and two of his friends found themselves in an article entitled 'Faces Without Shadows' in the September issue of Town Magazine in 1962. The piece centred around three clothes-obsessed youths from Stoke Newington in the form of 20-year-old Sugar, Michael Simmonds (also 20) and a 15-year-old Mark Feld (later known as Marc Bolan).

They talk of the days of riding scooters and wearing Levi jeans back in 1959. When speaking of where to go out, Feld mentions 'that all the Faces go to Le Discotheque in Wardour Street. Whilst talking clothes, Sugar insists 'All the faces go to Bilgorri's in Bishopsgate and call him a 'great tailor'.

It must be noted that there is no mention of the word 'Mod' in any of the article.

In August 1967, legendary writer, Nik Cohn, wrote an article for The Observer Magazine in which he spoke of the dilution of Mod from its purest form into a culture that was dying and waiting to be replaced by its successor, the Hippies. The piece contained a few photographs and even a cut out and dress paper doll of the new breed. Interestingly, Marc Bolan, then 19, talks about those days just five years earlier, when he'd made his debut in the Town magazine article.

Bolan stated: "When I was 12, I lived in Stamford Hill and there were about seven guys living there who were among the first Mods. They were mostly about 20 and they were Jewish and none of them worked. They just ponced and lived off their parents. All they cared about were their clothes and they had new things all the time.

'I thought they were fantastic and I used to go home and literally pray to become a Mod. I really did that. Then I started and I came to have about six suits. Suddenly people started to look at me and come up to me and then I was accepted as a Mod.

'At this time clothes were all that Mod was about. The music and dancing and scooters and pills came later. I'd say that Mod was mentally a homosexual thing, though not in the physical sense. I was too hung up on myself to be interested in anyone else, and, anyhow, I was still very young.

'I didn't think at all. The only thought I ever was, Oh I just bought one suit this week and I should have bought three. That was all. I was completely knocked out by my own image, by the idea of Mark Feld. Even though I was so young, I was regarded as very cool, very fast, and I was quite a figure. I still meet people who talk about Mark Feld like a great hero and they couldn't care less about Marc Bolan. It's as if we were two completely separate people.

'I remember when Levi jeans first came on the scene. It was regarded as an ultimate achievement to have a pair. They were very hard to come by but we heard there was a shop in Whitechapel that stocked them and we all went down there and stole a pair. I don't know what the shopkeeper did because we stole the lot. I just took a pair and stuffed them up my jacket and ran for the bus. It was completely uncool but I had to have them.

'Then we had our shoes hand-made for us by a man called Solly. They were elfin, absolutely tiny, and they crippled you. They cost £5 a pair and fell apart in a fortnight but they were really beautiful. I'd say they were almost the greatest kick of all.'

The article then shifts to the second-generation Mod, a product of Mod's popularity when it had become an established movement by 1964. Chris Covill, was 21, and from the Shepherd's Bush area. Chris reflected nostalgically about his recent past just three years earlier: 'I used to go to the Crawdaddy Club in Richmond when I was sixteen. I was working and selling clothes and I went to see the Rolling Stones every week. There was a great feeling if you were a Mod, you couldn't be touched by anyone else. You felt as if all the Mods were together and everyone else was outside.

'Then pep pills came in. The average Mod spent £4 10s. a week on clothes, £1 on clubs and £1 10s.on pills. They started on about five pills a time and a year later they'd be on 20. They only used to get blocked at the weekends and, out of all the thousands that were using them, I only ever saw one that was hooked.'

Bolan had been unimpressed with the newer species of Mods that had infested his once beloved scene.

'I'd been quite happy' Bolan had stated. 'I'd had an article about me in Town magazine – I got a stack of fan-mail and it was marvellous to have everyone dig me. Then Mod suddenly started to get out of hand. The new Mods were completely uncool and I wouldn't even speak to them. I took it all incredibly seriously and these new developments were like sacrilege.'

'Mod' may have raised its head in the late Fifties but it would only really start to get noticed in the following decade. By 1960, Britain had seen many fads come and go, including Rock 'n' Roll, skiffle, calypso, mambo, kwela, and cha-cha. The music weeklies though were still dominated by jazz, both traditional and modern.

Launched at Manchester's Theatre Royal on March 6th, 1960 and given its first London showing at the New Victoria

Cinema, Warwick Films' 'Jazz Boat' was released. Complete with jiving sequences in Chislehurst Caves and on board a Thames cruise from London to Margate (actually shot in June '59 on Jazzshow's 'Floating Festival of Jazz'), the film would show Anthony Newley as a jazz loving, suited Modernist getting into trouble alongside leather jacketed Teds. The film ends with a battle at Margate's Dreamland, scarily predicting the way Modernism would head.

At a Chris Barber concert in Victoria Park in Hackney on May 23rd, a mass brawl had erupted between the Trads and the Modernists. It was pretty fierce and included fighting with chairs and bottles. It was only broken up after the police turned up accompanied by dogs.

Trads were referred to as 'Mouldy Figs' by the Modernists, and there was often a cry of 'Ooblies' which was in reference to the scat-singing style jazz as in 'Ooblie Dooblie, scooby dooby shebop, shabam' type of lyrics.

On Saturday, July 30th, 1960. the third Beaulieu Jazz Festival was held on the lawns of the Palace House, in the heart of the New Forest. The Trads turned up en-masse with their stripy socks, bowler hats, and toppers. The BBC had decided to film the concert and broadcast it live. When Johnny Dankworth came on stage for his set, the Trads started booing him. A decidedly different atmosphere fell over the concert and there were chants of "We want Acker! We want Acker!" Acker Bilk entered the stage in a Model T Ford supplied by the Beaulieu Museum. The stage was pretty impressive and had a full-size merry-go-round complete with wooden horses.

Suddenly the stage was invaded by a lone figure who grabbed the microphone and shouted, "Free beer for the working man!". When the crowd realised that he was live on television, more people clambered on stage and the piano collapsed under their weight. Chaos swiftly ensued with people clambering up the metal scaffolding where the television lights were positioned. There were teenagers on the stage who began dismantling the carousel. And they began trying to shimmy up the lighting gantry with the unbolted horses. Before long the scaffolding began to collapse and bodies and wooden horses fell to the ground. The BBC were forced to pull the plug on the live broadcast and the following day the papers spoke of 39 people being injured, three of them seriously. There were reports of a storage shed catching on fire and two youths being arrested for assaulting the police,

August 7th, 1960, the Sunday People newspaper reported on the 'Beatnik Horror' which had befallen the previous weeks concert, with journalist Peter Forbes putting the blame squarely on the shoulders of four American writers and poets in the shape of Jack Kerouac, Allen Ginsberg, William Burroughs and Gregory Corso. The paper stated: 'These four beatnik "prophets" do not themselves preach violence. But they do infect their followers with indifference or outright hostility to established codes of conduct. Nothing matters to the beatnik save the "kicks" or thrills to be enjoyed by throwing off inhibitions. If you feel any urge, no matter how outrageous, indulge in it. If the beat of jazz whips up violent emotions, why not give way to them?'

Acker Bilk was distressed, and in Melody Maker two weeks after the incident, he told of his disappointment:

'For those still misguided enough to believe that our fans were responsible for the disturbance at Beaulieu, we would like to make it clear that the trouble makers were irresponsible exhibitionists.

'They didn't even know which band was on the stand. All they wanted was to show off in front of the television cameras.

'They were phoney, imitation beatniks. Real ones may be weird, untidy and excitable, but they're not hooligans.

Bilk then continued that it was 'The unfortunate exaggeration of national newspapers that must take a major share of the blame. Accounts of the scene were vividly written to make sensational reading.'

Two letters to Melody Maker, August 13th 1960:

PRIMITIVE

'The surest way to prevent a recurrence of the hooliganism at Beaulieu would be to have a Beaulieu Modern Jazz Festival. Surely Lord Montagu must realise by now that if he presents primitive music, then primitive people will roll up to participate.'

-        Peter Webb, Ashford, Kent.

OOBLIES

'Since, according to Lord Montagu, the Festival is not a financial but artistic venture, why book the bands which always seem to attract the ooblies?

-        Don Norman, Chichester, Sussex.

The Trads hangout was the 100 Club listening to the likes of Ken Colyer and Acker Bilk.

The holy trinity of Soho of clubs for the modern jazz lover was:

The Flamingo at 33 Wardour Street. Modern jazz was on the menu Fridays, Saturdays and Sundays 7.30 – 11.30 or 12pm. There were all night sessions on Saturdays till 6am. Membership was 10s 6d per annum. The all-night sessions were a real coup for the club, and this came about because Jeff Kruger who ran the club had been to see the Chief Constable of Savile Row Police Station and told him that it would be helpful to them if all the kids usually hanging around Soho were in one place. There would be no alcohol available on the premises, and they would stay open until the first tubes started running. He also handed the police an olive branch of telling them that they could implant a number of plain-clothes officers in the club, but only if they made the arrests outside. Jazz musicians loved smoking weed, but with the in-house police this wasn't possible, so pills became the drug of choice at the venue, mainly from the American selling their ration of Benzedrine tablets for sixpence each. Bands included the Tubby Hayes Quartet, the Tony Kinsey Quartet (with Bill Le Sage) and Joe Harriott's Quintet.

The Marquee in Oxford Street adjoining the Academy Cinema was Wednesdays, Saturdays and Sundays. 7.30-11.30pm. Membership was 5s per quarter. Sunday nights were hosted by the Johnny Dankworth Orchestra with supporting bands such as Shake Keane.

Ronnie Scott's had only opened in 1959. By 1960 it had already established itself as the epi-centre London's scene for modern jazz. Scott was a tenor saxophonist of international stature himself and he'd lead his Quintet through four sessions a week. One of the best attractions here was the West Indian alto sax player Harold 'Little G' McNair. Sunday evenings Tubby Hayes held court. There were live jazz sessions 7 nights a week until 2am except Sundays when the lights went out at 11.30pm. There were all-nighters on Fridays and Saturdays until 5.30am. Membership was £1 1s a year. Attractions included 24-year-old, Harold McNair, who'd worked in Paris alongside people like Bud Powell and the Quincy Jones Orchestra.

Back then you'd crave Cavelli shoes from Italy or maybe a wide weave corduroy Italian styled jacket. You looked as far away from the drab streets of Britain as much as possible and had dreams of exotic places in Europe such as France and Italy.

In Man About Town magazine in November 1960. There was a one-page article on the French designer, Pierre Cardin. In it, he spoke of a newer style of suit that was slightly more casual to suit the habits of the modern man.

'I did away with jacket collars, and I chose unusual cloths and made the garments as supple as possible by avoiding any padding or stiffening. Of course, I must mention that I avoided anything of English origin because the English style is perfect in itself and cannot be copied. I also didn't include any of the national styles like the Italian or the American – I wanted to do something typically French.

'I used sober cloths, but the lack of collars, the purity of the line, which follows the body closely, the absence of padding, and the narrow trousers give a very slender and elegant effect.'

It would be another two years in Britain before the collarless jacket was noticed on four lads from Liverpool known as The Beatles. But the continental styles that had been adopted by certain youths at the tail end of the Fifties continued to influence British culture.

Islington boy, Malcolm Sanders recalls "French Jiving was an art form. This is around 1960. I knew a couple of guys, I think Roy Wicks was one of them, and they actually went to France to study the dancing. It was that important. The French Jive was still big because The Twist hadn't come in yet. That's why I hate Chubby Checker for bringing that dance in. It killed The Jive, and you've got no contact with a girl anymore. She's now a distance away and it also meant that people who couldn't really dance can suddenly dance. You suddenly weren't noticed any more. At the time dancing was a great puller. A lot of the best dancers were ugly girls, but made you look good as well! I used to practice dancing at home using the door handle to substitute the girl."

To dance you needed to go to a club, but often it wasn't that simple. There was still quite a violent undercurrent that revolved around where you were from. It was all very territorial.

Terry Smith remembers "Me and Richard Cole met at The State in Kilburn in 1961. I saw him outside putting a bottle over someone's head. I remember he had a long green coat on. I'm from Edgeware Road, Paddington and Richard was from Wealden, Kensal Rise. We gravitated towards the other sharp dressers. People like Johnny Pearce who ended up later working at Granny Takes A Trip. It was half a crown to get in The Lyceum in the afternoon. It was the best dancehall in London. I always remember coming down the stairs to 'Duke of Earl' playing full blast."

"All the best dancers at the Lyceum worked at Smithfield meat market." says Richard Cole "All the bouncers, people like Georgie Morgan and Jesus all worked at Smithfield. Lots of the others were porters there and the boys who worked at Covent Garden, if you went in the afternoons there were guys in big boots doing the Twist. It was one of the few places that people from different areas would congregate but they still had their different places to stand. At the bottom of the stairs to the right there's be The South London, Elephant and Castle and some of the East End boys, to the left there'd be our crowd, to the back would be the Faclo and the North London mob, and anybody else, to the left of all of us, took a chance of getting stabbed."

Malcolm Sanders: "The neutral link up for all Mods was The Lyceum. We never went South of the river. The South London never went to the Royal because they were going to the Streatham Locarno. We wouldn't go there because if you did you might pull a bird from Croydon or somewhere, and that's a holiday isn't it? It's just not your manor, end of story. You think you're better than them and they think they're better than you. It's all part of the game."

Terry Smith adds "The beginning of the end for us going to the Lyceum was the trouble. It may have been Frankie Fraser, Little Frankie, or Little Rich, nobody really knows for sure, but they got a couple of gallons of petrol to burn the Lyceum down. It never happened, but because there'd been fights there and the fact that they were all Mecca places, basically all the Mods got banned."

At the time it was the main organises of mass dances were Rank, with their Top Rank Suites and Mecca, who owned Mecca Ballrooms all over the country. The punters at these mass-dances were usually from a working-class background, and it was usually what they worked all week for, so that on

Friday and Saturday nights they could look forward to a few drinks, dancing and meeting the opposite sex.

These organisations also had strict codes and rules. Any kind of claim to spontaneity or individuality on the dancefloor would be discouraged by the door staff and management who guard the dancehalls. Any form of straying from the normal accepted behaviour was seen as a form of rebellion that was to be dealt with immediately. The insistence of the club's respectability being guarded at all times was relentless. All dancers were expected to perform in civil manner. Ballroom attendants, as they were known, were like huge apes dressed in dinner suits and bow ties and they would scrutinize everybody coming in to the building, and also on the dancefloor. There were signs up on the entrance stating, 'NO JIVING' and later 'NO TWISTING'. The bouncers kept a close eye on couples during the slow dances section but then hated it when people started dancing on their own, especially when dances such as The Twist were seen as lewd.

In 1960, places such as the Ilford Palais introduced a smart dress policy which included the wearing of a tie and a complete ban on any form of jeans. Many of these dance halls insisted on males to wear suits. The theory being that they would be less likely to cause trouble and start a fight, and more likely to spend their evening admiring themselves and pursuing the girls. In reality, there was no let up, and after a few light ales there were usually a few punch ups that normally revolved around competition for a girl, territorial issues or simply "oo you screwin?" challenges after being looked at. The girls were usually fewer in number at many of these places, so they were competed for by the males.

The thing that the whole Mod ethos revolved around though, was getting the respect of your mates. The boys were too self-involved to care what girls thought anyway. The rules had changed completely. Unlike the Teddy Boys, the Mods didn't crave machismo and they didn't care much for adult opinion either. Their entire reason for existence was to impress their friends.

Some dancehalls also employed a 'No coloureds policy' but so as not to appear racist in any form, they would often employ black ballroom attendants and allow in a token quota of black people just to show 'they had nothing against black people'.

At The time it was Mecca's policy to refuse entry to persons who were identified being aligned to groups who had caused trouble in their establishments. In the past they had banned entire groups of people such as Teddy Boys, sailors, Jews, black people and even deaf and dumb mute people who had been involved in past disorders. This would lead to many Mods abandoning the ballrooms in favour of smaller clubs.

Georgie Fame, Flamingo Jazz Club,
33 Wardour Street, London, by Tony Frank, 1966

CHAPTER
TWO

FROM THE DISC TO THE SCENE

"The Scene was my favourite. Our mob were always by the piano in the corner. Jimmy West's mob, who were the Faces, were always opposite in the corner by the toilets. I was incredibly impressed one night when Dusty Springfield brought down Dionne Warwick."

TERRY SMITH

In 1960 La Discotheque opened above the Latin Quarter in Wardour Street. Above it was a casino with roulette and chemin de fer. The club had formerly been the El Condor Club ran by body builder Tommy Yearsley who at the time was boyfriend to Diana Dors.

The El Condor club was a very different place to La Discotheque. In the Winter edition of 1958 of 'Man About Town' magazine it is described thus:

LE CONDOR, A club with a difference, No. 17 Wardour Street, W.1, Tel. Gerrard 2740, is attracting a great number of the right young people and is occasionally visited by royalty. The club is run, with the exception of the kitchen, by amateurs. Raymond Nash, the proprietor, who is well known in the property world, holds a black belt in Judo, so, quite naturally, everyone behaves. Andrew, the receptionist, is a classics student from Oxford.

Even the decorations were carried out by amateurs, and very capably too. They are quite beautiful and original. There is a canopy over the dancefloor. Naturally the food is very good and almost entirely in the English manner. Prices, of both food and drink, are reasonable. A bottle of vintage champagne, for example, costs only Sixties.

There are two orchestras, a quartet for the conventional rhythms, and The Kings of The Caribbean Trinidad Steel Band for the exotics. There is always a first-class cabaret. The annual membership fee is four guineas, and members are very carefully selected, references being taken up in every case. No ladies are allowed in to the club without an escort. Altogether, this club provides a breath of spring air in Soho and anybody desirous of joining a really first-class night club would do well to apply to the secretary for further details.

An advert for the club in their 1959 Summer issue carries the tag line 'For Lords and Ladies, for debutantes and Dilettantes, Escalope Holstein or Eggs and Bacon, Dinner jacket or well, perhaps not Denims! But certainly for YOU.

John Taylor, who was the fashion editor of *Man About Town* magazine during that period described it as 'It is one of those small and sophisticated clubs, with a clientele that will include those interesting enough to be accepted without the hoohars of convention as well as those who have come on from somewhere that demands a dinner jacket and an evening gown.'

The El Condor was one of *the* places to be in the late Fifties and boasted a clientele that included royals such as the Duke of Kent and Princess Margaret. It certainly seemed to be a million miles away from how La Discotheque came to be known. Raymond Nash and notorious Notting Hill 'slum landlord' Peter Rachman were in charge and changed the whole ethos of the club. It was different in that it did not feature live bands but established itself as London's first real disco.

"In 1961, it was full of actresses and actors. Regulars were people like Kenny Lynch, Freddie Mills, Frankie Vaughn," remembers Alan Garrison.

Rachman, an overweight, balding, bespectacled man employed the bouncers including Norbert 'Fred' Rondel, a Jewish refugee from Berlin who had been a professional wrestler working under the name The Polish Eagle. Another doorman was Bert Assirati, a retired heavyweight wrestling champion. Others that graced the door were Pat Stapleton, an ex- Irish Heavyweight boxer and an ex–guardsmen named Dennis John Raine who was shot in the knee after refusing entry to a couple of wannabe punters. Norbert also owned his own club, The Apartment, in Rupert Street.

Alan Garrison was already a keen record collector when he first entered the Wardour Street nightspot.

"The first ever record I bought was 'Western Movies' by The Olympics, in 1957. I heard that on Radio Luxembourg because the BBC Light Pregramme only played crooners in those days and it was boring. I was tuning through stations on the radio one night when whoosh... I heard Radio Luxembourg. The flip side of the single was 'Well' which was pure black R&B Doo Wop, which was brilliant. In fact, Carol King copied it note for note for the flipside of Little Eva's 'Locomotion' and called it 'He's The Boy'. Through Luxembourg I discovered Chuck Berry, Bo Diddley, Muddy Waters and the Isley Brothers doing 'Shout' in 1959.

"The first album I bought was the Isley Brothers *Shout* LP. You couldn't get records on import so I used to go to a shop in Canning Town called Stereo Electronics. The guy there got used to what I was buying and they had a little booklet every month with all the new releases in Britain so I'd pick from that.

"Then I started going to clubs and went to La Discotheque. I was about fifteen when I went up the steps there wondering what I was going to hear. I could get in to X certificate films when I was about eleven so they thought I was older than I was. It was really dingy, I went into the café and just watched everybody dancing. Over a few weeks I got to know people and started chatting to the bird that did the records. I told her what records I had and she asked me if I ever played them out. When I said no she said she would let me have five minutes on the decks. It went well so she said she would offer me the chance of a DJ spot, nothing regular but if anybody went sick or whatever."

LA DISCOTHEQUE R&B PLAYLIST 1961

(SUPPLIED BY ALAN GARRISON)

OLDIES BEING PLAYED IN 1961

Fannie Mae	Buster Brown *(Fire 1008)*
This Old Heart	James Brown *(Federal 12378)*
The Twist	Chubby Checker *(Parkway 811)*
Road Runner	Bo Diddley *(Checker 942)*
Babalu's Wedding Day	The Eternals *(Hollywood 70)*
The Hunch	Paul Gayton *(Anna 1106/1107)*
How Deep Is The Ocean	The Isley Brothers *(RCA Victor 47 7718)*
Respectable	The Isley Brothers *(RCA Victor 47 7657)*
Shout (Parts I&Ii)	The Isley Brothers *(RCA Victor 47 7588)*
Tell Me Who	The Isley Brothers *(RCA Victor 47 7787)*
Come To Me	Marv Johnson *(United Artists 160)*
(Baby) Hully Gully	The Olympics *(Arvee 582)*
The Slop	The Olympics *(Arvee 592)*
It	Ron & Bill *(Tamla 54025)*
My Beloved	
(No Strings Version)	The Satintones *(Motown 1000)*
Money	Barrett Strong *(Anna 1111)*
Rockin' Pneumonia &	
Boogie Wooogie Flu	Huey (Piano) Smith & The Clowns *(Ace 530)*
A Fool In Love	Ike &Tina Turner *(Sue 730)*
Chains Of Love	Joe Turner *(Atlantic 939)*
Stay	Maurice Williams & The Zodiacs *(Herald 552)*

1961 RELEASES

Let's Twist Again	Chubby Checker *(Parkway 824)*
Pony Time	Chubby Checker *(Parkway 818)*

Whole Lotta Woman	The Contours *(Motown 1008)*
Ya Ya	Lee Dorsey *(Fury 1053)*
Do-Re-Mi	Lee Dorsey *(Fury 1054)*
I Need Your Loving	Don Gardner & Dee Dee Ford *(Fire 508)*
I Know (You Don't Love Me No More)	Brenda George *(AFO302)*
Little School Girl	Wilbert Harrison *(Fire 1037)*
Jamie	Eddie Holland *(Motown 1021)*
No Love	Mable John *(Tamla 54040)*
Mother In Law	Ernie K-Doe *(Minit 623)*
Please Mr. Postman	The Marvelettes *(Tamla 54046)*
Shop Around	The Miracles *(Tamla 54034)*
She Put A Hurt On Me	Prince La La *(AFO 301)*
Mash Them 'Taters	The Olympics *(Arvee 5044)*
That's No Lie	Gino Parks *(Tamla 54042)*
Buttered Popcorn	The Supremes *(Tamla 54045)*
It's Gonna Work Out Fine	Ike & Tina Turner *(Sue 749)*
Poor Fool	Ike & Tina Turner *(Sue 753)*
Quater To Three	Gary US Bonds *(Legrand 1008)*
Bye Bye Baby	Mary Wells *(Motown 1003)*

Peter Rachman died on November 29th 1962 following a heart attack. His wife Audrey appeared to take over the club with shares in the club belonging to Albert Grew (90 per cent) and the remaining 10 per cent owned by a bodybuilder, who had once been a contender in the Mr Universe competition, Norman Mann. However, the real owner was still tough Lebanese entrepreneur and West End gangster, Raymond Nash. Although Raymond only ever claimed to be the manager. Rachman and Nash's other club was the Last Chance Saloon on Oxford Street. These two establishments catered for a mixed clientele of suburban white kids, West Indian drug dealers, off duty stripper's and the upper-class Chelsea set.

Pete Gage: "The first time I became aware of Mods was around summer 1962. A bunch of World's End boys gate-crashed a rather tame party that I'd held at my mother's house. These blokes made quite an impression on me. Not least because they were wearing these fantastic Fred Harrison tweed suits, baggies with turn ups, narrow lapels etc. The jacket button was always done up until such time, as was also the fashion at the time, the blokes would undo the jacket button, put their hands in their trouser pockets with their jackets flung to the rear. The other impressive thing about them was that one of them, Bernie, had under his arm jazz LP's by no less than Thelonious Monk and Gerry Mulligan. I got to know Bernie from that crowd quite well as I too was developing a great love of bop and post-bop – so-called 'modern' jazz."

LA DISCOTHEQUE R&B PLAYLIST 1962

(SUPPLIED BY ALAN GARRISON)

Night Train	James Brown *(King 5657)*
Duke Of Earl	Gene Chandler *(Vee-Jay 416)*
Popeye (The Hitchhiker)	Chubby Checker *(Parkway 849)*
Slow Twistin'	Chubby Checker *(Parkway 835)*
The Fly	Chubby Checker *(Parkway 830)*
Wiggle Wobble	Les Cooper & The Soul Rockers *(Everlast 5019)*
Do You Love Me	The Contours *(Gordy 7005)*
He's A Rebel	The Crystals *(Philles 106)*
Soul Twist	King Curtis & The Noble Knights *(Enjoy 1000)*
Stubborn Kind Of Fellow	Marvin Gaye *(Tamla 54068)*
Hitch Hike	Marvin Gaye *(Tamla 54075)*
Happy In Love/Calypso Dance	Wilbert Harrison *(Fury 1047)*
Hide And Go Seek (Parts I&II)	Bunker Hill *(Mala 451)*
Twist And Shout	The Isley Brothers *(Wand 124)*
Twisting With Linda	The Isley Brothers *(Wand 127)*
The Loco-Motion	Little Eva *(Dimension 1000)*
Way Over There	The Miracles *(Tamla 54069)*
Everybody Likes To Cha Cha Cha	The Olympics *(Arvee 5051)*
The Wah-Watusi	The Orlons *(Cameo 218)*
Papa Oom Mow Mow	The Rivingtons *(Liberty 55427)*
May I Have This Dance	Seniors *(Sue 756)*
Let Me In	The Sensations *(Argo 5405)*
Mashed Potato Time	Dee Dee Sharp *(Cameo 212)*
Twistin' Matilda	Jimmy Soul *(Spqr 3300)*
Green Onions	Booker T. & The M.g.s *(Stax 127)*
Paradise	The Temptations *(Gordy 7010)*
The Argument	Ike & Tina Turner *(Sue 772)*

Dear Lady Twist	U.s. Bonds *(Legrand 1015)*
Twist Twist Senora	U.s. Bonds *(Legrand 1018)*
Seven Day Weekend	U.s. Bonds *(Legrand 1019)*
Contract On Love	Little Stevie Wonder *(Tamla 54074)*
I Call It Pretty Music (Pt 2)	Little Stevie Wonder *(Tamla 54061)*
La La La La La	Little Stevie Wonder *(Tamla 54070)*

Other hot clubs during this period included The Flamingo in Wardour Street that had switched over from jazz to R&B. In March '62 it had secured the services of Georgie Fame and the Blue Flames, as well as other likeminded artists in the shape of Zoot Money and his Big Roll Band and Chris Farlowe and The Thunderbirds. The Flamingo appealed to a funkier crowd. The Roaring 20's in Carnaby Street specialised in Jamaican music and there was Klooks Kleek at the Railway Hotel in West Hampstead, that had been started in January 1961 by Dick Jordan and Geoff Williams as a modern jazz club and didn't switch over to R&B until September '63.

A letter to *Melody Maker* dated 11th August 1962:

I feel I speak for many rhythm and blues lovers in this country by saying: don't let the spotlight fall upon this wonderful music.

Spare us the agonies that the real jazz enthusiasts must have suffered with the popularity of their music.

At present R&B is pure and unspoiled. It has depth and soul and is the expression of the way of life of a people.

What will it be in the clutches of commercialism? Diluted, decadent, the tattered remnant of an art form. And to what purpose? Temporarily joy for the teenagers and fat profits for the pop record moguls.

I feel that R&B will only survive by continuing in relative obscurity.

Let's leave R&B with those who really appreciate it and don't hand it on a glittering plate to the popsters.

Michael Salter, Husbands Bosworth, near Rugby.

Jamaican ska music was proving popular amongst more and more white kids who found rhythms so different to the usual styles of R&B. Clubs such as the Roaring Twenties club at 50 Carnaby Street and The Limbo Club in D'Arblay Mews were mainly aimed at West Indian regulars, but handfuls of Mods had started to take note too. Georgie Fame and the Blue Flames had built up a Mod following at The Flamingo, and Georgie would frequent The Roaring Twenties as a punter as well as eventually playing gigs down there.

In an interview in *Disc and Music Echo* Prince Buster reminisced how they had met in 1964 at the club: "Georgie knows what music is all about. He's a really great, man. I went down the Roaring Twenties Club in Carnaby Street, saw Georgie play and I was really excited by what I heard. I never thought a white organist could play with that feeling. I have great respect for him."

The Roaring Twenties, The Flamingo and La Discotheque were all attracting the Mod crowd now that the ballrooms had lost favour, but there would soon be another club to entice them.

Alan Garrison recalls "I never went to The Lyceum because it was kind of London united. Our main competition came in 1963 when The Scene Club opened up, and all the posers went there."

The Scene was at situated in Ham Yard, just off Great Windmill Street. In earlier days it had been known for its jazz links as the Club 11 and later as Cy Laurie's Jazz Club. Ronan O'Rahilly, who went on to found the pirate station Radio Caroline, took over the club and pointed it into the direction of R&B and Blue Beat. A blonde girl named Sandra was employed behind the decks.

Terry Smith vividly recalls: "The Scene was my favourite.

Our mob were always by the piano in the corner. Jimmy West's mob, who were the Faces, were always opposite in the corner by the toilets. I was incredibly impressed one night when Dusty Springfield brought down Dionne Warwick. To me, La Discotheque was for rich little Jewish boys whilst The Scene was much more for street people.

"Somebody came down the State, Kilburn one Friday night and said they'd got free passes for a new club called The Scene. So, we thought we'd give it a try. When we got there, it was still the leftovers from the Cy Laurie jazz club and they didn't like us, a little group of Mods, so they all left. When you went in the early days there were still women there in long dresses."

The thing that the Scene Club would later be known for was that it employed a maverick DJ that owned a great R&B record collection. Guy Stevens was way ahead of the game and had probably the finest collection of R&B records in the country at that time.

Meanwhile back at La Discotheque, Alan Garrison was in fierce competition with The Scene Club: "We used to go to The Flamingo and you'd get the US airmen and a few Marines, and they'd teach us the dances like the Mashed Potato, The Hully Gully and The Slop which was a line dance. Then we'd go back into La Discotheque and teach everybody the dance there. It helped pull the punters in as they'd be impressed. We started off playing all the dance crazes. Stuff like Chubby Checker, The Orlons and The Olympics. One of the first big dances was the Mashed Potato.

"It was in the Flamingo I got 'The Hunch' by Paul Gayten on the Anna label which was a rolling R&B instrumental off a US airman stationed at Mildenhall. I played that down the Disc and it filled the floor. Then 'Money' by Barrett Strong came out, which was also on Anna so we didn't even know about the Tamla label. Then The Miracles 'Shop Around' came out and that was on Tamla but it didn't have the reputation then, it was just another label. By the time 'You Really Got A Hold On Me' by The Miracles came out and I started noticing I liked that label more so I asked the airmen for anything on the Tamla label. Then Mary Wells came out and that was on Motown, and that is when we connected Motown with Tamla. London released a few Motown bits but then Oriole started the USA series with Motown and they released The Contours stuff. The Contours records in the clubs were huge… 'Do You Love Me', 'Get In Line' and 'It Must Be Love' some of their flip sides were better than the A sides, such a dance groove.

"I used to get *Billboard* magazine which was 2/6d and that was a huge amount of money in those days for a magazine which were usually something like sixpence. It had all the latest releases in America for that week. So you'd look down the list and you'd know by the label… you'd know Chess, Motown, Cameo-Parkway.

"I'd buy records from Transat Imports on a Friday. Singles were about ten shillings where a normal single would cost about 6/9d and an LP would be about three quid instead of £1.10s which was good value straight from America. You'd give him your list and he would have them the next week. A single like 'My Guy' by Mary Wells for instance we had that the week after it was released in America – three months before it was released over here. We'd play it and the people in the club would be loving it. Then there was the Jamie Holland album and we played the track 'Jamie' and that was the beginning of the Motown sound with the tambourine and snare lead.

"'In My Tenement' by Roosevelt Grier was a floor filler. It's funny but Cameo-Parkway is just seen as a dance craze novelty label now but at the time it was the nitty gritty, it really was the business, sadly when that teen dance craze phase ended they didn't know what to do so the label folded. The Olympics were massive, then they went to the Mirwood label and were rocking. They had the same producer, Fred Smith, and James Carmichael the arranger the whole time from 1957. Scepter Wand was great with The Shirelles , Tommy Hunt and The Isley Brothers.

"The first thing on Stax was actually Satellite 'Last Night' by The Mar-Keys then 'Green Onions' came out which I ordered blind after seeing the name in Billboard magazine. 90 per cent of stuff we ordered we'd never heard.

"When Martha Reeves and the Vandellas brought 'Quicksand' out after 'Heatwave' and it was an identical beat. So, as we didn't have headphones at the time, I was taking pot luck trying to play them joined together. Now and again I got it right on the beat but most of the time it was off the beat, so you just faded one out and brought the other one up hoping people didn't notice. Anyway, one guy came up and asked why I didn't use a slip mat. I didn't know what they were, so he explained you put them on the deck, then you cue it up via headphones and just hold it and just let go. We hunted all over for them but never found any so we cut circles out of Cornflakes packets and punched a hole in them! It worked perfectly with those two records and two others we did it with was 'Let's Dance' and 'Some Kinda Fun' and 'Glad All Over' and 'Bits and Pieces' by The Dave Clark Five.

"We boycotted anything white or English. The Beatles were taboo. If you played a Beatles record at La Discotheque or the El Toro people would have just walked off the dance floor. One of the rare ones was 'House of the Rising Sun' by the Animals because it sounded so black. Anyway, one night we were down The Flamingo to see them. Chris Farlowe was the support act. He did his set and I thought, he's pretty good and enjoyed it. After he finished he came back on stage and told the audience The Animals were delayed as their van had broken down he then asked if the audience wanted records or he offered to do his set again. The audience opted for his set, which he eventually had to do three times until The Animals turned up. I mean you've got to give it to the guy. He went up in my estimation and was brilliant. After that I bought his records and I played them in the clubs."

LA DISCOTHEQUE R&B PLAYLIST 1963

(SUPPLIED BY ALAN GARRISON)

R&B PLAYLIST

Twenty Miles	Chubby Checker *(Parkway 862)*
Da Doo Ron Ron	The Crystals *(Philles 112)*
Then He Kissed Me	The Crystals *(Philles 115)*
Tell Him/	
Hard Way To Go	The Exciters *(United Artists 544)*
Can I Get A Witness	Marvin Gaye *(Tamla 54087)*
Nobody But Me	The Isley Brothers *(Wand 131)*
Sally Go Round The Roses	The Jaynettes *(Tuff 369)*
The Monkey Time	Major Lance *(Okeh 7175)*
Heat Wave	Martha & The Vandellas *(Gordy 7022)*
You Really Got	
A Hold On Me	The Miracles *(Tamla 54073)*
Little Girl Blue	The Marvelettes *(Tamla 54088)*
Mickey's Monkey	The Miracles *(Tamla 54083)*
The Bounce C/W	
Fireworks	The Olympics *(Tri Disc 106)*
South Street	The Orlons *(Cameo 243)*
Denis	Randy & The Rainbows *(Rust 5059)*
What A Guy	The Raindrops *(Jubilee 5444)*
The Birds The Word	The Rivingtons *(Liberty 55553)*
Be My Baby	The Ronettes *(Philles 116)*
Slop Time	The Sherrys *(Guyden 2077)*
Zipp-A-Dee-Doh Dah	Bob B. Soxx & The Blue Jeans *(Philles 107)*
Walking The Dog	Rufus Thomas *(Sta140)*
Poor Fool	Ike & Tina Turner *(Sue 753)*
That's How Heartaches	
Are Made	Baby Washington *(Sue 783)*

| You Lost The Sweetest Boy | Mary Wells *(Motown 1048)* |
| Fingertips (Parts 1&2) | Little Stevie Wonder *(Tamla 54080)* |

ROCK PLAYLIST 1961 TO 1963

Smokie (Parts I&Ii)	Bill Black's Combo *(Hi 2018)*
Three Steps To Heaven	Eddie Cochran *(Liberty 55242)*
At The Hop	Danny & The Juniors *(Abc Paramount 9871)*
Dream Lover	Bobby Darin *(Atco 6140)*
Cathy's Clown	The Everly Brothers *(Warner Bros. 5151)*
Sherry	The Four Seasons *(Vee Jay 456)*
Alley-Oop	The Hollywood Argyles *(Lute 5905)*
Beatnik Fly	Johnny & The Hurricanes *(Warwick 520)*
Louie Louie	The Kingsmen *(Wand 143)*
Monster Mash/Monster's Mash Party	Bobby Pickett & The Crypt Kickers *(Garpa 44167)*
Brontosaurus Stomp	The Piltdown Men *(Capitol 4414)*
Piltdown Rides Again	The Piltdown Men *(Capitol 4460)*
Running Bear	Johnny Preston *(Mercury 71474)*
What A Guy	The Raindrops *(Jubilee 5444)*
Half Breed	Marvin Rainwater *(Mgm 12803)*
Martian Hop	The Randells *(Chairman 4403)*
(Ghost) Riders In The Sky	The Ramrods *(Amy 813)*
Little Latin Lupe Lu	The Righteous Brothers *(Moonglow 215)*
Be My Baby	The Ronettes *(Philles 116)*
Short Shorts	The Royal Teens *(Abc Paramount 9882)*
Oh Carol	Neil Sedaka *(Rca Victor 7595)*
Runaway	Del Shannon *(Big Top 3067)*
Get A Job	The Shilhouettes *(Ember 1029)*
To Know Him Is To Love Him	The Teddy Bears *(Dore 503)*
Poetry In Motion	Johnny Tillotson *(Cadence 1384)*
Rubber Ball	Bobby Vee *(Liberty 55287)*

Alan Garrison: "It was in '63 or '64 that Fred, the owner of El Toro contacted me to move to there. It was about 200 yards away from Finchley Rd tube station. You went down this rickety old staircase, past the pay booth, then there was a little corridor, the café was on the right-hand side when you turned in there was a dance floor and a stage right at the top. It was all ultraviolet lit on the dance floor. I got five pounds a night at La Discotheque and I got five pound a night at the El Toro until I told Fred I would go back to the Disc and he raised it to seven quid a night."

Things didn't go so well for Raymond Nash, the La Discotheque owner. In April 1964, Nash, craving legitimacy, bought Peter Cook's club The Establishment at 18 Greek Street which had hit hard times as the owner toured New York with *Beyond The Fringe*. But things didn't turn out because the intellectuals who used the club weren't keen on the new owners' background and abandoned the club. Raymond Nash was deported back to Lebanon.

Willy Deasy (seated) with Johnny Moke (in light top)

CHAPTER THREE

THE MODS ARE HERE!

"Ian Hebditch was studying Fashion at Portsmouth Art College in 1965 and apart from being extremely cool and stylish he was influential in changing my Mod style to a more flamboyant look. We had decided that times were changing, and we would change with them."

JIM LUSH

Whilst many in the early days of the culture never used the word Mod to describe themselves, the name became a lot more common around 1963. By 1964 it became the byword to describe a certain group of people. Whilst the culture had first started in areas such as Stamford Hill and Tufnell Park, there was a new breed being drawn in from areas such as Shepherd's Bush, Dagenham, Barking, Tottenham and Richmond. The early Mods were the first generation who couldn't remember the war so they didn't feel guilty about spending money. Initially they were only obsessed by clothes, and a little later came music and dancing. Some had had scooters but they were never seen as a fashion accessory, they were merely transport. The new Mods introduced scooters as part of the Mod uniform along with pep pills and pop music.

Steve Dench, from Manor Park, East London recalls: "I first discovered the world of Mod, by going along with a friend of mine to the local church Hall in Manor Park in 1963 when I was 14. It was the world of soft drinks back then. I saw all these boys and girls dressed in a way I had never seen before. The music got me, the dancing got me, the styles that the boys were wearing…chalk stripe, pin stripe, one or two double breasted…every suit had style. I just hadn't noticed this before. I was a bit of a streetraker and the boys I knew just didn't wear those clothes in the street, except my cousin Gary who would parade up and down the streets in these different colour suede jackets.

"All the boys were either suited or in Levis. So smart casual or smart formal. Young boys were in there, aged just 16/17, and they were in bespoke three-piece pinstripe suits with shirt and tie.

"But the guy who was playing the music was a rocker! There he was up there in his greased back hair and leather jacket. He was playing a lot of stuff like Howlin' Wolf and a lot of Blues, some really early Tamla. I didn't know how to dance, so I stood there watching the kids out there dancing."

Pete Gage: "I used to go on Monday nights to the Hammersmith Palais for about a year in 1963 with some lads from Chelsea where I lived (Wiltshire Close, Draycott Ave). The Palais required suits and ties, so my little crowd were always togged out in our made-to-measure suits, usually from Burtons in Sloane Square. Slanting pockets, 6 inch vent, narrow lapels, waisted jackets, often in a subtle Prince of Wales check, but more often in a herringbone fine tweed or, as in one of my suits, from Fred Harrison's at The Cut in Waterloo, a thicker herringbone tweed in a sort of light to mid-brown. We'd have button-down shirts, sometimes tab-collar shirts but always with a narrow tie. Sometimes we'd wear a Fred Perry polo with the suit but of course we'd have to put on a tie as we entered the Hammersmith Palais so the bouncers wouldn't turn us away. The irony was that at the Palais we'd be all togged up, standing with our hands behind our backs, as was the fashion for a while back then, back combed hair, eyeballing all the other lads and acting hard. Invariably we ended up in some face-to-face confrontation that would sometimes lead to a fist fight outside the Palais at the end of the evening, or in the underpass leading to Hammersmith underground station. All good fun, but quite painful, although I'd never admit to it at the time!"

Terry Smith: "We were all grafters and we had everything made so we were always a bit different from those around us. Everything had to be found. If you wanted to buy clothes you had to fuckin' know someone. There was a woman in Harrow who made our leather coats. Mrs Trot for our shirts. She should be documented. She seemed old to us but was probably only in her late thirties, early forties. She was based in a little terrace house in New Cross and she made shirts for 10/6d with your own fabric. So, we started experimenting. We used to go to Carnaby Street to get our trousers off the ankle. They started noticing our shirts and saying 'That's nice' a week later they'd have a similar looking shirt in the window. So, we were influencing them rather than them influencing us."

Steve Dench: "I really took a fancy to the shirts I saw that night I'd first seen Mods. I had never seen a button-down shirt before. I got talking to a boy in there who was a friend of my cousin and he told me that just up the road in Manor Park was a shirt maker where you could get a shirt made-to-measure for three quid – which was decent money back then. You could pick out the style of collar and cuff you wanted, and so I had a button-down shirt made in blue, and after that I must have 30 to 40 shirts made. You didn't pay any money until that shirt was made and then you settled up with them.

"I couldn't get Levis, as I couldn't go to five or six pounds which they were back then. So, I had to get mine for two pound fifty and they were called Cowdens. They looked the same, the same blue and all that, but that was all I could afford. The bottoms of those would range from 14 to 16 inches. Sometimes people frayed the bottoms."

Pete Gage: "There was another crowd from Pimlico, Churchill Gardens, Mickey and Brian Lovatt, Paul Beecham and a handful of others, including Nancy Urquart and Jill Davis. Nancy and Jill would dance together round their handbags, whilst the Churchill Gardens boys and my crowd would stand around somewhere in the middle of the dance floor in some sort of circle of protection for the girls. Inevitably we would end up dancing on our own doing something not too far removed of what would become to be known as 'The Block'. The first of the lads to dance would invariably be Paul Beecham. He had front did Paul; he had the audacity to wear a distinct middle parting, backcombed hair, great suits, and boots with Cuban heels from Anello and David in the Charing Cross

Road, later made famous by The Beatles. The trousers were always fairly narrow at the bottom and just a little short, as a sign of being a Mod. (Trousers the previous couple of years had been baggies, like the old Oxford bags, my old man used to say, "nothing new in what you're wearing"). I am recalling all this pre-Scene stuff because it is so relevant to why I first went down The Scene. I was slowly drifting away from my Chelsea crowd in 1963. There was a bit of friction between me and the self-appointed leader of our gang, and I was getting a bit bored with them as individuals anyway."

Steve Dench: "My first trip to Clacton was with my mate Johnny Murphy. He lent me his older brother's leather coat, I had no idea it was his, and I borrowed a pair of Levis, but I wanted them to have a faded look that was coming in then. I was told a lot of guys got into a bath of bleach, but Johnny said the best way was to wear them into the sea. He said, "as soon as you get down there, dive in, and that will sort them out." We thumbed a lift down there and the first thing I did was take off my shirt and in I went into the sea. It took about two days, but they did start to bleach out. All the salt-water, you see. I also had to stand around in soaking wet trousers for about four hours. I just about got a beer down there, because I was so small and then I slept in bus shelters till the police moved us on.

"I went to the youth club and the coffee bar for a further year and then when I had that other year under my belt I went to the The Lotus in Forest Gate. Which was a real Mod club. There used to be a couple of guys who came over from Paris, one of whom was a black guy who they called Frenchie and he would tell the older boys about the fashions in Paris, the hairstyles and the new dances, so everyone would crowd around this guy.

"I remember being in The Lotus one evening and he said to me "Spanish dancing boots are coming in…" Bloody hell I said, where am I going to get them? And he told me about Anello and David and that you could get them made to measure there. So off I went. They showed me all these different leathers and I told them I really wanted blue with a Cuban heel. They told me no problem. I had three fittings and then went in to pick them up.

MOD

The animal world's equivalent to mods are called sheep. Two more weeks of "My Generation" in the Pop 50 and the flower of our youth will develop bad stutters. And if Pete Townshend ever gets a wooden leg, Thursday nights at the Marquee will sound like a carpenter's workshop. ■ The trouble with writing about mods is they've probably all changed by the time you're finished typing. And there's nothing so pathetic as the mod who's a step behind — like the cat on the left. At this particular second mods like Bob Dylan, mohair, the Yardbirds, vents, Len Barry, scooters, Sonny and Cher, op art ties and Roy Head. The girls haven't started wearing Union Jack underwear yet, but they will. ■ There are no fat mods. So if you can't stick to the diet sheet you'd better get out to the Ace Caff with the rockers. Mods believe Britain is ruled from London's Carnaby Street. ■ They have more suits than their fathers had hot dinners. And despite nasty rumours spread by rockers, mods really do like girls.

Cost me forty pounds. Lot of money. I paid off it weekly. I had a full-time job and I did two paper rounds. I'd get ten pound a week in the car showroom, and if I got someone down to buy a car, I'd get a fiver a car. Some weeks I'd get fifty quid a week.

"Anyway, I get these boots and I'm over the moon with them. I get togged up to go down to The Lotus and as I walk in wearing them, everyone starts laughing. I asked what's up and they said looking at my boots "They went out of fashion two weeks ago." They were obviously clued up weeks before me, so by the time I got around to them and picked mine up, waiting two weeks to have them made, I was too late. It was a mania…"

The drug scene by 1964 was bigger than ever. Two of the main drugs being:

Amphetamines: These came in a variety of shapes, sizes and colours, with a variety of nicknames such as French blues, purple hearts, Dex, Bennies, Doobs, Leapers or just plain old pep-pills. More commonly associated with appetite suppression, these stimulants were often stolen by sons, daughters and grandchildren from the family medicine cabinet or bought illegally from pushers for anything from 1s to 7s 6d, depending on strength and type. One such type were 'bombers', usually about half an inch long, and could be all white which contained seven milligrams, half black/half white which contained twelve and a half milligrams or the most potent, all black (known as black bombers) containing twenty milligrams.

Amphetamines increase energy, and confidence, and induce a feeling of well-being. The habit of taking these type drugs could lead to increasingly large doses of up to 30 at a time as they were well known users gaining a tolerance for them. These doses could cause excessive elation, often giving the appearance of being drunk without alcohol, resulting in extreme fatigue the next day, referred to as 'comedown'.

Barbiturates: Which were often used to induce sleep. They were often nicknamed Goof balls, Sleepers or Yellow Terrors. They usually came in tablet or capsule form and had the effect of slowing down activity yet removing inhibitions. The general effects were similar to alcohol.

Within 24 hours of a dose the consumer could show anxiety symptoms – a tremor. Twitching with weakness, dizziness and a feeling of nausea.

Amphetamine/barbiturate compounds such as Drinamyil were popular because they produced more euphoria and less anxiety than just amphetamines taken alone.

Steve Dench: "The big thing back then were these things called purple hearts. I didn't take them to start with because I was scared of them, but my cousin said all they will do is keep you awake, that is all they will do. If you wanted to dance all night or go on to another club, these will keep you awake. So I started taking them, but I just didn't want to get into drugs"

Ian Hebditch also remembers the drug scene around Portsmouth: 'Not only did we know all the plain clothes detectives, but we had a list of all the unmarked police cars belonging to the Portsmouth Constabulary. I can only remember one raid on The Birdcage and that had something of the air of a farce, perhaps that is why it was never repeated. The Action were playing, when Rikki (Farr) interrupted to say that the police were outside. The band immediately broke in to the *Dixon of Dock Green* theme as the police trouped in like the Keystone Kops, they told us all not to move, giving us plenty of time to dispose of any narcotics we might have had in our possession, and they proceeded to search us all. It was absolute chaos, people were running about all over the show. In the end they just closed the club for the night and chucked us out. I think they nicked two people out of about a thousand, and they must have been so stupid they deserved to be caught.

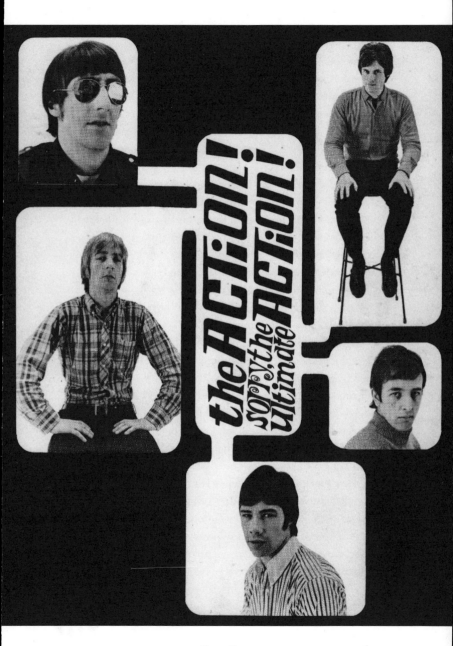

Rikki collected almost a bucketful of pills off the floor when it was swept. The police could never close The Birdcage for long because Rikki sat on the council and not only had he quite a bit of influence but also quite a glib tongue.'

Scooters gained more prominence. The scooters to have were the Vespa GS160 or a Lambretta TV175, which in turn, as scooters progressed, would be replaced by the Vespa SS180 or the Lambretta SX200.

Richard Cole: "Johnny Pearce was always ahead of the game in a sense. When he first got a scooter, he took it in and got it sprayed gun metal grey, when he got his first suit made it had the one button and when he painted his bedroom it was black. He was creative."

Phil Luderman remembers "It all started when I went to a church youth club. The Movement in Battersea, where I lived, had just started but I wasn't old enough. Some of the local Mods came to the church hall, and I was just fascinated by them. I knew once I was old enough to get a licence that I would join them. I got some money together by working at Cecil Gee's. I bought a Lambretta LI150 which was basic and quite cheap. Most of my Mod friends had TV175's, so they looked down on me a little bit and I didn't feel I was part of the scene with this early model. I saved and managed to get a TV175 locally in Battersea High Street. Most of the local Mods bought theirs at Naylor and Roots which was right in Clapham Junction near to Henry London's, where we got our suits made. It was a limey yellow colour, which was a standard colour for TV's. The first thing I got done was to get the side panels chromed at a place in Wandsworth. Some of the scooters up there were fully chromed, and there wasn't a painted panel on them, but I thought that was a bit OTT. At the time, Jaguar had a 3.8 Mark 2 in a lovely bronze colour, so I had it sprayed that colour. It's funny but up until I was about 16 I never had any experience with women, but after I got the scooter chromed, that changed."

Malcolm Saunders: "Haircuts for Mods in the Islington area, plus some of the Hackney boys, was done by a big Jewish bloke called Stanley Kaye. Six shillings and sixpence for a haircut. That was fucking dear, so you had to save up. You'd ask for a college boy cut or a 'Perry Como' which had a higher parting. You could get your haircut at a normal barber, and that would cost about a shilling or one shilling and sixpence but you just got a bloke with some clippers giving you a short back and sides. No thanks!"

Steve Dench "As I was now working, I saved up fifteen quid and wanted something special. So, some friends mentioned Cecil Gee over in Soho. I looked in the windows and yeah it was very very nice. I went in there all suited and booted and a guy came over, so I told him I had seen a shirt in the window that I liked, and straight away he asked how much money I had. I told him fifteen quid and he told me I wouldn't be able to buy anything in there. I told him I had come all the way up from Essex and he said, "I tell you what, how about this for thirteen pounds?" And he handed me a bottle of aftershave. I said, "I don't shave!"

"But I bought it anyway, and it was by Ralph Lauren, only it wasn't called that, it was called 'Polo' and you know what, I've still got it and it is still half full! I was frightened to use it... all that money, I was dead scared to use it."

Mod spread out from London, into the Home Counties and down to the south coast in to places like Southampton, Portsmouth and Brighton. Every little town getting its own scene.

Brighton had a pretty good Mod scene of its own. Kids would meet up at the one of the many cafes, including The Zodiac at the bottom of St James Street, situated just above Hilton's shoe shop. The walls were painted matt black with signs of the zodiac painted on them. Orange lighting adding to the atmosphere. There would be a mob of hip kids placing their two-shilling pieces on the glass of the Kings and Queens pinball machine, awaiting their go. Others used their money predominantly to play the great soul 45's stacked in the Wurlitzer Lyric jukebox that boomed out endlessly. Others places included the Scandinavian Coffee Bar in Western Road, referred to by regulars as 'The Scan', The Istanbul, also in Western Road and the Chateau Rouge in West Street. Another Mod stronghold was the King Alfred Bowling Alley.

The place to get the ultimate Mod machine was Blaber's

Scooter Centre at the bottom of Dyke Road. Spray jobs, accessories and that all important chroming took place there, with the place to be seen at night being Castle Square with parking outside Electricity House, where the riders would gather to show off their chrome-laden steeds. Wearing full length leather or suede coats from Esther and Ben Royce's shop in the Queens Road, they then had to decide the best place to go.

The clubs included The Regent, The Starlight Rooms in

Montpelier Rd, The Barn at the bottom of West Street tucked away down an alley, and of course The Florida Rooms at The Aquarium.

'Mods and Rockers dress as they do because of a deep-rooted psychological insecurity, and an emotional inability to impress in their own right.' Was just one of the findings in a nation-wide survey in the early months of 1964, into the clothing habits of teenage boys that was carried out by 54-year-old Brighton based clothing retailer Barnett Oberman, who owned 17 clothes shops up and down the country.

"Originally, the survey was to help us gauge market trends." Oberman told a *Brighton and Hove Gazette* reporter. "But we soon found that teenagers we questioned gave such similar answers to our queries that we realised that this survey had definite psychological value to everybody who wants to understand why teenagers dress as they do."

The survey took three months to complete and 500 boys between the ages of 13 and 19 were questioned.

In the survey, it is claimed that the sole aim of both Mods and Rockers when purchasing clothes is to find something that will make them stand out. Neither the quality nor the price really matters, as long as the item is sufficiently outstanding to draw attention to the wearer.

"For centuries it has been the women who have worn the fine feathers" said Mr Oberman. "But now it is the men who are vying with them. In parts of London we found that Mods actually came into a shop and chose a colourful shirt which matched their eye make-up. Not that there is anything cissy about these lads in the accepted sense. It is just that the wearing of cosmetics helps them to have that feeling of being somebody."

The survey also stated that Mods mainly buy clothes that they think will appeal to other Mods. Rockers, on the other hand bought clothes to impress everybody. It also claimed that neither Mods or Rockers generally paid any attention to what their girlfriends suggested that they should wear. Other teenage boys were usually the ones to help them choose their clothes.

In May 1964, the *Brighton and Hove Gazette*, upon hearing of the survey, decided to hold their own survey, based on the findings of the Oberman report, amongst the teenage boys present at the Starlight Rooms in Montpelier Road.

John Starr, a Mod, stated that "Good smart clothes definitely help make you feel important. But clothes are only the beginning. The clothes make you stand out, and then you start to feel more self-confident. You acquire poise and polish. After that you really begin to feel like somebody. But there are many teenagers who pretend to be Mods but aren't really Mods at all."

Lots of the boys agreed that nobody helped them choose their clothes, and definitely not other teenage boys.

18-year-old, Mark Jones was quick to add "None of us here ever use cosmetics, whether we're Mods or Rockers, and we resent the continual harping on about this sort of thing in reports and surveys of this kind. The suggestion that we buy shirts to match our eye make-up is just rubbish, and things like this are invented by people who want to cause a sensation."

Portsmouth had its own scene too with an array of cafes, shops and clubs centred towards the new Mod style. Jim Lush and Ian Hebditch were two likeminded souls who embraced it all.

Jim Lush: "Ian Hebditch apart from being extremely cool and stylish was influential in changing my Mod dress style to a more flamboyant look. We had decided that times were changing and would change with them. Backcombed, rollered and lacquered hair, satin shirts with beads along with our Tonik suits, smart shoes and accessories became more acceptable than collar and tie. We were obviously moving towards a more glamourous look. In fact, satin button-down then became my preferred shirt style and seriously comfortable to dance in.

"Ian was studying Fashion at Portsmouth Art College in '65, he then went on to get a BA in Fashion and Textiles and worked in the fashion industry before taking up teaching. He showed me some very cool designs for menswear he had done that were ahead of their time as he wanted to include more organic and natural fibres in his clothes design. His eye for textiles was second to none. I was putting my own style ideas together and was hanging around the girls from the Fashion Design course at the Art College. I had actually applied to Art College to enrol on the Graphic Design course, but because I had no 'O' or 'A' levels, I was told to re-apply when I had some qualifications. I completed my engineering Apprenticeship instead. Then became a graphic designer in my own right with my own agency!

"Our first meeting was a bit cheeky as there were girls at art college that Ian knew well and was good friends with and I was interested in them. So, I struck up a friendship so that I could meet them and asked one of them out. But then she dumped me but Ian and I remained buddies. What I hadn't realised was that Ian had been watching me and thought I was pretty cool so I was more than flattered when we got to know each other and would ride our scooters to gigs together and pick up girls."

Sadly, Ian Hebditch passed away in 2007. In 1971 he'd written a thesis on Mods entitled 'I Do Like To Be Beside The Seaside' in which he gave his personal recollection of the Sixties Mods. Thanks to his partner, Jane Shepherd, and Jim Lush, I am able to share some of his insights throughout this book.

It is essential to note that in the intro to his thesis he made it clear that they never referred to themselves as Mods, and that it was a word invented by the press. They themselves thought of themselves as individuals, who were involved. Obviously, these views are his own personal ideas, and are centred around the Portsmouth area during that period. Hebditch goes on to inform us that:

'It is important to know something of the complex hierarchy of the movement, so that no confusion exists as to who I am referring. First there were 'The Lads' who were really the true Mods in my opinion. They were looked up to, had the smartest clothes and the best images, they were seldom 'first in' in dance hall brawls, this was left to the next group down the scale who I term 'Heavies'. They dealt out most of the violence, encouraged by the first group, less intelligent and not as well dressed nevertheless they formed a useful and important part of the team. There were also the younger kids who hung around trying to get some of the glory, they were never accepted by the others. The people in parkas (U.S. Arctic Combat jackets) who rode around on tatty scooters were not Mods at all, the name for them in my area was "Feds" (Scooter Federation) — they were outcasts.'

Malcolm Sanders agrees: "I never wore a parka. That was for the other lot. I know it sounds wrong, but we were looking down on your normal Mods. You know, the quantity, the mass, we looked down on them. Don't ask me why but we did. Looking for new gear all of the time was what it was about. Willy Deasy was in the top Mods, so was Mokey (Johnny Moke)."

Ian Hebditch: 'I became completely involved with being a Mod, even at school I had a suit with big vents in it and was once caned for lacquering my hair in the toilets. I even got pilled up for P.T on one occasion for a bet, funny when I look back because the P.T master didn't realise anything was amiss, he just thought I was trying extra hard I think.'

On February 11th 1964, *The Daily Herald* ran a series of articles over four days entitled 'The Way-Out Mods'.

On day one, the feature was called 'The Mecca Of The Mods' and sub-titled with the words 'In a street in Soho – the most way-out world of people who keep one jump ahead.' It was written by Mavis Davidson and accompanied by photos from Chris Barham. The opening words of the article can be found at the front of this book. It starts with photos of Patrick Kerr and Theresa Confrey. In it, both are described as 'top Mods' that spend £15 a week. It is then followed by an article on Carnaby Street and in particular, John Stephen (the owner of many clothes shops), who, it points out, at 27, has been way-out so long he can afford a Rolls Royce. It estimates that he has turned a £300 investment over five years into a business worth £400,000. 'A suit bought today is guaranteed to last less than three months. A hat can be old hat before you are out of the shop.' writes Mavis Davison. It states that top Mods in Carnaby Street will happily pay out £5 on shoes, £30 on a suit, £5 for trousers, £10 for jackets and £4 for shirts. Then spend the same amount next month. An apprentice engineer, aged 17, informs them that he spends half of his £8 wages keeping up with Carnaby Street.

Day two of the series is probably the most interesting, but sometimes ill-informed. Entitled 'The Faces Way Out' it again mentions Patrick Kerr and Theresa Confrey but says that you don't have to be famous to be a 'Face'.

'But as often, a Face is just a Face. Copied, envied and anonymous. Someone in the crowd, but not of the crowd. The uncommon denominator. They are a Face because they were first, either with a new fashion, or a new dance. Colin Marriott, an 18-year-old London mathematics student, is a Face. Honoured as the Mod who led the way in the wearing of white plimsoles. At The Scene, London's top Mod club, Colin is a boy who is watched. An idol not only because of his dress, but because he can do the heel movement in the Face Twist faster than anyone else.'

The Scene, which it describes as 'a black-walled Temple of the Mods', is then somewhat inaccurately described by stating that the club has 7,000 members and crowds of 600 every night. It describes the Face Twist as having a hand movement somewhere between a High Noon gun-draw and a Hula dance. It goes on to say that 17-year-old Ann Merrington is an originator of the Face Twist, and she explains that old Bill Haley records are the best to dance to it.

The third day is devoted to Patrick & Theresa Kerr, explaining their hectic lifestyle now that they are the dancers on television's *Ready Steady Go!* Programme. Day four of the series concentrated on Patrick and Theresa's forthcoming wedding.

Not everyone agreed with the papers spotlight on the scene. A few days later *The Daily Herald* printed this in the letters page. It was headlined 'Too Old To Be A Mod – At 20!':

'The real Mods are the 15- to 19-year olds – teenagers who like to be different and yet keep in a circle of their own.

'They follow each other like sheep. They do not follow a Top Mod like Patrick Kerr (22), who is not a leader of fashion but has a fashion of his own.

'Anyway, except for a few who won't give up, you are finished as a Mod when you get to 20.'

John Casey (a has-been Mod), Battersea, London.

Carnaby Street appealed to the mass-consumer type of Mod because it was affordable. Items were relatively cheap because the emphasis was that in a months' time, it would probably be out of fashion anyway. John Stephen owned several clothing boutiques in Carnaby Street and he tapped in to the Mod market with ease. He charged £7-£10 for a jacket. £3 to £5 for a shirt. This is at a time when a hairdresser earned about £20 a week. Working class lads could not afford to shop in the Kings Road and were aware that John Stephen was at the bottom of the range for retailers in London in 1964. This is another reason the Mod scene boomed, because it became less about individuality and became more of a style uniform.

America had shown interest in the Mod scene in Britain. In an American version of *Vogue* magazine dated August 1st, 1964, English journalist Peter Laurie covered the culture over a three-and-a-half-page article with a tag of 'So young, so cool, so misunderstood'. It stated that: 'To be a Mod is to be young – from twelve to eighteen at the most' and told Americans the basics of the new cult and their 'enemies' – the Rockers. It also featured a striking photo of Colin Walsh in neat college boy style in white t-shirt, dark bomber jacket, dark trousers and desert boots.

Colin Walsh: "The magazine came out in '64 but the photo featured in it was taken in '63. I reckon it was at least nine months before. I think it was around the Christmas period '63. At the time I 'd been in The Scene Club dancing around, on pills. We used to take around 20 pills and another 10 in the morning. Always Drinamyl, not Dexedrine, sometimes 30 a night. I was buying tins of them from Hackney Road. A thousand blues from Bee's Chemist. I used to give her threepence each and sell them for a tanner (sixpence). Pete The Pill used to sell them too, he was the pusher in Wardour Street. We used to flit from The Flamingo to The Scene. Anyway, that night a fella came up to me and asked if I minded him taking photos for a magazine. He said he wanted Piccadilly behind me, with the Eros statue. As it was nearby, I agreed. Anyway, he took loads of photos of me, and I didn't think any more of it because I was so off my nut, I just went back dancing. Months later, a friend of mine, Johnny Hillman, who worked at a hairdresser's in Mayfair asked if I'd ever been in *Vogue*. I told him no, but they'd had a copy for the customers to read, and he'd ripped out the pages to show me. It was only then, that it all came back to me."

CHAPTER FOUR

THERESA CONFREY AND PATRICK KERR

"The killer was Ready Steady Go! If you wanted to dance on RSG, and you weren't a regular at The Scene Club or spotted somewhere, then you couldn't get on. You could walk on set, half an hour to it starting and have a coffee and chat to Marvin Gaye or Stevie Wonder."

DENIS CONFREY

CHAPTER

B ack in early 1964 there was no such thing as a celebrity Mod. Steve Marriott, Roger Daltrey, and Guy Stevens were relative unknowns. The nearest we came to it during this period was 22-year-old Patrick Kerr and Theresa Confrey (21).

Patrick, from Dartford in Kent, and Theresa, of Abbey Wood both made their name by becoming the dance demonstrators on Redifussion Television's *Ready Steady Go!* They weren't bandwagon jumpers though as many had thought. They'd both attended clubs in those early days.

"In 1961 or 1962 I remember one fashion where we went to The Lyceum. The girls had to wear tight, little dresses and carry a little basket" remembers Theresa. "You'd carry everything in that basket. The look was topped off with handmade shoes from Stan's of Battersea. There was a whole early scene of dancing but it was less to do with dance and more to do with clothes. We danced at the Railway Hotel in Dartford where Ross MacManus (Elvis Costello's father) played in a band. In those days it was all about live bands and jiving. Patrick was a face. The other places included the Welling Embassy, the Ilford Palais and the Tottenham Royal."

Patrick meanwhile got a job in Leicester Square with Arthur Murray, an American dance instructor. Through that both Patrick and Theresa found themselves at a newly opened dance studio in Bond Street called The Anna Neagle and Fred Astaire Dance Studio. The studio was very fashionable amongst the upper classes and they met British model Mandy Rice Davis. Party invites followed, and it wasn't long before Patrick found himself teaching Princess Margaret 'The Twist'. The Princess had a friend who owned a ship and explained that they were in need of dance demonstrators.

The couple soon found themselves in Tangiers about to be picked up by ship and setting off to a new adventure in America and the Caribbean during a three-month cruise. Whist there they got to meet young students every weekend in New York picking up the latest Latin American and Puerto Rican dance styles in clubs such as the famous Peppermint Lounge on West 45th Street. Here they learnt dances such as 'The Peppermint Twist', 'Hully- Gully' and 'The Bossa Nova'.

"When we came back with the Bossa Nova dance, television picked up on it. David Jacobs from *Juke Box Jury* and various TV shows had us demonstrating the dance which was great. Sometime around this point Elkan Allan who was Head of Entertainment at Rediffusion must have realised the new scene was all about dancers. He invited us to do a pilot show called 'Step Lively' and then we thought nothing more about it." says Theresa.

The couple began working for Radio Luxemburg and filming dance demonstrations for Pathe Pictorial News. During this period, The Beatles hit town. Soon they were mingling with the Fab Four as well as many of the up and coming Brian Epstein stable before setting off on their second visit to the U.S.

Theresa's younger brother was fifteen-year-old Mod Denis, he remembers it well. Denis was in the enviable position of getting into all of the best places through his sister's connections. Clubs, clothes and music became a way of life to him. "In '62, when Patrick and Theresa were on their first cruise, me and my sister used to write once a week. When she got to port she'd write me a letter telling me of her adventures. She'd tell me she was in Jamaica or wherever and ask if I wanted anything to bring back. I said a Beatles album. She wrote backing asking, 'who are The Beatles?' She returned with four albums, which I still have to this day; Barbara Lewis – 'Hello Stranger', Ben E King 'Stand By Me', Marvin Gaye 'Stubborn Kind Of Fella' and The Miracles 'Hi, We're The Miracles'. Music meant a lot to me. The first record me and Theresa ever owned we bought together. It was a 78rpm in 1956, 'I Don't Care If The Sun Don't Shine' by Elvis, and we didn't even have anything to play it

"Back in the States we picked up more dances. It was about then that we got a telegram from Elkan Allan which read 'STEP LIVELY GONE. STOP. *READY STEADY GO!* IS ALIVE.' says

Theresa. "He brought us back. So that's how we came to be on the show. We came back with a whole background of what now would be called 'Street Dance', you know, people doing urban dance that we picked up from these kids in America. The 'Hitch-Hike' was the first one, which we found on the streets really. It was a dance craze that was just hitting the States."

Elkan Allan was 40 years old but hip enough to realise the potential of the emerging teenage consumer market as an audience. *Ready Steady Go!* began life on August 9, 1963 and had On October 4, 1963 Patrick and Theresa found themselves doing their first RSG dance routine having been introduced to the audience the week earlier. After a brief chat with ageing presenter Keith Fordyce the pair perform 'The Hitch – Hike' in lines with audience members to 'Gonna Make Him Mine' by The Orchids. The show was bound to pull in big viewing figures as the show also featured The Beatles first RSG appearance, miming to 'Twist and Shout', 'I'll Get You' and 'She Loves You'. From that moment on, both Patrick and Theresa would become known through various Pop magazines and TV appearances.

Denis Confrey: "The killer was *Ready Steady Go!* If you wanted to dance on RSG, and you weren't a regular at The Scene Club or spotted somewhere, then you couldn't get on. It was way ahead of its time. It was 'have you met Stevie Wonder? Have you met Marvin Gaye? You could walk on set, half an hour to it starting and have a coffee and chat to them. During this period was the first time I went to The Scene Club myself. The first record I heard there was 'Monkey Time' by Major Lance, and the hair still goes up on the back of my neck when I hear it. Two of the things I remember about The Scene Club is that it introduced me to music I'd never heard before, and Mickey Tenner. Mickey had a clique around him. I never got to know him because he was older than me, but I was overawed by him. Crazy really, because I'd just been on *Ready Steady Go!* And met Stevie Wonder and Marvin Gaye."

Theresa Confrey: "At the time there was *Juke Box Jury*, *Six Five Special* and *Thank Your Lucky Stars* but they were just so old fashioned. To get on to RSG was a kind of elite club. There was a café next to Kingsway called The Kardoma. There wasn't a canteen in the Kingsway studio. You went in there and you'd be sat with Dionne Warwick. It was just completely normal for them to be there."

Denis Confrey: "I went down The Scene Club one night, and Theresa and Pat came down. They'd just come back from the States. Apart from albums such as the Barbara Lewis and Arthur Alexandra records they'd bought back for me, they'd also got me an Ivy League striped shirt and a white sweatshirt from Pitsburgh University with the word 'Pit' on it. I wore it down there on a Friday night. I got one step inside the door, and about 10 guys, including Mickey Tenner and all his boys, asked me how much I wanted to sell that sweatshirt."

Willie Deasy had actually made it on to the dancefloor for the very first episode: "The first night we heard *Ready Steady Go!* was on we shot down there. There was Marc Feld and his little Mob. I'd seen him down the Tottenham Royal a few times. Anyway, there were all these dancers down there. Out came the floor manager and she said "All the dancers from the Chelsea Dance College follow me" and turned her back. So, we pushed them all out of the way. We were first down there and picked where we wanted to dance. After that they asked us back the following week because all of these 'dancers' couldn't dance. They were dancing a Beatnik Jive thing because the Beatnik's had just finished. We were chancers, absolute chancers. I used to go to rehearsals and see my mates walking around the studio with empty film reel cases. If they were asked what they were doing, they'd say it was news for the top floor. They'd be just going up and down in the lift all day just so they'd be there from the kick off. That was *Ready Steady Go!* every week and it was getting more and more popular."

Ian Hebditch: "I reckon I was a bit brighter than a lot of the blokes, being at a grammar school but I was never conscious of it when I was out. Some of my mates were apprentices for instance but they all seemed the same as me at the time, there was no place for Latin or Geometry, it was what you looked like and whether you were a "good geezer" that mattered. It was all important to be able to dance well. Like the clothes, the dances were always changing with amazing frequency; there was one called the "Paint and Scrape" which resembled limbering up for ski-ing. It was especially popular for dancing to the Four Tops 'Can't Help Myself'. Some of the dances were very difficult and I used to practice at home in front of a mirror to make sure I could do it alright, not to be able to would be unforgivable.'

Patrick and Theresa found themselves in all sorts of teen magazines, newspapers and television programmes telling people how to dance. Once they were married though, Theresa retired to start a family. Patrick carried on, and even got his own weekly column in teen girls magazine *Mirabelle*.

Apart from established dances such as The Jerk, The Bang and The Block, Patrick Kerr's Mod Dance Column would introduce young teens to all sorts of weird choreography. Amongst the titles were The Modango (a Mod Tango), The Jet, The Jagger, The Loddy=Lo, The Eagle, The Froog, The Jamaican Froog, The Hollie, The Casual, The Foxx, Le Jimmy, Ringo's Dog, The Ad-Lib, The Ticket, The Troll. The Southstreet, The Climb, The Noo and The Sidewalk.

"It was like a recording contract." says Theresa. "We had to come up with a new dance every week. Some weren't great ideas really. The kids didn't think it was rubbish, so Patrick would rack his brains every week. When we were very good friends with Mike McGear (Paul McCartney's brother), he used to live with us. So, Patrick made up a dance called The Gear. It was like being an artist, in that you took the influences from around you. We were absolutely at the cutting edge of what was happening at the time, in both the music industry and the fashion industry. They were really related, they went hand in hand."

It was whilst at *Ready Steady Go!* That Denis Confrey got a story that he's been able to dine out on for years:

Step back into The Savoy with Patrick Kerr

Ready Steady

DANCE

STILL dancing? Great, because this week we're moving in on the last lesson of my current dance date . . .

THE SAVOY

This descendant of the Hully Gully and the American Slop certainly seems to be going down big with a lot of you now.

Of course, during 1963 the trend was to dance on your own. Partners were right out! But now changes are taking place. The Savoy can be danced with a partner . . . let's hope the dances stay this way for a while.

Last week, remember, I left you on the third basic movement. And that was: Step to the side with the right foot, cross left foot behind right, and then slide to the right—repeating the whole thing as many times as you wish.

You can see Patrick on A.-R. TV's *Ready, Steady, Go!* on your screens in London and the Midlands every Friday at 6.15 p.m.

Now, from there it's slightly more difficult! Starting with the right foot, begin to mark time (right-left-right). Then step slightly forward with the left foot without putting any weight on it, and bring it back to position. Now you mark time again—left-right-left. With me? Now step slightly forward with the right foot (as you see in the picture), and bring it back into position ready to mark time right-left-right.

Step forward with the right foot, heel pointing downwards. Now come down on it, and step forward again with the left foot, heel pointing downwards. But this time, as the weight is brought down, jump quickly, making a quarter turn to the right. (This you can see me doing in the picture.) Now you start to mark time again, (right-left-right), and repeat the whole movement. This step can be done as many times as you like, but normally it is only performed four times, so that at the end, you will find yourself back in the starting position.

And that's it! Next week I'll be giving you more gen on halts and dancers. See you then, all right?

"On New Years Eve 1964, the *Ready Steady Go!* Show was live from 11pm until 12.30am. It was the only occasion that it was on at a different time. I wore a green jacket from Carnaby Street. I remember that because it's the only thing I ever bought from there. Anyway, Theresa and Pat came over. I was there with my girlfriend of the time, Jennifer West. The show finished, and Theresa and Pat said that they were going upstairs to a party afterwards. We were staying at their place in Finchley, so we just said we'd get a taxi back there. The show finally finished around 1am. About 15 minutes later, a floor manager appeared and said "Great show! Here's a case of champagne." So, we got stuck in to this champagne, and by 3am I couldn't stand I said to Jennifer "Let's go upstairs to the party and see what the others are doing!" Theresa shouted "What are you still doing here?" I told her that

we'd finished downstairs and all the booze was gone. At about
4 or 5am Theresa said that they were moving on to the Ad Lib
Club, which at that time was *the* club in London. She told us that
we were going to be picked up, and to go downstairs to wait for
them. We were downstairs for about half an hour when in walks
the actress, Jane Asher. She led us to a waiting car outside, and it's
Paul McCartney sat in his Aston Martin DB5, which I think was
the only one in the country at the time. We get in the back, and
off we go. We got as far as Trafalgar Square and I feel sick. I said
to Paul "I feel ill" and he just replied "Fine, let's get you sorted."
He stopped the car, came around the back, and before he could
open the door, I was sick all over the back seat and fell out on to
all fours. Jane Asher was doing her bollocks, as you can imagine,
but Paul was brilliant about it. We got back in the car, and went
on to the Ad Lib. Once there, you had to go up these stairs, so
Paul and his brother, Mike McGear from The Scaffold, got hold
of me either side and helped me up the stairs. At the top, there
was John Lennon and Ringo Starr. I was so pissed I just shouted
"We've got to sing something!" We ended up all singing 'La, La,
La, La, La' by The Blendells. That's my claim to fame, I sang with
the Beatles. Obviously, once I got inside the club, I promptly
passed out!"

Ready Steady Go! had started life in August 1963. It quickly
established itself as the must see show for Mods, especially if you
lived outside London and wanted to know what the kids were
wearing and how they were dancing in the nation's capital. Apart
from the fact that the show would invite on some great American
stars such as James Brown, Martha Reeves and the Vandellas or Rufus
Thomas. Homegrown stars such as Georgie Fame and The Rolling
Stones would feature too. The real stars though were the audience.
This was made up of kids who were either the best dancers in their
respective clubs or the best dressed. People like Mickey Tenner, Paul
Beecham and Will Deasy were regular dancers.

CHAPTER

FIVE

RIOTS

"Yes, I am a Mod and I was at Margate. I'm not ashamed of it – I wasn't the only one. I joined in a few of the fights. It was a laugh. I haven't enjoyed myself so much in a long time. It was great – the beach was like a battlefield. It was like we were taking over the country."

JOHN BRADEN

On December 18th, 1963, which was a cold winters evening, the Prince Charles Theatre in London staged Britain's first ever 'beat' ballet. Staged by the Western Theatre Ballet Company, the company's artistic director, Peter Darrell had come up with the idea of 'Mods and Rockers'. The ballet was choreographed to a score arranged by Ian Macpherson from songs written by three of the Beatles, John Lennon, Paul McCartney and George Harrrison.

The 'Mods' were dressed in high-buttoned collarless jackets being the 'Shakers', whilst the leather clad Rockers were the 'Twisters'. The narrative being about a Mod girl being carried off Sir Galahad-style by a Rocker on his motorbike. It was obviously a mish mash of Romeo and Juliet meets West Side Story. Still, the ballet ran for three weeks, gaining quite positive reviews before disappearing.

At the time, most of the general public were unaware of the two cults. On Easter Bank Holiday 1964 that changed forever.

Many youths had descended on the east coast resort of Clacton. This included many Mods from London and the Home Counties, but this was just part of the traditional holiday beano. Many of the Rockers present that day were locals or came from East Anglian villages.

The weather was particularly unpleasant with a cold wind, and rain. Shopkeepers, cafés and other amenities were irritated by the lack of business but still refused to serve the teenagers. The dullness of the situation would soon spark unrest.

Willy Deasy: "We were in the vanguard of going down to the coast. When we'd gone down to Clacton at Easter there was maybe a dozen of us. Two car loads of us, with about five or six of us in each. They were big Humber cars driven by Johnny Moke (Mokey) and Billy Lampy."

Colin Walsh: "I'd never even heard of Clacton. We were all from South London. We would have gone to Brighton or

Folkestone. Clacton is the dreariest place in the World, and I reckon it must have been mentioned by the East End lot because Clacton and Southend were their places. It started off well, six of us went down there in a V8 Pilot which is a big American car. Later that night I slept under the pier beneath an upturned boat. During the night all I could hear was people shouting 'There they are!' and running around chasing these East End Boys and different firms. I think everybody was off their heads on purple hearts and bored silly. Clacton was dead by 9 o'clock."

Willy Deasy: "We went to go on the pier because we were bored. There was this old guy on the entrance. These guys were ex-army and they were used to obeying orders, and they expected people to obey theirs. He saw us coming towards him and thought to himself 'I'll give this lot the elbow'. So, he told us the pier was closed. I just thought, fuck it and jumped over the barrier, and everybody followed. We were just kids running along this pier. There was no fighting that day, just running along the pier. The bloke called the local police, and they came down just as we were walking off the pier because we'd had our laugh. Remember, we didn't drink or smoke or anything at this point. It was bank holiday, but the town was dead. We pulled some birds, but I remember there were people sleeping under upturned boats or in telephone boxes because it was absolutely freezing. If that bloke had just closed the gate and we'd just walked off, there would have been no riots, no police, nothing. After that though it all changed."

Terry Smith: "We broke into the caravans at Clacton. When all that rioting was going on we weren't interested in that. We were only interested in birds. Stuart Hill had the bed, and me and this girl were on the floor. When he finally got up, we got in to bed. I just finally got her knickers down when the police sergeant turned up and knocked on the caravan door!"

Windows were broken, some beach huts were wrecked and general petty vandalism took place. Fighting took place including against the police, and a detective was hit over the head with a pick-axe handle. The Police felt somewhat overwhelmed by the 'invasion' and called for reinforcements from neighbouring Colchester, Harwich, Brightlingsea and Thorpe. 97 arrests were carried out before peace fell on the town.

The following day every national newspaper with the exception of The Times carried a cover story that over-sensationalised the events. 'Wild Ones Invade Seaside – 97 Arrests' (*Daily Mirror*), 'Day of Terror by Scooter Groups' (*Daily Telegraph*), 'Youngsters Beat Up Town – 97 Leather Jacket Arrests' (*Daily Express*).

There was an emergency meeting by the Clacton Hotel And Guest House Association. They anxiously discussed how to stop these invading hordes from destroying the resort's businesses. Great emphasis was placed on the loss of trade over that weekend. The fact that the weather had been cold and wet was never brought into account. The 'Wild Ones' were the only obvious reason for their troubles.

Clacton's police chief, Norman Wood stated that: "For some reason, Clacton is attracting more than its fair share of these young thugs. It seemed that many young people were just going crazy." Whilst Councillor A. Hawkesworth, Mayor of Romford (from where some of those involved in the weekend's disturbances hailed from added: "I cannot condone their hooliganism, but I can understand their boredom. There is a lack of amenities in our district."

Sympathy was lacking from most of the general public but Fred Wiley MP declared: "They are Britain's most deprived age group. They come from vast housing estates with far too few social amenities and are expected to spend their time in amusement arcades."

FIVE

At Clacton's Magistrates Court Thomas Holdcraft was prosecuting 12 youths between the ages of 15 and 20. He laid down the law and told them: "There are vast numbers of Mods and Rockers, whose views on pop music and things of that sort are well known, but who have no serious views on really worthwhile matters. They have inflated ideas about their own importance in society, which perhaps explains the nonchalant attitude they adopt. Their behaviour shows them to be persons who are immature, inexperienced and irresponsible, lacking in any regard for the law, for the safety and comfort of other persons, and the property of others, and for the most part they did not have the excuse that they were acting under the influence of an artificial stimulant, such as alcoholic drinks or purple hearts."

Willy Deasy: "I remember that we'd been to this bowling alley in Southend, Mokey put on his bowling shoes and just walked out with them, so he had the perfect size. I just picked mine up but when I tried them on outside I'd got the wrong size so I flogged them to Reggie Vincent, I think. After that, everybody had to have bowling shoes. We went back again and got rid of all of our old shoes, swapped them, then walked straight out. Johnny would always be out, and people would ask where he got things from, and he wouldn't tell them. We went to Clacton in them, and I think that at the next seaside event loads of people had started wearing them."

One direct result of the Clacton disturbances was the publication of a bill designed to stop the use of drug peddlers pushing purple hearts and pep pills. The penalty for anyone caught in illegal possession of these drugs was six months in jail or a £200 fine.

The papers had also, in the time before the next bank holiday, printed articles describing the two different factions, Mods and Rockers. Whilst there had been slight indifference between the two parties before the troubles, the media accentuated the opposition between the two groups, setting the stage for future conflicts.

Whitsun Bank Holiday, and this time Clacton could breath a sigh of relief as youths targeted Margate, Brighton and Bournemouth. This time though it seemed as if the trouble was specifically between the two-opposing youth cultures.

In an extract from *Generation X* (1964) by Charles Hamblett and Jane Deverson they spoke to John Braden, an 18-year-old mechanic from London:

"Yes, I am a Mod and I was at Margate. I'm not ashamed of it – I wasn't the only one. I joined in a few of the fights. It was a laugh. I haven't enjoyed myself so much in a long time. It was great – the beach was like a battlefield. It was like we were taking over the country.

"You want to hit back at all the old geezers who try to tell us what to do. We just want to show them we're not going to take it. It was like a battlefield. I felt great, part of something important instead of just being something they look down on because you haven't passed your GCEs.

"I know some old men were knocked down but none of them were hurt. They might've got a bit of a shock but they deserve it – they don't think about us, how we might feel.

"It was great being in the newspapers – sure. We love reading about ourselves. Who doesn't. Blinkin' film stars and debs delights and social climbers hire publicity men to get their bleedin' names in the papers. We punch our way in, cost-free."

In Margate, at the amusement park Dreamland there was trouble with about 100 youths until the police manage to entrap them in the car park. Other teenagers outside the gates had noticed, and managed to rip off the gates, setting the others free. Once again shops, pubs and cafés were wrecked along the way and fighting between the rival gangs continued along the seafront.

Meanwhile along the coast Brighton was having its own problems as an estimated 3,000 Mods and Rockers came in to town.

Willy Deasy : "We went to Brighton. We got the train down there. Billy Lampy got this kid to get us half price kids tickets. When the conductor came along asking for tickets, we all pretended to be a bit backward until he got fed up and left us alone. Half of Islington was there. I think that there was a nucleus of about ten of our mob. Then there were girls who came along and brought others along, maybe a brother, so by the time we got there, they may have been twenty of us."

It was in Brighton that fighting took place all over the beach between the warring parties, then spilled over into Marine Parade, Palace Pier and around by The Aquarium.

Willy Deasy: "We were wandering along, me, Mokey and Terry Charles. We thought we've got to get away from this, because it all started kicking off. We went and found this part where holidaymakers were just sat down, and you could look down on the beach below. These old people were just sat in their deck chairs having a nice time. I looked around and saw this gang of Rockers coming towards us and I just thought 'Oh fuckin' hell'. I looked at Johnny and Terry, then I asked these old ladies "Can I borrow your deckchair?" These Rockers were getting closer, but you could see all these Mods following them. You could see what was going to happen. Suddenly these Rockers just flew at us. We had to get these people out of their deck chairs quick, I do feel sorry for them. I just said, "Please get your arse out of there!" I literally pushed her out of it. I needed it because somebody was coming at me. So, I whacked him with the deckchair and he fell…and then another. Terry Charles came over and joined in. We saw the photos in the papers…that was us."

Willy Deasy, Johnny Moke & friends

There were also disturbances at Bournemouth too that weekend with fighting around the bus station and Winter Gardens concert hall.

Paul Barker and Dr Alan Little wrote an article for *New Society* entitled 'The Margate Offenders; A Survey.' The information was obtained by distributing a questionnaire to the 44 Mods and Rockers that appeared in court at Margate. They received only 34 completed questionnaires back.

The majority were teens and single. None charged were fathers, with the average age of those charged, being 18. Only two were over 21, and only four of the 44 charged in Margate had been at Clacton in March.

During Whitsun 1964, although there were 56 arrests in Bournemouth, the damage inflicted was £100, in Brighton the damage was estimated at £400 with 76 arrests. In Margate with 64 arrests, the damage was £250. This has to be compared with Clacton on the Easter, which had cost £513 in estimated damage with 97 arrests. The damage costs are hardly breath-taking.

Willy Deasy; "We didn't get arrested. We did all the interviews for the paper next morning. I think Mokey had the *Daily Mail* and I had *The Sketch*. We just gave them a load of bollocks and they bought us breakfast 'cos we never had any money. We just made it up as we went along. All the old boys didn't like us fighting the war on the beaches. They'd all come out of the army, having been at war for years. Everybody bowed down to them, got told what to do in their jobs, but we thought we'd do as we wanted to do and it changed things. Just think, Rockers could be running the world now. There'd be people wandering around with tattoos all over them. Come to think of it, I think we lost!"

Obviously, Willy and his firm had gone through the whole club period of evolving, but there were now people literally becoming Mods because the seaside battles appealed to them. The new breed of 1964 Mod was a diluted, violent, and sometimes dim-witted product that was unrecognisable to their sartorially-obsessed Modernist forefathers.

"Teenage rebellion?" snorted the psychologist. "All my eye. Our memories are short. Mods and Rockers are exactly the same nine-day wonder as the Teddy Boys. The best thing we can do is to take no notice of them." London *Evening Standard*, May 19th, 1964

On May 22nd, 1964, Friday's *Brighton and Hove Gazette* ran with the headline 'What Makes Them Tick?' it is then followed by a report by Allen Ansell, chairman of Brighton's Council of Youth and based on a survey carried out among some of the young people of Brighton. The results resulted in the following disclosures:

- Sixty-two per cent of Brighton's professed Mods who were interviewed took drugs.
- Forty-two per cent of Rockers interviewed are drug takers.
- Twenty-eight per cent of the Mod girls said that they had had sexual intercourse.
- Seventy-three per cent of boy Mods also admitted having had intercourse.
- Only twelve per cent of the Rocker girls, on the other hand, admitted having had intercourse.
- Sixty per cent of Rocker boys confessed to having had intercourse.

THIS IS WHAT A WELL-ARMED HOOLIGAN CARRIES THIS YEAR

WHAT is the well-armed Mod wearing and carrying for the holiday season?

Wardrobe-wise there is a lot of difference of course—the Mods perch elegantly on their scooters showing off their sophisticated suiting, the Rockers hunch deeper into their leather jackets and roar off on ton-up bikes.

But when it comes to acquiring an armoury the distinctions fade.

Magistrates at Brighton and Margate were given a list of weapons yesterday which included: a cricket bat, a golf club, beach pebbles, broken bottles, deckchairs, a hammer shaft weighted with lead, and knuckledusters made from coins wrapped in newspapers.

Allen Ansell, a 20-year-old assistant to a factory managing director, carried out the survey with his 17-year-old girlfriend. They had talked to youngsters aged between 14 and 21 in coffee bars, dance halls and in the street declaring "I have not set out to paint a pretty, or a bad, picture of the young people questioned but simply to give the facts about local youngsters.

The piece seemed to bear no link to the previous weeks disturbances in Brighton and was totally irrelevant, but it was good for yet more sensationalist headlines. Inside the same paper there is also a feature about setting up a vigilante force made up of the general public to curb further violence from Mods and Rockers. Supposedly this was the brainchild of 52-year-old George Winston, a local restaurateur.

"There are enough good boys in Brighton only too willing and keen to help their own town," he declared. "I have already spoken to many of them. They think it's a wonderful idea, and I bet every trader in Brighton would be willing to contribute."

He then stated that local cadet corps, youth clubs and boys organisations would be drafted in and paid a small fee to patrol the town. Issued with armbands, they could take on the might of any would be invader.

"These Mods and Rockers are just a lot of yellow bellies." he said angrily. "They are cowards. I saw thousands of them come swarming across the road in front of the new restaurant, pushing elderly women and children. Nobody mattered to them. Last year we had trouble with beatniks. I saw a crowd of them one night running naked from the beach across the road. But these riots are the worst Brighton has ever seen."

Luckily, the chairman of the Brighton Watch Committee Aid, Leonard Knowles poured cold water on the scheme, suggesting that if people really wanted to help they should join the special constabulary. "I appreciate most fully any sort of willingness, but this country does not tolerate private armies." said Mr Knowles. "If the idea was sanctioned, it would act as a provocation more than anything else," he continued.

On the same day as the article there were questions in Parliament, questions on radio and television. The constant mass media coverage led to a situation of deviancy amplification. The fact that these youths had chosen to play out their skirmishes in front of camera seemed to be an affront to the old order of retired colonels, ex-servicemen and the tourist- orientated tradesman who dominated the local councils for their specific area. Many couldn't understand the Mods especially. Whilst the Rockers had all the traits that the older generation detested; long hair, leather jackets, big boots and motorcycles. The Mods had confused them totally by being smartly dressed with short hair. They had seemed to invert the social values associated with being smartly dressed.

During the Margate disturbances the windows of the buffet at Margate Railway Station were broken. Mrs Stott the manageress was interviewed, and she told the papers. "The boy who started it was so good looking and nicely dressed; you wouldn't have thought he was a nasty type."

There was still one more Bank Holiday to come. This time though the police had the upper hand because they already knew that the meeting place was going to be Hastings in August.

69 police officer were on standby at Northolt Aerodrome waiting to hear if they were needed. When they got the call, they boarded an Argosy of RAF Transport Command. After a short flight, they landed at Lydd Airport where a bus took them to Hastings.

Donald Brown, the chief constable of Hastings Police, stated: "For some time now, we have been receiving reports – some direct from the public and some through police channels – that Hastings was to be the next place for the hooligans to visit. We made detailed plans to meet such an emergency. Arrested hooligans were to be taken straight to the town hall. We must use a show of force in order to nip any trouble in the bud."

Windows were broken, traffic was disrupted, holiday-makers were pelted with stones. When around 500 teenagers assembled in the town centre looking where next to strike. The police began to herd the crowd away from the town centre and kept them on the move. In temperatures of seventy degrees they marched them up a steep hill to the borough boundary, three miles from the town centre. The kids realised that even if they wanted to start trouble again, it was a long walk back,

"We intended to knock the trouble out of these kids." said one police officer. "And a six-mile walk was just the thing to do the trick!"

During the weekend there were 64 arrests for acts such as wilful damage and threatening behaviour. Many were fined and 16 youths were sent to detention centres. In all there had been around 300 police officers on duty and their operation had largely been a success.

"It's been a rotten time." stated one would-be rioter. "The coppers kept on at us. If we sat on the beach they made us walk along the promenade. And when we got to the prom, they made us go back to the beach!"

Over the summer months there was also trouble in the northern coastal resorts including Skegness and Great Yarmouth. The newspapers must surely take much of the responsibility for fanning the flames in the first place for their over-reporting of the incidents.

Even television would not miss out on such opportunities. The actor Michael Crawford could even be seen on the television as a mouthy, opinionated, Vespa-riding Mod, Byron, on the BBC1 comedy programme *Not So Much a Programme, More a Way of Life* which was screened between November '64 to April '65. It was this character that Richard Lester had noticed and auditioned Crawford for the role of Colin in the 1965 film *The Knack... and How to get it*.

Chris Covill, in his interview with Nik Cohn in 1967, would state: "Mods were mostly peace-loving, and they were alright with their clothes and their clubs and their pills. But a lot of what I'd call False Mods came along, just ordinary kids who weren't dedicated. They wanted to be cool but there was violence in them and they couldn't change. That's when the bother with the Rockers started. The Rockers didn't exist when Mod began. They started up just to make a war. There were souped-up Teds with motorbikes and leather jackets and they were sick, but I don't think there would have been any trouble if it hadn't been for these False Mods."

Much has been talked about the seaside battles of the Mods and Rockers of the late Sixties. Far less common, is the subject of Mod gangs of the period.

South London Mod Colin Walsh says: "I don't know how the gangs got together. It was just mates growing up in different areas. I can't remember exactly how it all got together but it wasn't copied from North London. We were in it during the early stages. I think there were two or three areas such as Mile End, North London and us in South London. I don't know what fashion they had in West London but I can't remember them having trendy fashions. Our hero locally was Barry Chapman. He was the first to dress in the new style. He looked the perfect Mod around '61 or '62. We went along to Carnaby Street but back then there were only two or three shops then which were Vince's, John Stephens and Donis. We also had a shop in the Old Kent Road called Lewin's, which was an old outfitters."

Willie Deasy: "Our biggest threat wasn't Rockers, it was the younger Mods, the next generation coming up. They were nothing but trouble. A girl I knew was having a party in the Nightingale Estate in Hackney. So, me, Terry Charles, Johnny Moke and a couple of others went along. Anyway, we got there and in came this bird's new boyfriend, Johnny Weedon. He said, 'what are you doing hanging around my bird?' He's with all his little firm and says, 'let's have a straightener.' So, we go outside. BAM, BAM, BAM. Then my mob dragged me away. Later that night we drove up the West End. We didn't go to The Scene Club because we knew they'd track us down there. So, a gay guy we knew was having an opening night for a new club called The Harlequin with free booze, so we went there. A couple of weeks later I bumped into a mate of mine, Jackie Ruby, and he said "Fuckin' hell Willie, lucky they didn't find you that night. They had guns. They raided The Scene Club, La Discotheque and a few more. They would have shot and killed you that night if they'd found you." That gay club saved my life."

Ian Hebditch: "Violence was seldom, if ever, directed at the general public, fights were usually between rival groups of Mods, like the fights we had with the blokes from Southampton, or between Mods and their traditional enemies, the Rockers. It was always a case of hit or be hit, although I will admit we used to bait the Rockers a bit, a favourite trick was for a few of us to ride out to one of

their cafes quietly. Then short-out the spark plugs on their bikes (very easy with a soft pencil), then rush in and shout abuse at them and ride off at speed. The look on their faces when their bikes wouldn't start!

"However, if a group of Rockers caught us on the road they would force us in the ditch, we couldn't do the same to them because they would always outrun us. A great crowd of Rockers once tried to break into The Birdcage, everyone stood shoulder to shoulder, even Rikki, who was at the front, we fought them off with broken up chairs and anything else we could lay our hands on. This gives an idea of the kind of *esprit de corps* which existed amongst us. All Mods no matter where they were from would pull together when faced with the Rockers.

"The inter-Mod fights were a bit different. The only ones I experienced were those between my home town, Portsmouth, and Southampton. It was expected as I've already said that if they came over to Portsmouth we would do them over, if we went over there they would do us. What usually happened was that one of us would get knuckled by Southampton blokes when he was passing through, then we'd all go over on a Friday night (this was the favourite night for this sort of expedition for a scrap). The Southampton crowd always went to the Mecca Pier Ballroom on Fridays. So we'd filter in, in ones and twos so as not to be too obvious. When we were all in there would be a massive brawl, no-one used to get hurt much, there were too many of us for that. The police would break it up, pinch a few blokes, usually from the "away side" then we'd all go home until the next time. Why we fought the Southampton lot I don't know, we didn't fight with Mods from any other town, perhaps it was because they were so close. Strangely enough I have talked to some of them, and they don't know why they fought with us either."

Colin Walsh: "It was all gangs back then. There was the 'Mile End' with Billy Curbishley, Dave Stanley, Kenny Skingle, and they'd go to the Poplar Civic. There was also Les Paul, Yankee and Peter Champ, and they'd use the Upper Cut and the Chez Don. North London had a fella called Johnny Doughnut. His mob used the Tottenham Royal and later Club Noreik. The Junction Boys were Latchmere/ Battersea and Clapham Junction. Their leader, if they had one, was a black guy called Coco. They were a right heavy firm. They were naughty. The Mile End were bad, Deptford mob were bad, as were the Elephant firm – but the Junction were worse. They'd be at The Lyceum, but they had their own clubs like the Bali Hai above Streatham Ice Rink and the Streatham Locarno. My mate, Johnny McDermot got 48 stitches in the Bali Hai simply because it was like postal, off the manor. It was their club. Let's get it straight, there was no Mods and Rockers stuff in London. You never even saw Rockers in London, and if you did it was because they were changing their spark plugs on their bikes by the kerb. It was all just postal, Mods against Mods. Even at Clacton, Mods used to fight each other, and my mate Danny was knifed there. Mile End and us was like West Ham versus Millwall football stuff, exactly the same. There wasn't enough Rockers to go around and fight. We outnumbered them about twenty-five to one. In '62 or '63 there was a riot in Leysdown, and there was one just before that in Dartford. That was wild. Mods versus Mods. Just bored silly, no Rockers. Two people I know called Mickey and Ray went to Prison. There was a club in Dartford called La Scala. Paul from our firm had been beaten up there the week before, so we got a big team together in motors, pulled in and got the Elephant mob, then went down there and smashed the gaff up. It was all Art Deco, and we smashed all the mirrors. It never opened again."

Don't think, for one moment, that men don't count down here in a girl's world: her choice could be his. For himself, though, he picks a suit that wears the Woolmark. And it counts.

'Paris Northfield' from the <u>SUMRIE</u> 'Golden Grade' range: a single-breasted glen check two-piece, hand tailored with a softly natural shoulder line. In pure new wool worsted: about 29 gns. This is the very best wool in the world: pure new wool that's been tested to international quality standards and wears the Woolmark to prove it. Look for the Woolmark whenever you buy clothes.

<u>When it matters, people wear pure new wool</u>: Wool that wears the Woolmark.

PURE NEW
wool

It wasn't just the boys who could be aggro. South London Mod, Tony Foley, remembers a group of girls in the north-west London district of Somers Town: "If you crossed over to the right side of Eversholt Street, you were trespassing. The narrow strip between Euston and St. Pancras Stations was Somers Town territory. One of north London's hardest firms, led by the Warrens, lived here.

"The kids from the council estate on the wrong side of the railway lines, the Mornington Crescent side, where a girl called Vicky grew up, mixed mainly with Somers Town kids, so most of the teenage girls went out with Somers Town boys. Not Vicky! She was too much trouble even for them!

"And so, she gravitated towards probably the only firm of girls on the scene in the early sixties. The Angel Firm. This exclusive bunch of working-class north London girls were hard as nails. They fought like boys; punching from the shoulder and trunk, kicking, kneeing, nutting, and without a peep, without so much as a high-pitched whistle. They were efficient, awesome, and frightening in action. They ruled the Lyceum and the Royal and caused panic wherever they showed up."

THE SMALL FACES

Decca Records

CHAPTER

SIX

1965 AND ONWARDS

"One day a friend of mine gave me a Spanish guitar he no longer wanted. So, I'm walking round in Manor Park with the guitar over my shoulder and Stevie Marriott and Ronnie Lane came over and said, 'Can you play that?' I told them I was getting rid of it and they said 'nah, learn to play it, we're forming a band.'"

STEVE DENCH

The year 1965 would see a rise in a more uniformed Mod look. By now, white groups such as The Who, The Spencer Davis Group and The Small Faces were getting regular pop chart hits and gaining a mass appeal.

Whilst The Who had been influenced by their early manager, Peter Meaden, to become Mods, The Small Faces had come from the street.

Steve Dench recalls: "When I was 16 I got to know Steve Marriott who, back then, lived in Manor Park. Top of my road was Lawrence Avenue and you crossed over to some new sort of maisonettes and Steve was up there. I met him through some other mates and he was just Steve Marriott the kid that lived 'up there'. He had done a bit of acting and he seemed like a nice enough kid and I hung around with for a little while. Then one day a friend of mine gave me a Spanish guitar that he no longer wanted and asked me to get rid of it. So, I'm walking round in Manor Park with the guitar over my shoulder and Stevie Marriott and Ronnie Lane came over and said, "Can you play that?"

"I told them I was getting rid of it and they said "nah, learn to play it, we're forming a band." They then told me about a little back alley pub, near another pub called The Rose and Crown over in Ilford and they told me a time to go there, and said they were always in there. So, I went over and noticed one of my friends' brothers was in there, a guy called Alan Elliot, who played the piano in a sort of boogie woogie style, like Jools Holland. Anyway, he wasn't wanted. I must have seen at least four of the very early gigs they played. Steve kept saying to me, you've got to learn to play that guitar, cos you are the same age as us, virtually the same haircut and the same height! But it never happened.

"I then went to work in a car showroom and I was working there one day when this limousine pulls up and the window comes down and its Stevie Marriott. He calls me over and says "we've made it. We're on *Ready Steady Go!* and here you are there, here's two tickets." Cathy McGowan and all that. That was unbelievable. I had seen it on TV and never imagined I'd be there. It was packed. That night, I think The Supremes were there, and Long John Baldry who I had already seen in and around Soho.

"Obviously, we began to lose touch as his career moved on. A lot of people said he was loud. I don't think he was loud, he was just confident; a very confident guy.... All that acting experience I think made him the perfect front man."

CHAPTER

In 1964, America had witnessed the start of the 'British Invasion' with The Beatles and The Dave Clark Five leading the way for other British bands. What was crazy, especially in the case of The Beatles, is that, in a way the Brits were selling the Americans back their own music. America just didn't see it because most of the early R&B groups that the four boys from Liverpool were quoting, happened to be black. When the Beatles first went to America they told everyone they wanted to see Muddy Waters and Bo Diddley; one reporter asked: 'Muddy Waters... Where's that?' Paul McCartney laughed and said: "Don't you know who your own famous people are here?" John Lee Hooker understood, when he said: "it may seem corny to you, but this is true: the groups from England really started the blues rolling and getting bigger among the kids – the White kids. At one time, fifteen years back, the blues was just among the blacks – the old Black people. And this uprise started in England, by The Beatles, Animals, Rolling Stones, it started everybody to dig the blues"

Almost as if in retaliation, America launched its biggest ever campaign to bring the American sound back in to the British charts at the end of March 1965. Top artist such as The Supremes, The Marvelettes, Smokey Robinson and the Miracles, The Temptations, Martha Reeves and the Vandellas and Stevie Wonder flew over to take part in a 21-date mammoth package tour that started at the Astoria, Finsbury Park, London and ended at the Guildhall Portsmouth taking in both southern and northern cities, plus Wales and Scotland along the way. As it turned out The Temptations appeared on 'The Sounds of Motown' a *Ready Steady Go!* Special. Poor advance ticket sails led to Georgie Fame and the Blue Flames being added to the bill to entice young British fans in.

Britain had already seen hits in the charts by The
Supremes, Martha Reeves, Marvin Gaye and ex-Motown
singer Mary Wells, but not that much longer before,
British record companies didn't want to know anything
about the Tamla-Motown label. The Miracles had managed
to get a couple of singles out on London, and there were
releases by Barrett Strong, and Marv Johnson, but the
contact expired, and wasn't renewed. Motown executives
then proceeded to hawk around the songs until finally
they did a deal with the Fontana label. Singles were issued
by The Marvelettes, The Miracles and Eddie Holland
but never sold in big numbers. Except for the DJ's and
collectors who were trying to lay their hands on anything
Tamla related.

The Tamla contract with Fontana expired, and once
again not one British record company showed interest in
continuing Tamla releases. Another Tamla label, Motown
was set up, named after Detroit known as the Motor-town.
Then another, Gordy, named after Tamla boss Berry Gordy.
But still no luck in issuing them in Britain. In Summer
1962, there was finally a big break through when the
Oriole label began to release lots of singles and LP's. Once
that contract expired. There was lots of interest and the
bidding for it was high. Eventually, EMI's Stateside label
won and released several Tamla tunes.

By 1965 there was the Tamla-Motown label which would
release singles, EP's and albums galore. The first singles
were known as the 500 series with The Supremes 'Stop In
The Name Of Love' kicking off the series as number 501.

Boutiques continued to boom. The tendency was for
even quicker fashion changes, and this meant cheaper, but
often less well-made clothes.

For girls, the 'dolly' look was out. The trend had begun for simple lines in plain fabrics. Pinafore dresses with zips three-quarters of the way down the front, and zipped hip pockets on A-line skirts. Corduroy was an in material all year, and as the year progressed the width of the cord got wider.

The summer was pretty poor weather-wise with plenty of rain, so shiny vinyl rainwear in either black and white, light blue, or bright red colours such as yellow or red were fashionable.

The mini skirt was seen on the streets, although Cathy McGowan, compere of *Ready, Steady Go!* introduced a range of dresses with mid-thigh- length skirts. Mary Quant, meanwhile, made A-line hipster skirts way above the knee.

T-strap shoes and sandals were a trend that lasted the whole year.

For boys, peaked caps as worn by Donovan and John Lennon proved popular, as did US cavalry hats.

A more casual look of T-shirts proved popular too. The Who had popularised 'op art' for boys (and girls) in the form of appliqued shapes such as bullseyes. The Ricky Tick in Windsor were printing their own T-shirts with slogans on. Amongst the designs there was one with Prime Minister Harold Wilson's cartoon face with 'I Love Harold' in a heart, one had Batman on it with 'I'm A Good Guy' written above and even one with a cartoon of Hitler's face and the words 'It Was Either This Or A Milkround',

There was a trend for less tight trousers, but practically all remained hipsters. Jackets got a much more military-style look, as they were longer, with patch or button=down pockets and epaulettes: many were double-breasted and belted. Shirts went the same way with pocket flaps and epaulettes appearing on them too. Two-tone shirts, with dark green front and back, with light green sleeves, collar and cuffs became popular. Even plain shirts with floral collar and cuffs, or that look reversed. Plain shirts were worn with floral ties and matching handkerchiefs. Check shirts were popular still but had been superseded by the floral look. Pure silk knitted ties for the less flamboyant dressers.

Herringbone tweed was very desirable, and Tattersall check was made into jackets and three-quarter length coats. During the summer, Madras cotton jackets, as worn by The Small Faces, proved very popular.

Boots went out altogether, and shoes and moccasins in lightweight suede, mock croc and elephant sold well. Toes were squarer, whilst the leather was either, usually, punched and embossed, not shiny and smooth.

Hair was worn longer, the French crop look was long gone, and the new styles could be seen on bands such as The Action and The Small Faces.

By the later part of the Sixties some of the plusher clubs gained in popularity. These were the venues that drew in people from the music world, hustlers, general punters and stars from the world of entertainment. There was The Scotch of St James, which was hidden in Mason's Yard, SW1, Blaises in Queensgate, The Cromwellian on the Cromwell Road and the Bag O'Nails near Carnaby Street.

One of the most popular of these clubs was The Speakeasy at 48 Margaret Street, just off Oxford Street. The club was owned by David Shamoon, an Iraqi-born entrepreneur, along with Blaises and The Revolution Club, and managed by Roy Flynn. Opened in December 1966, it soon established itself as the late-night meeting place for people involved in the music industry. Entrance came via a mirrored door in a wardrobe. The cash desk was a coffin.

A visually striking feature was the huge painting of Al Capone by Barry Fantoni that hung by the bar. Open seven nights a week from 10pm – 4am, membership was four guineas and admission nightly was 10s. Live acts playing there included Ben E.King and Mary Wells.

The Bag O'Nails opened in 1965 at 9, Kingly Court. Yet again, this was another popular club for musicians to meet. Regulars included members of the Stones, The Beatles, The Who, The Animals, plus Georgie Fame and Zoot Money. Membership was three guineas and nightly admission ranged from 7s 6d to 12s 6d depending on the night of the week. The newly formed Jimi Hendrix Experience had held a press concert and gig here, In 1967, Rik Gunnell took over management when the Flamingo closed that year.

CHAPTER
SEVEN

THE ARRIVAL OF STAX IN THE UK AND THE DEATH OF OTIS

"I was walking over Duke Street bridge in Reading, there was a small newsagent just over the other side, a placard outside read 'Otis Redding killed in plane crash' I went into shock, bought a paper and went into The Star, opposite. Everyone was in a state of disbelief. I remember I got very drunk."

TONY EDWARDS

J ust before Hippies and white pop banged nails into Mod's coffin, there was one last blast of black music from the states.

When Steve Marriott of the Small Faces was interviewed in *Melody Maker* in February '66 he told them 'We're still playing roughly the same old stuff but we relive it. It's the Booker T kick really. He plays twelve bar numbers, but they are fantastically hip sounds. We dig Booker T & The MG's and the guitarist Steve Cropper is the guv'nor.'

By September that year, the UK audiences would really get to know Stax, when on Friday September 16th, Rediffusion recorded an RSG Otis special. Otis looked great, sporting a four-button double breasted jacket. His performance pulsated as he ran through 'Satisfaction', 'My Girl' and 'Respect'. Then homegrown guests Eric Burdon and Chris Farlowe added a dash of blue eyed soul with renditions of 'Hold On I'm Coming' and This Is A Man's World'. Otis then came back for 'Pain In My Heart' and amazing up-tempo versions of 'I Can't Turn You Loose' and 'Shake' joined by Eric, Chris and the RSG dancers, including Sandy Sargent. Also joining them on the set are hordes of dancing crop haired kids, that give a little glimpse of the future look of Skinheads.

The following year, the Stax label from Memphis, Tennessee had decided to follow on from the Motown tour by making their own invasion of Europe. At the time, whilst Otis Redding recorded with the usual MG'S plus Isaac Hayes, he travelled with his own band which often ranged between 12 to 14 members. On this trip to England though, to reduce costs, he brought nine with him including drums, bass, guitar and six on horns. The Mar-Keys were a three horn section that replaced the usual glamorous girl backing singers.

For most of the Stax stars, the trip to Europe was a dream come true. In truth, many of them had never even left the

ARTHUR HOWES in association
with PHIL WALDEN and STAX RECORDS present

The Otis Redding Show

with

OTIS REDDING
ARTHUR CONLEY
SAM and DAVE
EDDIE FLOYD
BOOKER T. and the M.G.'s
THE MAR-KEYS

compere
EMPEROR ROSCO

March 17th
Astoria, Finsbury Park Only
CARLA THOMAS

March,	17th	Astoria, Finsbury Park
,,	23rd	Palace, Manchester
,,	26th	Empire, Liverpool
,,	27th	Fairfield Hall, Croydon
,,	28th	Colston Hall, Bristol
April,	2nd	Birmingham Theatre

southern states. In America they had usually been forced into booking a hotel on the outskirts of wherever they were performing just so they could stay together as big cities usually had coloured separation.

Otis then surprised *Melody Maker* fans by stating "Yes I like Dylan, he's my favourite singer now. I love The Rolling Stones as well."

On a grey Monday morning, March 13th 1967 Booker T & the MG's, Carla Thomas, Eddie Floyd, the three Mar-Keys, Arthur Conley and Dave of Sam & Dave arrived at Heathrow airport. A fleet of Bentley limousines had been sent to escort them to their hotel by none other than the Beatles. Sam Moore arrived later that evening. Otis had already landed on Saturday 11th. The whole feeling of everybody is one of pure excitement. Carla Thomas will only be with the tour a short while as she had a previous engagement in Chicago due to singing at a civil rights movement benefit with Harry Belafonte.

It's Tuesday March 14th 1967, two young girls, Janet Martin and Judy Webb, who run the 'Uptightan'Outasight'- the Atlantic label fan club, are excited. The Polydor building at 17 -19 Stratford Place, London W.1 is expecting visitors. Nobody else in the offices seems particularly bothered. After all Jimmy Hendrix is a regular sight here as are Cream, The Who and a whole host of big names from the world of pop.

One by one the visitors arrive. Booker T & the MG's, Carla Thomas, The Mar-Keys, Arthur Conley, Eddie Floyd, Sam & Dave and the big guy Otis Redding. The American visitors are here to use the Polydor Records studio to rehearse for the big tour that starts on Friday at the Astoria in Finsbury Park.

The studio is sound proofed but actually you can still hear the music from outside. As soon as the opening bars to 'Green Onions' begins, the clattering of typewriters stop. Important documents are suddenly not being filed to their destinations as staff members seek out the most amazing noise coming from the little control room. Booker T, the epitome of cool, his fingers producing the most amazing sounds from the keyboard. Suddenly the air is filled with this loud twanging noise as Steve Cropper's guitar springs to life. All the time Al Jackson keeps the beat going, perfect drumming, timing impeccable. Donald 'Duck' Dunn is sat in the corner on a stool making chords sound like rolling distant thunder. This is all quite amazing as none of the artists present have played this material since it has been recorded and none of it was written down.

Nobody wants to leave the room, but as deadlines beckon some have to....and are instantly replaced by new bodies. By now Wayne, Joe and Andrew, The Mar-Keys captivate the audience with 'Philly Dog' and 'Last Night'. All through this Arthur Conley has been grooving around to the sounds but now he grabs the microphone and asks the million dollar question 'Do you like good music....that sweet soul music?' The bouncing bundle of energy was then replaced by Eddie Floyd. Eddie just sat relaxing on the stool roaring out the words to 'Knock On Wood' before going into a rather unexpected cover of 'If I Had A Hammer'.

Carla Thomas is next up and sends the whole studio audience into a saddened state as she gives her own mournful but beautiful take on Paul McCartney's 'Yesterday'. Before you can catch your breath Sam and Dave have their chance but decline the microphone and choose to sing naturally. Dave lying on the floor whilst Sam is on a stool. Nobody at this point have any idea of the sheer dancing capability of this duo that will later be witnessed when the tour finally begins.

Three hours have passed, and boy the temperature is getting hot! The Coke machine is emptied to quench the searing thirst. As the clock strike 6.30pm Otis Redding, the main man, is vocally holding court. Hollering out and demanding

'R-E-S-P-E-C-T'. It is now 7pm and a band who have booked the studio to record find the Stax gang and most of Polydor's staff including the managing director huddled around a great giant of a man telling everybody that he can't get no satisfaction. The band don't mind.... they just want to stay and witness this musical goldmine. People start calling their family and friends explaining they will be late home. Dinner dates are cancelled, evening plans altered, as nobody wants to leave. Al Jackson, who has been pounding the drums throughout, needs a break. The Coke machine that had been topped up is emptied once more. Booker T is sat on the floor playing Cropper's guitar going through some new material as Otis lends himself vocally. The evening draws to an end as Otis has ploughed through 'My Girl', 'Daytripper' and 'Try A Little Tenderness'. It is now ten past nine, everybody files out of the room knowing that the Stax tour will be a roaring success. It is time to go and head off to The Speakeasy for a night out.

Judy Head:"The rehearsals were in Polydor studios on the 3rd floor in Stratford Place. Yes, the Speakeasy gig was press reception, but I really don't remember if the Bag O'Nails was a public gig. We spent half a day in particular going to Buckingham Palace, Westminster Abbey/Big Ben and Houses of Parliament. I believe they made a separate trip to Windsor and Tower of London, but I didn't go that time. I think some of the guys went to Carnaby Street. Some of the less we'll known faces did find their way around London after rehearsals bearing in mind only a few were instantly recognisable then!! It wasn't only the sights they were seeking, some with more luck than others - but that's another story!!!"

The following day, after a relaxing day sightseeing around London. The members of the 'Hit The Road Stax' tour arrived at the Speakeasy Club in Margaret Street for a reception party laid on to welcome them. Frank Fenter from Atlantic Records and Arthur Howes, the co-promoter of the tour, had arranged it.

Jan and Judy had arrived at 6.30 and stood behind the coffin that is used as a reception desk to greet the guests as they entered. The Who arrived, followed by Cliff Bennett, Eric Burdon and Alan Price amongst many of the famous faces from the world of entertainment. Then of course were the DJ's, BBC producers, press people and the people from the music industry.

Booker T, Steve, Al and Duck are sitting with the Mar-Keys on a big round table chatting and sipping their drinks. Conley and Floyd are seated too, digging the sounds being spun. Sam and Dave are checking out the club, whilst Carla has been given a daffodil and is proudly showing it off. Otis is stood chatting to his manager Phil Walden. All of them are nervous and not really sure what to expect from this critical crowd.

Around 7.30pm 'Le President Rosko' is introduced and on he walks. Velvet jacket, frilly shirt and looking like a proper host. 'Ladies and Gentlemen.....Booker T and the MG'S!'. Booker stands up from the table, walks to the Hammond, bows to the audience and soon the opening bars to 'Green Onions' is wafting around the room as one by one the other band members are introduced. The band captivate everybody and before they can catch their breath Rosko is back introducing The Mar- Keys. 'Last Night' has got the whole place funky and the applause seems never ending. Carla Thomas is then introduced and enters the stage with a green sequined jump suit. Carla began with 'Baby' and followed it up with 'Something Good'. Sharon Tandy is sat in the front row and knows it is her job to replace Carla later in the tour as she has to return to the states to continue her studies. Rosko introduces 'Arthur Conley' who leaps onto the stage and is straight into 'Sweet Soul Music'

Pete Townshend of The Who is clapping wildly, as is just about everybody in the room. Eddie Floyd is centre of attention now and he gets everybody to put their arms in the air and clap along to 'Knock on Wood'. By now it's cooking, and Britain is about to witness for the first time Sam and Dave's dance routines. They had brought with them a reputation. The rumour was that they were like two James Brown's....only better! 'Hold On I'm Coming!' screams through the air, with 'You Don't Know' hot on its heels. They attempt to leave the stage, but the audience won't let them. 'I Take What I Want' fills the air. Sweat pours down their faces and the jackets have to come off. They close with their dance routine. As they go to leave the stage, the audience is still begging for more, so they come back on stage and reprise 'Hold On'. It seems that it will be impossible to follow such a sensational act.

The stage is suddenly platform to the giant frame filling the stage as he stomped back and forth singing his take on 'Daytripper'. Redding gave a performance worthy enough to show why he was topping the bill and culminated in 'Try A Little Tenderness'. Otis had proved he had soul and at least five encores showed he was the king.

After the performance all the entourage headed off for dinner at a place called 'Stones' where roast beef and Yorkshire pudding was a speciality.

The tour starts on March 17th at the Astoria, Finsbury Park, and is due to return home on April 9th taking in Britain, Paris, Stockholm, Copenhagen and Oslo.

The Uppercut, March 18th, 1967: The Uppercut was at the time one of the largest clubs in London. Situated in Forest Gate Centre, Woodgrange Road, E7. The club was open most nights between 7.30 until 11.30 and general admission was six shillings. It could easily hold 1,500 people in comfort and had a licensed bar for members. It had opened around Christmas time 1966. Brian Tilney the manager told *New Musical Express* in April '66 that 'most of his customers are aged between 15

and 20'. Friday nights would feature cabaret acts and big bands such as Eric Winstone and Denny Holland. Sunday nights was dedicated to new bands, competitions and dancers on stage.

On entrance, punters were greeted by a huge life-size painting of Billy Walker facing you in the ring. Sadly this was stolen not long after the club had opened. There was a room decorated with boxing posters that teenagers could relax in, full of pinball machines and a table top football game. The snack bar boasted a large hole in the wall so that a few hungry patrons could still watch the live acts on stage.

The audience mainly made up of young white Mods found it fantastic to mix shoulders with young black American GI's. When Booker T and the MG's finally hit the stage to 'Red Beans And Rice', many are unsure of the authenticity of the group, believing the two white members, Steve Cropper and Donald 'Duck' Dunn to be substitutes for black originals. Up until this point most people who had bought the single had no idea what the band actually looked like as their picture sleeve EP's and LP's had never featured a photo of the band. At the time Stax was used to racial tension in the states so made sure their products never featured the artists, but usually women (Otis Blue) or even vegetables! (Green Onions). The band were equally shocked with their reception finding an atmosphere of total non-prejudice.

Sam and Dave hit the stage wearing pastel coloured suits that will soon be showing off huge sweat stains as they plough through their dynamic set of 'You Don't Know Like I Know', 'Said I wasn't Gonna Tell Nobody', Hold On, I'm Coming', 'You Got Me Hummin', 'When Something Is Wrong With My Baby' and 'Soothe Me'.

Rosko then enters the stage and declares "the Ambassador is here". He then spells out his name in letters. Otis comes on and immediately goes into 'Respect'. 'I Can't Turn You

Loose' follows, then 'I've Been Loving You Too Long', during which he ad libs 'that much too long' and measures it out on his arms. Then it's 'My Girl', 'Shake', 'Satisfaction', 'Fa Fa Fa', 'These Arms Of Mine', 'Daytripper' and ends with 'Try A Little Tenderness' with Otis bellowing "Sock it to 'em, sock it to 'em!"

The audience left, dazzled and sweaty.

The tour continues: Leeds, Manchester, Liverpool. Rosko accompanies them on the tour bus. Sam and Dave argue a lot, others spend their time writing songs. It is just a normal bus, there is no room to stretch out, and the bus doesn't have toilet facilities.

Along the route, the entourage think they are being ripped off with the small food portions compared to those they receive in America at truck stops.

Croydon, Bristol, Birmingham, Cardiff and Leicester.

At Glasgow Locarno, Otis is pulled into the audience and gets rescued by security. Security have it tough as American GI's are having fights with tough locals.

In Europe, at the Paris, Olympia gig, the owner has to stop the show because the balconies are moving too much.

They fly back to two final shows held at the Hammersmith Odeon. Then fly home to America the next day. None of the bands had ever received the responses from an audience like they had just witnessed throughout Europe.

Sadly, the year would not end well for Otis Redding.

On Saturday December 9th, 1967, Redding was eager to get back to work after a three-month break after suffering from throat polyps. As the first stop of his Winter tour the band were scheduled to appear on the locally produced television show 'Upbeat' at WEWS studios at 30th and Euclid Avenue. The show was rehearsed in the morning from around 9am to 12 noon. After a break for lunch the show would then be recorded from around 1.30 to be broadcast at 5pm later that evening.

Otis apparently turning up an hour late, blaming the delay on electrical problems with his plane.

The band dressed all in yellow, whilst Otis himself chose a black shirt, and dark trousers perform 'Respect'. Host Don Webster then interviewed Otis before the show closed with Redding being joined by Detroit soul shouter Mitch Ryder performing 'Knock On Wood' until the credits appear.

Otis and the group had performed three concerts (8pm, 10.30 and 1am) at Leo's Casino in Cleveland the night before. The 700-seater club was owned by Leo Frank and was based at 75th and Euclid. The band were then flying to an engagement at The Factory in Madison when the crash occurred.

The Factory was located just off the intersection of State and Gorham Streets, It was advertised in the Wisconsin State Journal on Friday Dec 8th 1967 and described Redding as 'Redding whose popular music experts say 'dishes up a plateful of soul'.

The show was presented by Kaleidoscope Inc. who had already presented shows in Madison by Junior Wells and Paul Butterfield. Concert planner Ken Adamany of Last Coast productions paid William Barr to design the poster. Barr would produce 100 posters and based his design on the theme of 'Try A Little Tenderness'.

The support band for the Factory gig was the chillingly prophetic 'Grim Reapers' from Rockford, Illinois.

Despite adverse weather conditions, Otis famed for being both conscientious as well as keen on earning money was determined to fulfil his contractual obligations. They took off in foggy conditions. Whilst attempting an instrument landing, the aircraft lost power and plunged into the icy waters of Lake Monoma at 3.28 pm. Otis along with his pilot Richard Fraser and four members of the Bar-Kays with exception of Ben Cauley who was aboard the plane and was the only survivor, were killed. Reasons for the crash remain a mystery.

Two days later a telegram was sent from England:

WESTON UNION TELEGRAM
EST 11.42 AM   DEC 11 67
PHIL WALDEN
533 COTTON AVE MACON GA
DEEPLY MOVED BY THE TRAGIC NEWS OF AIR
DISASTER STOP ON BEHALF OF HIS THOUSANDS OF
FANS IN ENGLAND AND EUROPE
PLEASE ACCEPT OUR SINCEREST CONDOLENCES
STOP HE CAN NEVER BE REPLACED AND
HIS MEMORY WILL LIVE ON ALWAYS
JANET MARTIN AND JUDY WEBB

Redding's body was recovered from the lake late on Monday night and flown back to Macon, Georgia on Tuesday. Arrangements were made for his body to lie in state from 7.00 to 11.30am Monday, December 18th at The City Auditorium in Macon. A public funeral was set for noon the same day, followed by burial at his ranch outside of Macon.

Over four and a half thousand mourners crammed themselves into the City Auditorium in Macon, Georgia to pay their respects to Redding. The venue absolutely over spilling as it is designed for 3,000 seated. It started to fill at least three hours before the brief fifty-minute service. Eulogies delivered by Jerry Wexler, vice president of Atlantic Records; the Honourable Ronnie Thompson, Mayor of Macon and the Rev. C.J. Andrews, pastor, Vineville Baptist Church.

Wexler broke down as he described Redding as a 'human prince... whose performances were original and powerful'.

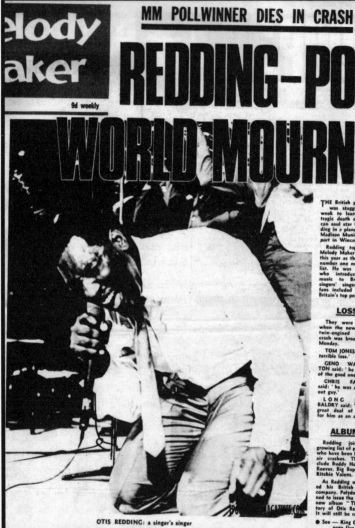

MM POLLWINNER DIES IN CRASH

elody aker

9d weekly

REDDING — POP WORLD MOURNS

THE British pop world was staggered this week to learn of the tragic death of American soul star Otis Redding in a plane crash at Madison Municipal Airport in Wisconsin.

Redding topped the Melody Maker Pop Poll this year as the world's number one male vocalist. He was the man who introduced soul music to Britain, a singers' singer whose fans included many of Britain's top performers.

LOSS

They were shocked when the news of the twin-engined plane crash was broadcast on Monday.

TOM JONES said: 'a terrible loss.'

GENO WASHINGTON said: ' he was one of the good ones.'

CHRIS FARLOWE said: ' he was a knock-out guy.'

LONG JOHN BALDRY said: ' I had a great deal of respect for him as an artist.'

ALBUM

Redding joins the growing list of pop stars who have been killed in air crashes. They include Buddy Holly, Jim Reeves, Big Bopper and Ritchie Valens.

As Redding was killed his British record company, Polydor, planned to issue the singer's new album "The History of Otis Redding." It will still be released.

● See — King Of Soul, page five

OTIS REDDING: a singer's singer

Thompson vowed that Macon would never forget Otis and described him as 'Macon's Ambassador of Goodwill'. The Rev Andrews said: 'Redding has been looking to live, but expecting to die'

Johnnie Taylor and Joe Simon sang hymns during the service and joined Joe Tex as pallbearers after the rites.

People attending included James Brown, Jamo Thomas, Don Covay, Gene Chandler, Mabel John, Eddie Purrell, Sam and Dave, Carla Thomas, Johnny Williams, Sugar Pie Desanto, Wilson Pickett, Percy Sledge, Rufus Thomas and others.

His 300-acre ranch at nearby Round Oak, Georgia remained his home, as many of his other showbiz buddies fled the south for seemingly warmer racial climates in the North. Most people from the mid-Georgia city, over 25, never having even heard of him.

Reading Mod, Tony Edwards, remembers:" I was walking over Duke Street bridge, there was a small newsagent just over the other side, a placard outside read "Otis Redding killed in plane crash" I went into shock, bought a paper and went into The Star, opposite. Everyone was in a state of disbelief; how could it be. A lot of very upset people that day, seem to remember I got very drunk, we all did. So talented, so young, so much more he would have achieved, a tragic loss!"

London Mod, Mickey Modern: "Probably a couple of days after Otis actually died, I was up top on a bus coming back from the west end, when I spotted a news stand below at The Elephant & Castle... the headline read Otis Redding Dead! That's how I found out... these days, one would find out in an instant online."

To some Mods, the death of Otis was also seen as the death of soul music. Whilst there were still fantastic sounds coming from black America. Some chose to hang up their sharp threads and embrace the sounds coming from America's west coast. The drugs had changed too, uppers and speed were replaced by cannabis and LSD.

CHAPTER
EIGHT

THE SEVENTIES AND NEW BEGINNINGS FROM THE DEATH OF MOD

"You'd be looking through the Quadrophenia booklet thinking 'this is great, this is great, what the fuck!'. I thought I was on my own I thought I'm a Who fan, I'm a Quadrophenia devotee. No-one else gets this. Everyone else is listening to KC and the Sunshine Band, Queen and Brotherhood of Man."

BUDDY ASCOTT

B y the end of the decade, Mods were all but forgotten about in England's capital. Short hair was frowned upon, and as men's faces got hairier, lapels on jackets and bottoms of trousers got wider, and music got heavier.

Meanwhile, in the North of England, there were still small remnants of the Mod dream to be found.

Throughout the heyday of Mod, places such as the Twisted Wheel in Manchester, The Esquire and King Mojo in Sheffield, the Nite Owl in Leicester and the Dungeon and the Beachcomber in Nottingham had very established Mod scenes. This was partly due to the fact that they had Roger Eagle (Manchester) and Peter Strinfellow (Sheffield) influencing some of the kids music choices.

However, by December 1967 the Mojo was no more.

The Twisted Wheel in Manchester had relocated from its original venue at Brazennose Street to another site in the city centre, at Whitworth Street. DJ Roger Eagle was long gone too. He'd started out attracting the local youths by playing the likes of 'Shake Dancer' by Little Walter and 'Don't Start Me Talkin' by Sonny Boy Williamson. By the time Eagle left in '66, he was bored of DJ'ing to kids demanding fast soul numbers, as their drug intake of amphetamines necessitated a different rhythm. Although, Roger's tastes had moved on too, the last time he dropped the needle on a record at 'The Wheel' it was Dyke and The Blazers 'Funky Broadway'.

The Twisted Wheel legacy continued though as DJ's like Paul Davis, Brian Rae, Brian '45' Phillips, Phil Saxe and Les Cokell continued to spread the black music gospel. Tunes such as 'Girls Are Out To Get You' by The Fascinations, 'What's Wrong With Me Baby' by The Invitations or Bobby Hebb's 'Love, Love, Love' filled the floor.

But other places came along as fast as the tunes. As the years moved on, new venues became the 'in' places to be.

Maybe you'd be at the Blackpool Mecca grooving to 'Competition Ain't Nothin' by Carl Carlton or Sandi Sheldon's 'You're Gonna' Make Me Love You', or the Catacombs in Wolverhampton to 'One Wonderful Moment' by The Shakers, or The Torch, Tunstall, Stoke On Trent to 'Wanting You' by April Stevens, maybe the Wigan Casino or Va Va's in Bolton to 'Stranger In My Arms' by Lynn Randell or Gloria Jones 'Tainted Love'. Then back to the Mecca in Blackpool for 'Double Cookin' by the Checkerboard Squares or 'Seven Day Lover' by James Fountain.

Old Sixties soul swapped hands for big money on labels such as Shrine, Mirwood and Golden World.

Lesser known clubs such as the String O'Beads in Bradford, The New Broken Wheel in Retford or the Bin Lid Club in Dewsbury enticed kids away from mainstream pop music.

The association to any kind of Mod legacy being that some kids still had scooters and belonged to scooter clubs, the tracking down of records that had to be American, black or rare, but preferably all three, and lastly the culture of drugs to keep you dancing all night. What had been lost though, was the worship of clothes. And in the world of Mod, that is a big deal.

By 1976, Kids up north involved in what had been termed

the 'Northern Soul' scene were shaking their arses at the Blackpool Mecca, Wigan Casino or The Winter Gardens at Cleethorpes to Lou Pride's 'I'm Comun' Home In The Mornun', Paul Humphrey's 'Cochise' or maybe 'So Is The Sun' by the World Column.

The pop charts in Britain were dross at this point. 'Save Your Kisses For Me' by Brotherhood of Man, Showaddywaddy 'Under The Moon Of Love'.... then there was Abba, Demis Rououssos, Silk, Leo Sayer and The Wurzels. But not everybody was listening to them, some were investigating old tunes.

Mick Talbot: "Between the ages of 17 and 20, I worked in the city at a shipping agent. I was basically a junior gofer in the late Seventies. Whilst there, in an open plan office of 10 people, it was noticed that me and this bloke called Barry, used to go down the record shop in our lunchtimes. I used to buy oldies, and a few of the older lot in the office, I'm talking about me being 17 and they're 38, which was about a 100 to me in those days, would say things like "I've got a Who album at home," So he brought me in an original copy of The Who's 'My Generation' and said "You can have it if you like, I never play it." Then someone else pipes up "Do you like all that Moddy stuff?" and he brings me in the first Small Faces albums. They're giving them away, but they're fascinated by someone not from that world, and its part of their youth, and they think that they're locking in to something from another generation. It's really sweet. Y'know, it's really nice. It's amazing how these things cascade. OK, The Who and the Small Faces were quite mainstream but the next thing I know this bloke's going "Have you heard of someone called Doris Troy?" Then, you're getting really deep."

If you were a Who fan, that looked longingly at their 1973 album *Quadrophenia* and wondered about the old days of the Sixties Mods, there wasn't a lot on offer.

Buddy Ascott: "By 1976 everybody is wearing flares, everybody has long hair. You can't find the clothes you want anywhere. You might as well live in Outer Mongolia, it was a cultural desert. When you at how The Who looked in the *Quadrophenia* booklet, that is one anachronism! You'd be looking through the booklet thinking 'this is great, this is great, what the fuck!'. I thought I was on my own I thought I'm a Who fan, I'm a *Quadrophenia* devotee. No-one else gets this. Everyone else is listening to KC and the Sunshine Band, Queen and Brotherhood of Man. I felt terribly isolated, which fitted in with my psyche of the time, a highly strung 16-year-old."

Mick Talbot: "Even though my dad was a modern jazz man, he used to work with a couple of geezers who DJ'd. So he said to me. "So, you're into rhythm and blues and soul eh? Johnny does two nights a week DJ'ing. Right, you know my mate Eddie, he's gonna get you one of those cassette machines, and we're gonna borrow all of Johnny's singles. You'll have to record them from Monday to Wednesday, because he's got to have them back for Friday and Saturday nights gigging. So we got every single that this Johnny had. I wish I could remember his surname, because he's one of my biggest influences.

"That's where I first saw the Pye R&B label. It was just amazing. Some of it was Chicago R&B, plus there was stuff like The Impressions, New Orleans R&B, Lee Dorsey…it wasn't just Motown and Stax.

"Those half a dozen cassettes I made were just running around in my brain for ages. I used to just put them on and sit at the piano and jam to them."

Whilst the north had their own underground scene, down south, there were alternatives too if you knew where to look.

If you liked black music there was The Lyceum on a Monday Night, or The Global Village on Fridays. There was Gossips in Dean Street or Spats in Oxford Street, where a young DJ called Paul Murphy stood at the decks.

The most notable though was a tiny club in Dean Street in Soho called Crackers. The club ran a session on Friday lunch-times between noon to 2,30, just like the Mods had at The Lyceum and Tiles had back in the Sixties and just 50p bought you entry to this other world taking place below the Oxford Street shoppers.

The crowd at Crackers were hip. They were the most knowledgeable about music and could dance better than anyone else. Nobody cared what you were. Black and gay people were still treated unjustly in the outside world, but here they could reign supreme if they could dance on the battleground of the small sprung wooden floor.

The DJ's such as George Power, Mark Roman, Nicky Price and warm up DJ Paul 'Trouble' Anderson would get things moving with tunes such as:

Express — BT Express
I Need It — Johnny 'Guitar' Watson
Hot Pants Road — The JB's
Street Dance — Fatback Band
Life On Mars — Dexter Wansel

The other major eruption against conventional music and clothing styles came in the form of punk Rock. The style and music had exploded throughout the long, hot summer of '76.

That summer the Sex Pistols played at the old Mod stomping ground of The Lyceum on the Strand. Advertised as 'Midnight Court Summer Rock Festivals' that ran from midnight until dawn on Friday's. The 9th of July saw The Pretty Things, Supercharge and Sex Pistols.

In the audience that night is a young Paul Weller, from Woking. The night would have a great effect on him. Weller was speeding and mesmerised by watching a young band with short hair, straight trousers and powerful three-minute songs.

Mick Talbot: "I always think that the mid-Seventies pub rock scene is easily looked down on. punk kind of took the plaudits for all that led to the Mod revival, but there was a lot going on in the 18 months leading up to it. I think that a lot of the pretention that was around in the early Seventies was despised by a lot of the pub rock bands. A lot of those bands couldn't get the gigs they wanted, so they went to pubs and went back to grassroots. I think there was quite a Sixties sensibility. A lot of those people were almost like Mods anyway. If you look at Nick Lowe when he was in Brinsley Schwarz, he's got a gingham button-down shirt and a great crop. Dr Feelgood had a bit of that too, with their early Stones ambience. Even bands like the Kursaal Flyers had a bit of stage presence like the Sixties acts. I think that kind of rubbed off on us a little bit. "

On 20 and 21 September 1976, The 100 Club in Oxford Street held Punk Special. It is sometimes referred to as the 100 Club Punk Festival. The gigs showcased eight punk rock bands, most of which were unsigned.

Monday, 20 September: Subway Sect, Siouxsie and the Banshees, The Clash and the Sex Pistols.

Tuesday, 21 September: Stinky Toys, Chris Spedding & The Vibrators, The Damned and the Buzzcocks.

Paul Weller was in the audience here too on the Monday. He had his own band, The Jam, that were playing old R&B standards. He'd been heavily influence by Dr Feelgood's 'Down By The Jetty' LP released in 1975, and he'd discovered a love of Mod having heard 'My Generation' by The Who on a compilation borrowed off his sister. The Sex Pistols would act as a catalyst to take his band to a different level.

Mick Talbot:" I went to see The Jam pretty early on at the Red Cow in Hampstead. I think they had a month's residency on a real slow night, maybe Tuesdays. We went on their second week, and there was a big queue. When I first saw them, I thought they were kind of Dr Feelgood sounding. I thought the Feelgood's were always entertaining, particularly the Wilko incarnation. My heart sank when Wilko left the Feelgood's (in April '77), but it seemed, hot on the heels of that, The Jam were breaking through. I mean the B-side of 'In The City' is 'Takin' My Love', and I thought that was very close to the Dr Feelgood sound.

"It was nice to see them before they had a record out. Most of their set was covers, they did 'Ride Your Pony' by Lee Dorsey, 'In The Midnight Hour' by Wilson Pickett, and The Who's 'Much Too Much', which was on the 'My Generation' album, and I knew it because I'd been given a copy about six months earlier by someone at work. I think they played 'In The City' but they didn't have many originals at that point."

Pete Downs is a good example of somebody in the street who had decided to 'opt out' of conventional life back in those fertile days as he remembers: "Having been born in Windsor in the last few days of 1957 I was too young for the original Mod era and even the following skinhead era. Even if I had wanted to become a mini-skin in 1969-70 my Mum and Dad would never have entertained the cropped hair or boots.

"The earliest pop groups that I remember seeing on TV and hearing on the radio when I was five years old were The Rolling Stones, Manfred Mann and of course The Beatles. In fact, my Mum bought me the single of 'She Loves You' as I was always singing it.

"Of course, the term 'Mods and Rockers' was familiar to me, although I had no idea at the time what the difference was. I would sit on my front door step in Windsor asking any passers-by if they were Mods or Rockers. That soon stopped when a teenage girl answered back that her boyfriend was a Rocker and if I didn't look out he would smash my face in! At which point I quickly ran indoors and gave up that particular line of questioning. Perhaps it was that incident that swayed me towards the Mod cause.

"Towards the end of 1964 we moved to a new house in Reading and I was delighted to discover that our playground was directly opposite the house that Marianne Faithful lived at. At this time, she was going out with Mick Jagger and it was not uncommon to see Mick pulling up outside in his Aston Martin. He even came across to the railings for a quick chat with us kids on one occasion which was a big thrill for a Stones fan.

"I can't really explain my move towards the Mod way of life without bringing up the arrival of punk in 1976/77. Most documentaries on TV or radio these days that look back on seventies Britain tend to paint the picture of everything being grey with strikes, power cuts and a dull music scene where everyone listened to twenty-minute drum solo's just awaiting the arrival of something new to come along and sweep away all before it. Personally, I loved growing up in the Seventies and never had any problem finding records to spend my money on whether it was pop, rock, soul, reggae or jazz.

"When punk arrived, I loved it but also carried enjoying the music I had enjoyed previously. Which meant I had no qualms about going into a record shop to buy the latest Stranglers or Jam LP alongside Santana or Steely Dan. Although I was excited by the arrival of punk, there was no way I was going to adopt the punk style of dress although it did influence my decision to cut my longish hair short and wear straight leg Levis instead of flares or baggies. This in itself was enough for my mates and most other people to label you as a punk rocker for looking a bit different from the norm."

Tom McCourt: "In 1976 I walked in to the Marquee to see Eddie and The Hot Rods. I had long hair and was wearing a Levi's white denim coat with a big fur collar and flared trousers. The Sex Pistols supported them, and I just thought, fucking hell… it just changed everything. I was fifteen years old and six foot, three and a half inches tall. From there I got in to The Flamin' Groovies and MC5. I'd go to Rock On in Camden Town, that was the best record shop in the world. They would say "Listen to this…" and then play you The Ramones. So, I walked in to punk by accident, and it was great. It felt like you were changing things. You had great nights out, and people looked at you like spawn of the devil. I suppose it sounds elitist, but you were all involved in something different from the norm. I started to make my own shirts and stuff. Then, suddenly, punk started to become the new 'normal'. 'New Wave' started and you'd hear stuff like Blondie. Then, one day in Camden, I saw this bloke, I think it may have been Suggs, and he was wearing a Crombie coat, Staprest trousers and brogues. I thought he looked great and just so different."

Gary Wood: "Embarrassingly, I was a Quo fan and I was at college in '76 and '77. There was a bloke and a girl there who were punks and they asked me if I wanted to go down The Vortex and I said "Ooh no, that ain't for me. All those weirdos dressing up and all that." So, I missed all that punk, and I regretted it within a year. All of a sudden, The Jam were on Top of the Pops, and they played down our way but I didn't know anybody who wanted to see them. My mates weren't interested. In September 1977 The Jam played at the 100 Club with the New Hearts. I got a ticket for it, and went with a mate who was 14, I was 18 at the time. It was full of punks, ordinary's and longhairs. It was rammed, and it was really exciting. The only trouble was that I got my arms burnt by a punk who was pogoing. His leather jacket was rubbing against me. The New Hearts came on, and they were the first live band I'd ever seen. They were really good. Ian Page was Ian Payne then, he had an attitude. Dave Cairns was a great guitarist. The Jam then came on, suited up. I was hooked."

Tom McCourt: "We used to go down to Liverpool Street to fight the Teddy Boys. They were a lot older than us. In Hoxton there was only about ten punks, maybe not even that. We'd all meet at The Roebuck, and then we'd go off to The Kings Road to fight them. We were all aged between 15 to 20. The Teds were 22, 23, even some in their 30s. It felt great because we all kind of felt together in it."

Buddy Ascott: "In 1977, I joined a punk band called The Meat. In honour of Keith Moon, I'd be wearing a white boiler suit. I'd cut the sleeves off and my mum had sewn Union Jack panels in. We were playing all over London at venues such as The Vortex and Roxy. Seeing the Pistols on the LWT programme had been a big influence. I'd never seen anything so threatening or exciting. They just looked like violence on stage, and that reminded me so much of The Who."

Pete Downs: "My first 'punk' gig was seeing The Jam at Reading Top Rank in June 1977 and was blown away by their energy. Up until that point most concerts I had been to, involved sitting on the floor at Reading University or massive events like The Stones at Earls Court plus a few festivals in Reading and Knebworth. But this was something very different, the nearest thing previously was seeing Dr Feelgood a couple of years earlier. Overnight The Jam became my favourite band but still no mention of a Mod revival at that point, not in Reading anyway."

Neil Barker: "My first clues to what Mod was came from Robin Potts, a Woking legend, who had been an original Skinhead/Suedehead. When I showed him my handful of punk 45s Robin said, "The Jam are not punks, they're mods!" I was 14 years old in 1977 and had no knowledge of mods, but he showed me the original *Quadrophenia* album and I was fascinated by the images and so my journey began."

Tom McCourt: "We went down to Liverpool Street one Sunday. I met up with my brother who told me he'd seen some Skinheads. I walked on down past The Raven, which was the Teddy Boys Pub, and about 20 of these Skinheads came out. They were all looking proper smart, not Boneheads, but proper geezers, really done up. I had a chat with them and that was it. I mean I already knew people like Terry Maddon and Binsy, who kind of dressed like that because they'd had clothes handed down. Money was tight, my mum had four or five jobs to look after me and my brother.

"In Becontree it was like a cultural thing and they formed a mob called Chartools. Chelsea, Arsenal and Liverpool – The CAL. There were a lot of families looking kind of normal, fighting these skinhead mobs. This Beacontree mob were all around the same age as us, 15, 16, 17. They had people like Dave Lawrence, Mark Nelson, Danny Thompson and Bob Baisden. These were a lot of the people who would later become known as The Glory Boys when they became mods, but at this point they were Skinheads."

Pete Downs: "I suppose I was a bit of a late starter as far as deciding to become a Mod is concerned as I had already turned twenty. Probably too old to be getting into another youth cult but as there was realistically no chance of being a Mod or anything else for that matter when you are twenty-five and settled down I thought I would grab one last chance to hang on to the teenage dream.

"In fact, it was the skinhead revival of late 1977/early 1978 that I got into as it was like being given a second chance. I had always worn Dr Martens and jean jackets anyway so apart from getting a number two crop it wasn't such a great leap."

Tom McCourt: "If you were a skinhead then, you'd be in a pub like The Greengate, then you'd go down Bethnal Green hunting down clothes and records on the stalls. I got my hair cropped and got in to that whole Sixties look. I suppose we evolved from it. My Uncle told me to check his bedroom, and in there I found piles of records and wardrobes full of clothes that fitted me. He had staprest, suits, Ben Sherman and Brutus shirts. Even better than the clothes, was the music. Even though I'd been a punk, I'd never listened to reggae really. But the best stuff I discovered was the Atlantic soul, Stax records and that compilation *This Is Soul*. All my mates were getting in to reggae but I loved the soul. I had found a treasure trove, and I was hooked on soul music."

Mick Talbot: "By now I was playing working men's clubs in a band which was more or less what became The Merton Parkas. We were called Colt for a while, before we became The Sneekers, by then Danny, my brother, had replaced the original guitarist.

"We had kind of twin lives in that band because we played very long sets with breaks at working mens clubs, which involved a lot of varied covers, and we'd also play pubs where we could play what we liked. You'd earn more money playing the working men's clubs, but your set was a bit more compromised compared with your tastes. We used to like to think we did it our own way, and kept our own identity, but there's no doubt looking at it from a distance that you had to compromise yourself.

"Somebody would come up and slap you on the back and say, "Elsie and Ted, it's their 50th today, can you play the 'Anniversary Waltz' please?" We'd have to pretend we could or play something that sounds a bit like it. But it was good in a way, because you learn a lot of different things. You learn that you're not as important as the bingo, the raffle, or even the geezer with the basket full of sea food. You are just a mere support to all of that.

"I never told anyone at work. The first time anybody knew that I did that, at work, was when the band (The Merton Parkas) I was in got a review in *Sounds*, and the bloke next to me went "That's your name ain't it? You in a band?" That was about a month before I left work because we got signed, and it looked like there was a chance we could make a living out of it. I was always very low key about it. It's just something I liked. It's not that I wasn't proud of it, but I wasn't gonna ram it down people's throats because it's never made me feel anything special."

Tom McCourt: "We used to go to Huntingdon and find old tailors' shops and army surplus stores. They'd have stuff that they'd never sold, so you'd go in and ask for button-down shirts or staprest, and you could get three pairs for a quid. You'd go back the following week and they'd sussed you. And they'd want a fiver a pair. We'd go to places like Hoxton and Fulham. You'd go to Wells Street Market and there used to be a little Jewish tailor and he had boxes of Ben Sherman's. He sold me 3 or 4 shirts for a quid. So I pulled out all the best ones he had there, and they were all brand new. He was selling flares and star jumpers at the time. I then found a jean shop in the Angel, so I went in and asked about button down shirts, so he took me out the back and he had boxes full of original American button downs. There was also this place in Petticoat Lane by the underground market that used to sell American suits for £10-20 each. They had dogtooth, sharkskin, Prince of Wales checks, it was everything you wanted. Clothes meant a lot, and if you were going to do it, you may as swell do it properly. At the time there was only a couple of hundred of us in London doing something different. I'd seen Grant Fleming, but I didn't really know him at that point.

Grant was with a lot of the West Ham mob. Kilburn had a lot of Skinheads, as did Swiss Cottage, Ladbroke Grove, West London. In Hoxton there were probably about fifteen of us and it grew more and more. I also met Tony Cummins, known as Panther, he used to be immaculate. He looked like he'd been zapped out of 1969 on to the streets of London in 1977."

Pete Downs: "There were a lot of smartly dressed Skins around at the time as well as the scruffier bald-headed type's that were mainly ex-punks that just wore army trousers or bleached jeans with a t-shirt. This led to the music press labelling all Skinheads as boneheads and the right wing following of some groups such as Sham 69 meant a lot of bad feeling towards any Skinheads, genuine or not."

Tom McCourt: "We'd go to punk gigs and Sham gigs. We had a disco at the youth club in People Street. I started taking my Uncle's records up there. A lot of these people were listening to modern reggae and we were taking up old stuff or punk records. We took a lot of Pama and Blue Beat stuff. Plus, we had compilations like the *Rocksteady Cool* as well as the *Tighten Up* and *Club Reggae* series. If you went to Rock On in Camden, they had some great singles. I used to be in there for hours. There was also this little shop in the Caledonian Road where I managed to buy loads of Stax 45's. This was around 1978. I was doing this myself and you start thinking 'are you on your own?"

Pete Downs: "I wrote a letter to one of the music weeklies at the time sticking up for the non-Nazi genuine Skins and after they printed it had a letter from another Skin in Cornwall who I later met up with for the 1978 Reading Festival."

Tom McCourt: "A couple of my mates who were in to punk but weren't in to the skinhead thing started talking about the Mods thing. One was a bloke called Ian Curry, and his brother was a Mod and Who fanatic, so we started talking about Mod bands. Next thing, we were buying Hush Puppy shoes."

Long
Tall
Shor

in time

with '79

CHAPTER NINE

TONY MANERO — THE ACE FACE?

"Quadrophenia was released and it felt like the end. You could see that when it came out everybody was going to be a fucking Mod. It would be in The Sun… 'Get your parka here!'. It felt like it was becoming another cult on the production line."

TOM McCOURT

' Faces. According to Vincent himself, they were simply the elite. All over Brooklyn, Queens and the Bronx, even as far away as New Jersey, spread clear across America, there were millions of kids who were nothing special. Just kids, Zombies. Professional dummies, going through the motions, following like sheep. School, jobs, routines. A vast faceless blob. And then there were the Faces. The Vincents and Eugenes and Joeys. A tiny minority, maybe two in every hundred, who knew how to dress and how to move, how to float, how to fly. Sharpness, grace, a certain distinction in every gesture. And some strange instinct for rightness, beyond words, deep down in the blood: 'The way I feel,' Vincent said, 'it's like we have been chosen.'

From 'Tribal Rights of The New Saturday Night' by Nik Cohn.

The film *Quadrophenia* was mainly centred on a group of teenagers in London. It covers ten days in the life of Jimmy Cooper before, during, and after the climax of the Brighton riots. Jimmy himself is supposedly representative of dominant characteristics in each of The Who's band members: Roger the fighter, Moon the mad man, Entwistle the romantic and Townshend the seeker.

The advert in the Brighton Evening Argus dated September 14th, 1978 read as follows:

'THE WHO Film Co. requires film extras as Mods and Rockers (boys and girls age 16-20) plus Mods with scooters (models between 1963-1970) and Rockers with British motorbikes to film from September 26 for three weeks in Brighton. Interviews at the Pavilion Job Centre'

The money handed out to the multiple extras didn't seem that much; £10 a day or if you had a bike or scooter, £15. Bearing in mind though that they used at least 600 extras over ten days of filming, and suddenly you realise that the cost of production was pretty high.

The filming of the Brighton scenes took place in the first week of October 1978. The assembled recruits include Mods from areas such as Barnsley and Preston, whereas the Rockers were from London and the South.

The music papers had been covering the build-up to *Quadrophenia* bit-by-bit, especially after the fight scenes had taken place. Brian Rock had written a small piece about it in the 'Thrills' section of the *New Musical Express* on October 14, 1978 and the *Melody Maker* gave it a three-page spread on the same day.

On the 6th of June 1979 three members of the cast were interviewed, Phil Daniels, Leslie Ash and Sting, by Den Heggarty of the group Darts for the ITV programme *Alright Now*. Whilst chatting to Sting and discussing the plot, Heggarty responds with: "Sounds just like *Saturday Night Fever* to me." Sting replies: "It's the same."

Stranger still then was the *Melody Maker* review on October 27th, 1979. Simon Frith wasn't impressed by the film. He viewed it as 'shoddy', he then compares it to the film which had been released two years earlier, but he says, was much better. 'An English remake of *Saturday Night Fever* — same plot, same cynicism, same soft core. It's the old story: humdrum teenagers, bored at work, bossed at home, chased by cops, lured by ads, escaping into style — kicks 'n' tricks, sex and drugs and rock 'n' roll.'

It is unsure whether both Heggarty and Frith knew that the actual foundations of *Saturday Night Fever* lay in the original Mod scene of West London in the Sixties.

Writer Nik Cohn had been born in Derry, Northern Ireland. He'd been raised in the Protestant area where Rock 'n' Roll was viewed as sinful, but at the age of 11, he'd ventured into the heart of the Catholic area and heard magical music and saw wonderous sights. The music was Little Richard's 'Tutti Frutti' and the sights were the local Teddy Boys. From then on, Cohn would have a lifelong obsession for working class gang culture and a love of hip music, especially Elvis, James Brown and rock 'n' roll.

At the age of 17, he was living in London, and the year was 1963. He took it all in, observed every detail, wrote it all down as if his life depended on it. This would lead to writing what could easily be the best book on music *Awopbopaloobop Alopbamboom* in 1968. He also captured Mod at its purest level in his writings of the article 'Ready, Steady Gone' for *The Observer Magazine* in 1967 and his book, *Today There Are No Gentlemen*, published in 1971, where he talks of Sixties purists such as Thomas Baines 'who refused to have sex at parties unless there was a shoe- tree available and a press for his trousers' and the sartorial adventures of Bernard Coutts.

In 1975 Cohn found himself in America working for *New York* Magazine where he asked if he could write a feature on modern American working-class subcultures. Having been granted permission, the writer met up with disco dancer named Tu Sweet who took Cohn from the cosy surroundings of Manhattan into the much tougher area of Bay Bridge in Brooklyn. One venue they visited on their travels was a disco named Odyssey 2001. On arrival, there was a drunken fist fight already taking place outside the venue, and one of the participants ended up rolling into the gutter and was promptly sick on Cohn's trousers. Horrified, he returned to the much safer environment of his Manhattan apartment. One thing he had observed that night though was a cool-looking clubgoer stood outside the disco calmly watching the brawl. The following day Cohn returned to the venue but could find no trace of him, so he spent the time taking in the surroundings and observing the local youth's mannerisms and their street talk.

THE WHO
QUADRO-
PHENIA

THE NOVEL BY
ALAN FLETCHER

When the article named 'Tribal Rights of The New Saturday Night' appeared in *New York* Magazine on June 7th, 1976 complemented by a set of paintings by artist James McMullan, nobody would have any idea that the piece was largely fiction. In his despair of not being able to find the mystery figure, he based the main character 'Vincent' on a teen gang member who he'd known in Derry and a 'one-time king of Goldhawk Road' and Shepherds Bush Mod called Chris that he'd known in 1965.

The article was used as the basis for the 1977 film *Saturday Night Fever*, and Vincent was the model for the super cool Tony Manero character played by John Travolta.

It's strange but if you watch the film knowing these facts, it does indeed have many 'Mod' moments, from the opening shots of the film where the cool-struttin' Manero spots a 'must have' shirt in a shop window to sitting around the family dinner table where he shouts at his father for messing up his hair.

You can also notice that 'Tribal Rights of the New Saturday Night' isn't that dissimilar to a piece written by US author Tom Wolfe called *The Noonday Underground*. Written in 1968, it was part of a collection of essays written by Wolfe for a book *The Pump House Gang*. The story revolves around a 15-year office boy called Larry Lynch who, when free from the shackles of the dull office world, goes out to live 'the life' by dancing during dinnertime sessions at the Mod club Tiles. The difference here being that you have an American writing a piece on English subculture based on real life characters and places using their real names, compared to somebody who had been based in England writing a piece on America subculture mixing fact and fiction together.

With this in mind, the film version of *Quadrophenia*

brilliantly captures the whole teenage angst of trying to fit in and could be a film about any teenager trying to find themselves in a world of peer pressure and racing hormones. The fact is that it sadly lacks the golden rule of mod: attention to detail.

Strangely enough, as early as October '78, Franc Roddam was quoted as saying that he wanted original music in the film by the likes of Geno Washington, Georgie Fame and The Small Faces but it never materialised.

In fact, the film could have been very different if other proposals had worked out. Firstly, John Lydon AKA Johnny Rotten of the Sex Pistols had become close friends with Pete Townshend and Townshend offered him the part of the lead character, Jimmy Cooper. It seems a bit muddy as to why Lydon never got the part. Stories abound from Johnny failing the audition to the distributors of the film refusing to insure him for the part, so he was replaced by Phil Daniels.

Jimmy Pursey of Sham 69 was also rumoured to be involved. In fact, when Paul Weller was interviewed by *Sounds* in November 1978, he was asked about the impending effect of *Quadrophenia* turning a grassroots revival into a full-scale Mod comeback, and Weller replied: "Yeh I can see there's gonna be a big Mod revival in the summer which'll be really boring cos it'll be the beach fights all over again, just like the Punks and the Teds last year." And the piece ended with him saying "I think Jimmy Pursey's gonna do it better..."

Grant Fleming: "When I was working with Sham, there was talk of the film *Quadrophenia* happening, which obviously I loved. Incidentally, I put myself up for the lead role. Obviously, I never got it but they did offer me a bit part. Anyway, when they were doing the filming in Brighton, West Ham were playing Sunderland away so I decided to go to the game and got my head cut open for my sins, so I never went to the shoot.

"The production company sent over a copy of the film synopsis. They wanted a band for a scene, and to record some songs for it. I went along with Jimmy Pursey and Dave Parsons to Eel Pie Island to meet Townshend and Daltrey. They kind of got accepted, so they wrote a couple of songs for the film, and they were going to be in it. I don't know what happened, whether they were dropped or just couldn't do it, but it never happened. If you look at the scene with Sting dancing and Jimmy jumping off the balcony, as they go in to the venue, there's a poster with Sham 69 on it."

One thing that the film certainly got correct though was the fact that the old school generation of adults treated young teenagers as mere children. Even if they'd had the money to pay, no teenager would be allowed to stay in a hotel or B&B without their parents. Kids ended up sleeping under the pier, in changing rooms, under upturned boats, anywhere that was dry and shielded you from the wind.

In a feature on Mods in *Record Mirror* dated August 18th, 1979 it states: 'The Mod movement has been brewing up for the last six months but this film is going to be the turning point. It should turn Mod from being a cult culture into a mass marketed product. Still. That's one of the penalties of success.'

On August 23rd 1979, the *Daily Mirror* gave a hint at the atrocities that the film might inflict on the small but established Mod scene. In a two-page centre spread 'March of the New Mods' the piece, written by

Marcia Brackett, she states 'The hub of the new revival is, of course, London. And in the vanguard are the acknowledged leaders of Mod…The Who.'

Using two of the film's stars Phil Davis and Leslie Ash as models the article tells of The Who getting involved with the fashion business by forming a company with the Succhi chain. The band not designing but approving each item to be involved in the Succhi-Quadrophenia label. The band had also stated that the reason that they'd got involved in the fashion side of things was 'to protect their fans and their name, and to avoid unapproved use of our labels and symbols'.

If anything was going to reel in the poseur brigade it was the offerings of a black nylon parka (£12.99) or purple suede parka (£125) both complete with a large circle and arrow on the right arm, or maybe a catsuit (£9.99) or a grey slub-weave silk mixture suit (£79.99). Bearing in mind these were 1979 prices, it certainly wasn't aimed at the kids in the street. To be fair, the article did also involve three girls who had got into the look recently and their clothes were mainly secondhand or Oxfam.

In September, just prior to the release of the film, there was a Succhi-Who fashion show held at The Lyceum in London. The free bar had most of the music business liggers getting legless whilst the fashion parade people posed.

The room was full of middle-aged funkateers and soul boys. DJ Chris Hill was present and was just getting the taste for more gratis hooch, when the bar was suddenly closed. There's a large crash, and lasers lit up the room, models sauntered along the catwalk whilst wearing Succhi's usual range of clothing. It was all padded shoulders, miserable pouts and slow strutting to the sound of disco.

The fashion victims clapped whilst the music types sat there bewildered.

The set suddenly swung around to reveal the *Quadrophenia* logo, with a lone target above. Models then entered the stage in satin parkas and Carnaby Street-style catsuits with holes cut out in strategic places and hooded Italian-style T-shirts. The show closed to cries of "rubbish" from former Sixties Mods. Sadly, members of The Who didn't join them in doing so.

By the third week of September, the film *Quadrophenia* had hit London, was being shown at the Plaza in Lower, Regent Street, the Classic in Qxford Street, the ABC in the Fulham Road and the ABC in Edgware Road. It went on general release on September 23rd.

Tom McCourt remembers: "*Quadrophenia* was released, and it felt like the end. You know when you feel like you know everyone, and you knew what was happening. You could see that when *Quadrophenia* came out, that everybody was going to be a fucking Mod. It would be in *The Sun*... "Get your parka here!" It felt like it was becoming another cult on the production line. Here comes another revival. It felt like you were losing it all. It was quite sad at the time because the thing was that you went to gigs and the people in the bands would be talking to you in the pubs. I fucking hated what happened."

It later transpired that there had in fact really been a guy called Tony Manero who danced at the Odyssey 2001, but apparently, he was an okay dancer, nothing particularly special, and the disco itself had just been average until the production company put in the crazy lit-up dancefloor. On its release *Saturday Night Fever* brought in all the fake and phoney types that Manhattan could offer. They invaded Bay Ridge in search of that elusive coolness. And in doing so diluted and killed-off the original scene in the process. Much the same could be said for *Quadrophenia* and the early British Mod-revival scene.

A lot of people ask if there are any other films with Mods in. Well there have been a couple of American independent films revolving around the subject, *We Are The Mods* (2009) set in modern day Los Angeles and *Young Birds Fly* (2011) set in present day Southern California. Both are teen dramas. There is also a sub-plot of Mods and Rockers in the 2010 remake of Graham Green's *Brighton Rock*. Although in truth, I'd stick to the original.

In the Sixties there were various glimpses of Mods in films, including *Georgy Girl* (1966) (two Mods on scooters), *Up The Junction* (1968) (Dennis Waterman turns up on his Lambretta) and the horror flick *The Sorcerers* (1967) (Disco scenes with original Mod Face, Mickey Tenner, as a dancer). Special mention must be given to *Performance* (1970) for James Fox's portrayal of Chas, the Mod looking gangster (that would later influence the band, Secret Affair's, look).

For visual references to the very early days of 'the look' you should check out the documentary *We Are The Lambeth Boys* (1959), or *The Boys* (1962), and for scenes of early Soho, it has to be *The Small World Of Sammy Lee* (1963).

To me, the best visual depictions of the archetypal Mods on scooters can be found in the Picnic-Nik advert from 1966, an episode of *Gideon's Way* called *The Rhyme And The Reason*, which features a hapless Mod on his Vespa 6S, and believe it, or not, an advert for Lucozade made in

1998 featuring the best one-minute nod to Sixties Mods going (and featuring Eighties Guy Joseph). The best by far though is a little-known film by Ken Loach that was made for the BBC Television series *The Wednesday Play* in 1965 called *The End Of Arthur's Marriage*' and features some superb footage of Mods on their scooters. All of these are available on YouTube at the time of writing.

THIS IS A MOD EVENT
NO ROCKERS!
* * * *

THE FIRST BIG MOD EVENT SINCE THE 60's

ALL DAY

AT TRIAD

TRIAD LEISURE CENTRE
SOUTHMILL ROAD, BISHOPS STORTFORD, HERTS.
— PHONE BISHOPS STORTFORD (0279) 56333
BY SCOOTER (OR CAR) TRIAD IS A HALF HOUR RIDE
DOWN THE M11 MOTORWAY FROM THE REDBRIDGE
ROUNDABOUT ON THE NORTH CIRCULAR ROAD. OR TAKE
THE A11. OR TRAINS FROM LIVERPOOL STREET STATION.

THE PURPLE HEART
the crooks · the mods
back to zero · squires

PLUS 60's SOUNDS DISCO – BRING YOUR FAVOURITE DISC AND WE WILL GIVE IT A SPIN

sunday 20th may

DOORS OPEN 2.30 PM – FINISHES APPROX. 11 PM.
TICKETS ONLY £1.50 – PAY AT DOOR
LICENSED BARS & FOOD AVAILABLE
LARGE SCOOTER PARK AT REAR OF BUILDING
* * * * * * * * * *
PRIZES FOR BEST SCOOTER (SHINE THOSE LAMBR
PRIZES FOR SCOOTER WITH MOST MIRRO
PRIZES FOR BEST DECORATE
PARKERS. PLUS MAN
MORE PRIZE.

CHAPTER

TEN

LIFE AFTER QUAD

"The Mod thing did go towards giving a typical teenage London kid like me an identity although it was one I shared with loads of others of course. It gave me confidence and certainly if nothing else gave me an idea of how to travel around London on public transport going to gigs and events."

MARTIN GAINSFORD

CHAPTER

The prophet had spoken the truth. *Quadrophenia* had indeed gathered a whole host of new faces (with a small f) who were willing to don a parka in the name of Mod. The sad fact was that they could often buy a parka from those 1977 and 1978 young somethings who were quickly scrambling for the exit door.

In October, The Chords, one of the shining lights of those early days, would reach the dizzy heights of 63 in the UK charts with 'Now, It's Gone'. The lyrics of the song almost perfectly capturing the feeling of that period amongst the early crowd.

Buddy Ascott: "After The Chords signed to Polydor, we were compared to The Jam by fucking everyone. As much as I loved that band, The Who were still the be all and end all, and The Clash were more important to me. The Jam had taken influences like R'n'B, a bit of black soul and The Who. That was the problem, we had taken the same influences. Billy Hassett was from Deptford and sang in a London accent. He got accused of singing like Weller, who was from Woking trying to sound like someone from London.

"In fact, back in 1977 I'd read that interview with The Jam standing by Big Ben in the *New Musical Express*. Paul Weller said that they covered 'So Sad About Us', and that was it. I went to see them the following week at Ravensborne College in Bromley. I'm in the crowd shouting out for 'So Sad About Us'. Weller's gone "At least I've got one fan here tonight." And I've shouted back "No you haven't. You've got a Who fan here who just wants to hear 'So Sad About Us!"

November would see The Purple Hearts, whose first single 'Millions Like Us' had got to 57 in the charts back in September, now sign a long-time deal with Fiction (distributed by Polydor) and release 'Frustration' with album to follow in the new year. Meanwhile, Secret Affair's *Glory*

Boys LP was released to a five-star review in *Sounds* by Garry Bushell. In the same issue, The Jam would have to be content with Pete Silverton's four-star review of the *Setting Sons* LP. However, *Glory Boys* would peak at 41 in the UK Album chart whilst Setting Sons spent 19 weeks on the UK album charts, rising to No. 4.

The magazine *Fab 208* did a Sixties/Mod special in November '79 that ran features on Beatlemania, a colour spread of the Merton Parkas, an article on Mods and Rockers, a pull-out poster of The Jam and features on the Sixties. One page entitled 'A Day In The Life Of A Mod' saw *Maximum Speed* fanzine editor Goffa Gladding describing a typical Saturday in his life. Whilst covering clothes he gives out these nuggets: "I catch the tube to Oxford Circus to have a look around Carnaby Street and can't help but grin at the idiots walking about sweating in parkas. Well it is 65 degrees! There's a bit more to being a Mod than having a parka with THE WHO written on the back, y'know!

"I wear a black mohair suit which I had made-to-measure in a tiny tailors in Finchley, North London. The old bloke who works in the shop has still got a lot of the old patterns left from about 15 years ago, and although the suit cost me £80, it's a really worthwhile investment. It's cut in the classic three-button style, with five-inch (12.5 cm) side vents, ticket pocket, and trousers with 17-inch (43 cm) bottoms. My shirt is a button-down collar which I picked up in a jumble sale for 5p, and my knitted Terelene tie was the same price. I can't decide which shoes to put on, but eventually go for a pair of suede pointed Chelsea boots bought secondhand from a stall in Beaufort Market, Kings Road (which has now unfortunately, closed down). I'm just about ready, I think, and the final touch is some black eye make-up just to make people stare!"

TAM PACT

SPRING TOUR 1979

Coventry, 1978
Pic: Denis O'Regan

Tour Dates

F·I·C·K·L·E BOOKLET

4th May, 1979	SHEFFIELD	University
5th	SHEFFIELD	University
6th	NEWCASTLE	City Hall
8th	SALFORD	University
10th	LONDON	Rainbow
11th	LONDON	Rainbow
12th	LOUGHBOROUGH	Auditorium
14th	EXETER	University
15th	LIVERPOOL	University
16th	LIVERPOOL	University
18th	GLASGOW	Strathclyde University
19th	GLASGOW	Strathclyde University
21st	BRISTOL	Coulston Hall
22nd	BIRMINGHAM	Odeon
24th	PORTSMOUTH	Guildhall

Truth be though that people like Goffa were in the minority.

Grant Fleming had become despondent, the cult that he loved was being diluted in front of his eyes. He even sat down and penned his thoughts at the time in a series of private notes on a pad: "Ashes to ashes. Dust to dust. Here lies the desecrated body of Mod. Yeah, I agree there's thousands of Mods parading the streets, battling the winters in their ill-fitting parkas but Mod as a scene, as a meaningful movement has long past. People think that because all the early Mods disassociate themselves from it that they're just being elitist, but at first it was good other people getting in to it but we had it so right, our own little scene and then along came hundreds of kids with a parka, tie, Who patch etc. Look, if they had got it right it would have been brilliant, but they put no thought or ideas into it, so it became another stereotyped image. Now you see little kids marching about sporting targets, union jacks etc.'

Grant was a true original of that early revival period. A shining star, lighting the way, but now he was fading. It seemed the party was over.

Names and faces would gradually disappear into the mists of time; Dave Lawrence, John Lawrence, Danny Meakin, Ricky Meakin, Danny Harrison, The Crank (Steven Borg), Boris (Tommy Russell), Dave Smith, Scotty, Waitsey, Norman, Large Al from Hayes, Bethnal Bob, Hoxton Tom, Gary Crowley, Wembley Tony, Vaughn Toulouse, Goffa, Clive and Kim of Maximum Speed, Rhino from St Albans, The Millwall Mafia, Barney Rubble and his firm....one by one the lights went out.

By 1980, Back To Zero had split after less than a year together as a working band. The first Mod fanzine *Maximum*

Speed had folded too. Even though the year saw great releases such as The Chords 'Maybe Tomorrow' single and their album *So Far Away*, The Purple Hearts LP *Beat That*, Secret Affair's anthemic single 'My World' and their second LP *Behind Closed Doors*.

By November 1980, Billy Hassett had left The Chords in what the record company would describe as 'intense musical and personal differences', whilst the band cited Billy's 'lack of musical dedication'. Either way it was the beginning of the end for the band.

The bands had also found that the 'Mod' tag around their necks had become a millstone, especially Secret Affair, who had tended to be so outspoken in their interviews. Most of the music paper critics, from the very start, had mocked the new Mod bands, blaming them for the commercialisation of the culture and a lack of musical originality.

In truth, bands had lost their popularity amongst many of its followers too. Lots of the kids involved found themselves far more interested in the original music of the Sixties era, and many vinyl-only clubs sprang up over the early Eighties including 'Cheeky Pete's' in Richmond, The Mildmay Tavern in Dalston, the Beatroute in Greek Street (ran by Dick Coombs and Ray 'Patriotic' Margetson), Sebright Arms, Hackney (Ray Patriotic), The Bush Hotel, Shepherds Bush (Tony Class), The Greyhound at Chadwell Heath (Dick Coombs), 'Rascals' Rhythm & Soul Club at Scamps, Southend (Chad Fredericks and Del Reeves), Orpington Civic Hall (Andy Ruw) and the Hercules Tavern, Lambeth North (Tony and Robin Class). There were lots more, but too many to list.

Martin Gainsford: "The crowd I mostly knocked about with were from The Elephant And Castle not too far from a pub called The Hercules Tavern in Lambeth. Funnily enough my grandfather was born just off of Hercules Road and whenever we went passed it on the bus when I was a young kid I would have it pointed out to me so when we heard there was a 'Mod Night' taking place there I knew exactly where it was. By late 1979 bands who maybe only six months earlier had been at the hub of the burgeoning London Mod scene were now taking part in nationwide tours, appearing on telly and signing record deals so the early grass roots scene that had first drawn me in me was changing dramatically. Up to then live gigs were what it was all about until Tony Class and his brother Rob decided to get a sort of 'club scene' going.

"I lived in the same street as Rob another early 'revivalist' who I recall in 1978 driving around locally with 'English Rose' emblazoned on the side panels of his scooter. He was a bit of a local 'Face' and would often pull over and chat to kids of a similar type and word began to spread about The Hercules Tavern. There were however a couple of other local pubs frequented on certain nights of the week by Teddy Boys. Lambeth has long enjoyed a connection to this early British youth movement and it is looked upon by many as its birthplace. With this in mind it is hardly a surprise that conflict soon began with many 'Teds' considering that their 'patch' was being invaded. The Hercules was to be the first of maybe half-a-dozen South London pubs that Tony and Rob would use for their 'nights' but the story was always the same. Mods from all over London would come on foot, scooter or public transport to enjoy fantastic music and camaraderie only to be met by violence and antagonism by local yobs, Teds or Skinheads. The 'guvnors' of the various pubs enjoyed a full house on what were generally quiet nights during the week and I remember well how much the bar staff enjoyed hearing all the hits of their own youth and seeing smartly dressed young kids behaving as they perhaps had done themselves fifteen or so years earlier. However, generally, within a few weeks word spread and we would leave one of the pubs at the end of the night only to be faced with a mob of opposing youngsters out for blood.

"I try not to think too much about that side of it all but it became a worry for my family as stories hit the local newspapers about the violence. After one particularly unpleasant affair I was caught up in both inside and outside at the famous boxing pub The Thomas A Beckett in The Old Kent Road a young scooterist was killed when hit by a lump of paving slab hurled at him. A violent time it was.

"Despite such tragedy Tony and Rob forged ahead undeterred and simply looked for another venue. They tried to remain positive clearly recognising what so many young Mods were getting from events they were staging in pubs such as The Fort in Grange Road, The Gloucester Arms in Bermondsey and The Walmer Castle in Peckham. Rob would begin the evening playing contemporary stuff by The Jam, the Two-Tone bands, Secret Affair, The VIPs and such like. Later Tony would take over playing what is now regarded as standard 'Sixties' stuff ranging from The Monkees to The Yardbirds with a healthy dose of Motown – but to a teenage kid like me it was about as good as it could get. On some nights there were a hundred or more scooters parked outside.

"Scooter clubs I recall in regular attendance were The Lambeth Roadrunners, The Forest Hill Chappies and The Viceroys. I also remember an all-girl club called The

Rosettes and Tony would play Marv Johnson's 'Rose For My Rose' for them. What impressed me too was the care and concern Tony had for these kids he kind of took under his wing. If he heard a particularly large or nasty mob was planning to come down he'd finish things a little early or advise a safe route back to different parts of London if he got wind there was a mob gathering in a certain local area. He and Rob relished telling those in attendance where other Mods planned to meet up for a tea at a cab drivers hut or lorry drivers stop-off point.

"Even then Tony was laying the bedrock for what he and others have built upon ever since. I remember the early Tony Class era as being a time when things began to get a little smarter and more authentic clothes-wise too. Early '79, certainly for me and most of the kids I saw or knew, was all about parkas, 'Jam Shoes', Target T-Shirts or Fred Perry tops. By late '79 and into 1980 I had a couple of suits, albeit Carnaby Cavern ones, a leather three button blazer and a number of decent shirts and roll neck jumpers. Almost everyone in attendance at these events began to shift towards a smarter look and only wore parkas to ride their scooters. Again, for me some of my most cherished memories of the whole Mod thing is of that period and for that I thank Tony and Rob."

Ann Griffin: "I was living in East Acton, West London and think had just turned 15, this was mid-1981. A friend from school wanted to go to a Mod club she had heard about up the road in Shepherd's Bush. I was into rockabilly at the time and wasn't too fussed but went along with her. Anyway, we turned up at this club, and were hanging about outside not sure of whether to go in or not. The bouncers on the door were a couple called Mick and Lil, some old Teds who used to do the doors of rock 'n' roll clubs and they let me in for nothing to have a look. I met some people in there I knew from school – Ela and Georgia – and that was that! What attracted me is that a couple of blues tunes were played that I recognised from rock 'n' roll clubs so it was familiar even though it was a 'new' scene to me."

Martin Gainsford: "The Mod thing did go towards giving a typical teenage London kid like me an identity although it was one I shared with loads of others of course. It gave me confidence and certainly if nothing else gave me an idea of how to travel around London on public transport going to gigs and events. I learned to keep my head down at times and my eyes open. A sad way to grow up but it has held me in good stead all of my life. It opened my eyes to people from other areas who I felt an affinity with through Mod whereas previously they may have simply been 'Norf London', 'The East End lot' or whatever. Of course, sometimes friction arose with other groups of Mods which was regrettable but sometimes *boys will be boys* despite you all wearing the same clothes and listening to the same music.

"As a schoolboy I never really excelled at anything aside from English. With fanzines popping up all over the place I thought I could try my hand at my own and put out two editions of *On Target* in 1980. Issue two contained an interview I conducted with Paul Weller after he had invited me to Stratford Place where Polydor had a demo studio. It is hard to believe now that as a 16-year-old I was in the company of the driving force of what was then England's biggest band. I was one of the fortunate kids of the period who had gone to sound checks, signings and other events when I met the band including a charity football match on one occasion organised by Gary Crowley. But here I was having a one-on-one chat with Paul Weller.

"I was also part of a small group of other lads in the studio Paul asked to provide backing vocals on the demo of the song 'Dream Time' from *Sound Affects* too. In honesty if I were to do similar today I'd still be thrilled so the effect it all had on me as a teenager is almost incalculable. Weller, Foxton and Buckler along with of course Paul's dad John are to be applauded for staying so grounded as they handled themselves with no airs and graces or saw any divide between them and their fans."

THE JAM 'POP ART'
THE JAM B/W No.2
SOUND
AFFECTS
THE JAM 'START'
THE JAM 'GOING UNDERGROUND'
THE JAM 'DREAMS OF CHILDREN'
THE JAM 'TUBESTATION'
THE JAM B/W No.1
THE JAM RED

20p EACH + 15p p+p

BETTE
BADGE

CHAPTER
ELEVEN

THE TRIP TO CARNABY STREET 1984

"Around 1984, one of my first jobs was at the men's clothes shop Woodhouse. There were a lot of gay guys working there and they took me under their wing. I was really into the Mod scene at the time and they took me to the WAG Club. I remember I was wearing a Prince of Wales check suit and a black roll neck."

JONATHON COOKE

B y 1982, as press coverage dried up, tastes amongst the scene were beginning to change and more and more Mod-related bands began to break up. The charts at this time are full of the likes of the Human League, ABC, Depeche Mode and Haircut 100.

At the Morecambe rally that year, many Mods who had attended, seemed to have completed the transition to Scooter Boy by the time the weekend was over. The Scooter Boy culture is exactly as it sounds in that the whole ethos is based around that mode of transport. That said, they still had their own kind of uniform which was loosely in the shape of army greens, flight jackets and Dr Marten boots. There was an air of despondency amongst those that remained loyal to Mod.

Then came the bombshell, on October 30th, 1982. The Jam announced that they were splitting up. To many, The Jam had been instrumental in their decision to become Mods in the first place.

It didn't seem possible; the band had five years of unbroken success. The Jam had toured their recent UK No. 1 album *The Gift* around the world, following British dates with tours of Europe, North America and Japan. Paul Weller, then 24, followed that with a summer holiday in Italy and returned home to let it be known that he wanted to break the group up. His band mates Rick Buckler and Bruce Foxton were devastated and so, obviously, were the thousands of fans.

On the 5th of November The Jam appeared live on the first-ever edition of the Channel 4 TV series *The Tube*. At the end of November, they released their final single 'Beat Surrender,' which became their third to go straight to No. 1 in the UK. The band announced their final tour, which included five nights at Wembley Arena, and on December 11, culminated in an emotional farewell at the Brighton Centre. Then they were gone.

Over the next two years, the Mod scene quickly saw who was in it for the long run, and those who had seen it as a passing phase. A weekly information sheet, known as *The Phoenix List* was handed out at various Mod related clubs and shops. It was published every week by a Mod Society called The Phoenix – London, and was written and edited by Canadian Mark Johnson who wasn't popular with a lot of Mods. For most the real Mod grapevine continued to be the fanzines written by those actually involved. Both *The Phoenix List* and the fanzines could be picked up at the Rockafella Center in Carnaby Street.

Strolling down Carnaby Street from the Great Marlborough Street end, you'd breeze past the Shakespeare's Head on the right and on to the stairs that led up to the Flea Market. As you ascended the stairs you had to try to not catch the eyes of the Neanderthal Boneheads that tended to congregate on them with the sole intent of parting young Moddy Boys of their hard-earned dosh with their cry of "Ave you got 10p?" Onwards and upwards to the top where you'd find Jimmy. Jimmy was the Chinese guy who ran a shop called Robot. There'd be lots of Mod and Skinhead clothing hanging up, but you went there to pick up the latest Mod fanzines, records and trawl through their bootleg live recordings on cassettes such as *The Jam Live at the 100 Club '77* or whatever.

Back on the street there were rubberised coloured paving slabs that were a faded testament to a bygone age. Westminster Council had spent £60,000 on giving the street a facelift back in 1973 but the colour had become muted and defaced with chewing gum and dirt.

On the right-hand side is a short street known as Fouberts Place. A few shops in on the left-hand side brought you to The Cavern at number 22. The shop tried to trade off the heritage of the original Carnaby Cavern (which closed in 1978) but I'm not sure if they were related. Prices were cheap – a suit there at the time would cost you £39.99 in colours such as Dogtooth or Charcoal Grey. Trousers were £15.00 or £25.00 if you wanted mohair ones. Mohair suits were available in two colours, Silver Grey or Air Force Blue, and would set you back £65.00. For the same price you could order a custom-made three-button leather or Hush Puppy-coloured suede jacket. For the girls there were ski pants available in black, navy or silver grey for £9.99 or maybe Prince of Wales or Dog Tooth mini skirt for the same. The shop also sold various tops such as Fred Perry's, jean jackets, target T-shirts, cycling shirts and tops featuring chevrons, arrows and stripes all for affordable sums. All items featured a small Cavern label with a Union Jack motif. A smaller Cavern shop was also to be found at 19 Ganton Street.

On the corner of Carnaby Street and Ganton Street was a huge red-painted shop called Melanddi which dealt in similar styles but featured their own exclusive designs as well. Red, white and blue Jam tour jumpers at £11.99, 'Modern World' arrow crew necks for the same, boating blazers in various shades at £19.99 and different styles of shirts featuring tab collars, pin collars or long points. Their button-down range was available in various shades, polka dots, paisley or op art designs. Melanddi was never exclusively Mod as they also sold a range of bondage trousers, New Romantic styles and Fifties-style suits. They also stocked a huge range of shoes that would range from boots with far too many buckles for Goth-related fantasies to their own styles of two-tone brogues and Jam shoes. Most young Mods though preferred to buy such shoes from Shelley's at 19 Fouberts Place, practically opposite the Cavern. They also sold bowling shoes, black and white Jam Gibsons and Jam 'badger' stage shoes, but Shelley's ones had 'As made for The Jam' inside each of them.

These shops based their ideals on those of the original off-the-peg Mod shops of the Sixties such as Male West One where

the trousers were pre-made to a certain length. After trying them on, the assistant would pin them up and would alter them for you within the hour. Although shops such as these did a great service to young Mods on tight finances, they were frowned upon in many of the Mod clubs. To many, only original vintage clothing (which was still quite easy to pick up in charity shops) or tailor-made clothing would do. Shops like the Cavern were seen as entry level Mod clothing retailers. The fact is that anybody slightly interested in Mod styles at the time could visit them. Whilst you could maybe forgive a young kid of 13 or 14 parading around in a badge covered parka and burgundy coloured Sta-prest. Anybody old enough to earn a wage would be generally laughed at by the older contingent of Mods.

You came to realise that on a visit to Carnaby Street during this period, there were two completely separate sets of Mods making their presence felt. One group completely oblivious to the fact that they were seen as clueless by the others. In the Sixties they'd been known as 'Scooter Boys', 'Tickets' or as Ian Hebditch said in his thesis on Portsmouth Mods, 'Feds'. They probably had half a dozen names in other areas too, but in Eighties Britain the derisive word for them was 'Moddy Boys'

In the mainstream world at this time popular suits had padded shoulders and were one-button baggy linen suits, that may have looked fine upon a vice cop cruising around Miami but on the dancefloors of London's underground Mod scene you'd be shot. What you needed was a tailored classic-cut suit. This is where Charlie Antoniou came in to play. Charlie became the tailor of choice for many Mods because not only was he fairly cheap, he knew exactly what you wanted. He understood three-button jackets, four-button jackets, double-breasted jackets. He knew all about stepped-bottoms on trousers, splits at the seams, frog mouth-pockets, covered buttons… he was the man. Finally, you had a great reason to be roaming Carnaby

Street. You'd press the small bell beside the door to get buzzed-in, up the stairs to the small room filled with busy sewing machines and stacks of cloth. Likeminded Mod friends all chatting and checking the clothes hanging on the rack. It was all about individuality. Anybody could wear a three-button jacket from The Cavern, but a tailor could make you a beautiful eight-button double-breasted number.

Of course, not everyone used Charlie's. Others favoured Paul The Tailoring Stylist in Berwick Street, Crawford's in Ilford, Stan Price in Walthamstow or Dave Wax in Hammersmith, to name a few.

Handmade shirts became popular amongst a select few. That meant a trip to see Katy Stevens in Archer Street. Katy was an elderly lady, who'd come originally from Budapest. Katy, along with her husband, had ran Star Shirtmakers back in the day. Now all these years later, she was on her own, apart from the company of a cat, and she'd regale young Mods with tales of making shirts for The Small Faces and The Beatles in the Sixties. Many, including myself, never really believed her, but she was telling the truth.

Alan Handscombe discovered Mod through two of his mates, Rob Murphy and Ian Jackson, who he'd met at Two Tone Gigs. The First Mod club he'd been to was at the Phoenix in Cavendish Square and run by Tony Class in around late 1981.

"I sort of fell into it as I'd seen *Quadrophenia* when it came out and been to see The Jam four times. It didn't make me want to be a Mod though as I wasn't into Parkas, Mod Revival etc. I was a 16-year-old Skinhead into ska, rocksteady and soul music, and to be fair, a lot of the Mods I saw about were not particularly sharp. As a young Skin and living in Camden Town I was able to get tons of great clobber. You could still get Brutus Shirts in the packets for a fiver down Brick Lane market and great tonic trousers, so I was well turned out by the time I discovered

Mod. My first tailored suit was by a tailor called Paul's on Berwick Street, before you hit the market. It was a lovely suit, but expensive. I'd heard about Charlie on Carnaby Street and Katy Stevens in Soho for shirts as well. I started to use them and carried on using them for a very long time. Katy sadly passed away and Charlie then stopped tailoring, so I use George of Haringey right up to this day."

By 1984, Mods also had a new enemy in the form of Casuals. The Casual movement had started to evolve in the early Eighties, building up on the football terraces from Liverpool, Manchester, London and the Home Counties. It was based around a love of modern European and designer clothing and had replaced that whole Skinhead/Bootboy look of the team scarf wrapped around your wrist. Boots were replaced by the latest trainers Adidas, Puma, Fila, Reebok, Nike and clobber ranged from Pringle golf jumpers to Armani coats, taking in Lyle and Scott roll necks, Sergio Tacchini tracksuits, Pierre Cardin, Benetton, Robe di Kappa, Elesse, Burberry and Aquascutum.

Whilst many of these kids, liked rap and dance acts. there was no specific style of music allligned to the cult, although there were attempts to have two bands represent their culture, in the same way as The Who and The Small Faces were attached to Mod. One band, Accent, were a Chelsea-supporting band who fancied themselves as some kind of Casual Jam wannabes, who managed to talk the legendary clothing shop, Stuart's, in the Uxbridge Road to give them free clobber. The other band was called The Sines.

Either way, Casuals was just another name to add to the growing list after Rockers, Teds, Punks, Boneheads, New Romantics, Rockabillies, Psychobilly's, Goths, Soul Boys and generally everybody else who seemed to hate Mods.

In an interview with *Sounds* in September '84 Dennis Greaves of The Truth was interviewed, and whilst talking about his band he said: "Casuals, Smoothies, Soulboys…they're all getting more like Mods all the time, which is great."

Unfortunately, somebody had failed to tell this to the Casuals and the violence continued.

Jonathon Cooke: I remember, around 1984, one of my first jobs was at the men's clothes shop Woodhouse in their Oxford Street branch. There were a lot of gay guys working there and they took me under their wing.

"I was really in to the Mod scene at the time, and they took me to the WAG club. I remember I was wearing a Prince of Wales check suit and a black roll neck. They gave me some poppers, and I had a brilliant time with those guys.

"Anyway, you were supposed to wear the clothes from Woodhouse when you worked there. There was lots of Armani and that kind of stuff. We'd get loads of Casuals coming in to buy jumpers from there. I wasn't into that at all but I had to buy a few items of clothing to wear there. They told me that if I came dressed in my own clothing that they would have to let me go because I didn't fit in and Woodhouse wasn't about youth cults.

"I remember that I'd convinced them to sell *The Face* magazine in the shop. When the first issue they ordered arrived, it was the one with a feature they'd done about a Mod run to Clacton. They were saying: "Why are we stocking this magazine?" I told them that just happens to be in this one issue.

"One Friday night I came off my scooter, and I had to stay at a friend's house, and he was a Mod. I'd ripped my clothes in the accident, and I had to borrow some of his clothes to go to work the next morning. I couldn't do anything else, but that morning they sacked me because they were convinced I was trying to turn their place into a Mod shop!

"It was a shame, because I loved working there, but I went to work for Stiff Records just after."

Apart from run-ins with these perm and wedge-haired firms, buying records was also a huge part of Eighties Mod life.

Dave Edwards: "Camden Market used to be great in the early Eighties, there were loads of record shops and the markets had a couple of stalls. Record fairs were in their infancy then too. There used to be some great ones at The Bonnington Hotel in Bloomsbury and that's where I first met Mick Smith, still my favourite record dealer. There were also a couple of shops in Hanway Street, a small road at the end of Oxford Street leading to Tottenham Court Road. One of the shops had sales boxes in there from Ady Croasdell and Ian Clark. You could always find some great soul and R&B in them. Best find for me was probably 'I'm A Lover Not A Fighter' by The Brand on Piccadilly for £4. The person I was with offered me £100 straight away. I've still got it with the price sticker still on the sleeve."

Another person who would help shape the Mod scene through various records in the mid-Eighties was Paul Hallam.

Paul Hallam grew up under the flight path of Heathrow near Feltham in Middlesex. When all the cool kids at school were trying to be pre-teen David Cassidy's or Marc Bolan's, Paul was at home listening to Tommy Steele and George Formby. That may sound quite cool now to some, Paul assures me that it was not, in mid-Seventies suburbia.

Football replaced music as was his big thing from 1974, first Liverpool, then Walton and Hersham and then finally, around 1977, Millwall.

Another big love of his was vintage horror films (the UK was enjoying a big horror revival at the time with comics like *Monster Fun* and crisps like Fangs, Bones and those pickled onion adverts with Vincent Price. Paul's mum used to let him stay up in the summer of '77 to watch re-runs of *The Mummy, Creature from the Black Lagoon* and the cross over films such as *Frankenstein meets the Wolfman, House of Dracula* and so on.

Around the same time the first official Beatles live album was released – *Live at the Hollywood Bowl*. With no footage available of the fab four in concert the ad men used old Universal clips to promote the album.

Paul Hallam: "They would play 10 seconds of 'Help' - to a clip of Fay Ray screaming in King Kong's arms, 'Ticket to Ride' - to a clip of Dracula's carriage driven fast through Carpathian Mountains. I liked the clips and I started to like the sounds. My sister was (and still is) 13 years older than me so had grown up a Beatles fan in the Sixties. I remember going around her house aged 11 and 11/12ths and asking if i could borrow some of her old albums. She agreed, and I did. Within two weeks I had borrowed and taped the lot - home taping did NOT kill the music industry. Far from it in my house.

"She suggested I listen to some more stuff of hers - mainly Sixties pop like the Tremeloes and Cliff Richard ('The Day I Met Marie' is good, honest). And so, it started. I borrowed some Rolling Stones, Kinks and a random Who single that was wedged between Pickettywitch and Edison Lighthouse.

"In the September of 1979 I turned 14. I had no sense of style, but I did have a party. The deal in those days was you had a party and everybody who came bought you a single. Colin Hanna bought me a copy of 'Time For Action' by Secret Affair. I had been keeping an eye on the Mod Revival but it was all a bit too punky for me and a lot of the kids at my school who had turned Mod seemed to become Rude Boys before I had time to ask them about it. And I was still only 14.

"I had put the Manfred Mann *Semi-Detached Suburban* compilation album on my birthday wish list, but my mum seeing a bargain bought me another one from Record Scene

Sunbury as it was a quid cheaper. This one had some of the hits on it but also some cool R'n'B jazz tracks including a vocal version of 'Watermelon Man'.

"A year moved on and I was still buying up Beatles solo albums – including all the Ringo ones, but I was also getting some Kinks and Troggs ones of my own.

"Then around my 15th birthday a distant cousin called Barry moved down from Wales to live with us. He was 21 years old, had a job at a tax office in Ealing, and the biggest record collection I had at the time ever seen in my life. My parents forbade me from playing 'Taxman' by the Beatles loudly on the day he arrived so I got around the ban and played 'Sunny Afternoon' by The Kinks instead "the tax man's taken all my dough etc etc".

"He asked me if I liked this sort of music, and if If I did, how did I feel about bands A, B, C and D? I hadn't heard bands A, B, C, or D, so when he returned to his parental home a few weeks later he bought me copies back to listen to and tape. These included early Bowie, *Motown's 20 Mod Classics* and a Phil Spector compilation album. I loved 'em.

"Two months later everything changed. John Lennon was shot dead and my dream of a Beatles re-union was off the table. I mourned and wore a black armband – worn with a black shirt and black jumper – to school. I decided if there would be no Beatles gig for me to go to I had better find something else to do. I knew of a venue nearby to me called Feltham Football Club. As many places did back then it hosted different music nights each week – Skinhead Monday, Heavy Metal Tuesday, Punk Wednesday and Mod Thursday.

"A few of my mates claimed to have been before, though this turned out to be false, so I decided that week in early December 1980 this was it – I was gonna go to a Mod night. I borrowed a Fred Perry top from school mate Nigel Mitchell to go with my peg trousers and tassle loafers, and off I went.

"I loved it. I knew quite a lot of the songs they played and even had a bit of a dance in the corner where nobody could see me. We'd got a lift to the club in the back of a van driven by one of the bigger boys, but they refused to take me all the way home, so I was dropped off in Ashford with a 30-minute walk on the cards and I was late home already. One of the blokes on the scooters that had driven behind the van offered me a lift and had a spare helmet. So that was it. 15 years old. On the back of the scooter after my first Mod Club experience.

"I woke up the next day and re-wrote my Christmas present list crossing out. 'Venus and Mars' album by Wings and replacing it with a pair of Sta Press and Hush Puppies. I was on the road to Mod obsession."

Paul Weller hadn't been idle after his break-up of The Jam, and he'd teamed up with Mick Talbot of the Merton Parkas to launch his new venture, The Style Council. Whilst Weller was happy to embrace a far more soulful journey into music with his new band, many old Jam fans really could not get where their beloved spokesperson was coming from and found it hard to relate to Weller's new, impassioned, vision. Opinion was divided. Some would say that he had abandoned his Mod ideals, whilst the more perceptive ones thought he had embraced the true Mod ideology even more.

Some of the better bands that carried the thankless torch for the Mod scene during this period included The Direct Hits from South London, Small World. Fast Eddie, The Times, The Moment, The Blades, The Scene (originally 007 and featuring Gary Wood on guitar) and a band called The Jet Set, who based themselves around the late bubblegum pop acts like The Monkees.

Probably considered to be one of the best bands were The Truth who'd formed in 1982 and included Dennis Greaves of the R&B band, Nine Below Zero. They'd adopted a quite soulful pop sound and had even had chart hits with 'Confusion Hits Us Everytime' (No, 22 in '83) and the brilliant 'A Step In The Right Direction' (No. 32 in '83) plus other minor hits in '84.

The Prisoners were probably the most widely respected band around then. Not strictly a Mod band, but more of a Sixties garage band, their Hammond organ-filled tunes crossed over to a much wider appeal than just the Mod scene. Graham Day (Vocals and Guitars), James Taylor (Vox Continental and Hammond Organs), Allan Crockford (Bass) and Johnny Symons (Drums) filled a gap for a whole bunch of Small Faces addicts who had never seen their heroes. The band had already released its first album, *A Taste of Pink*, in September 1982, filled completely with the band's own compositions including 'Better In Black' and 'Come To The Mushroom'.

There seemed to be interest in Mod again, so much so that *The Face* magazine ran a feature on the Clacton rally that year, and *Sounds* had even run articles on bands that were representing 'Mod 84' and the first ever National Mod Meeting in November that year to decide the following year's scooter rallies.

Bands may have been playing, but the scene gravitated towards rare vinyl. In the early to mid-Eighties, London was a treasure trove of record shops. Hanway Street, a tiny offshoot from Oxford Street boasted three shops dealing in old vinyl, Rocks Off, Vinyl Experience and On The Beat. In Camden there was Out On The Floor and also Rock On by Camden tube, plus loads of stalls and small shops around Camden Market. Sounds Original was by Northfields Tube Station and Vinyl Solution in Hereford Road. In Portobello Road there was Intoxica and the nearby Plastic Passion. There were tons of other outlets dotted all over the capital.

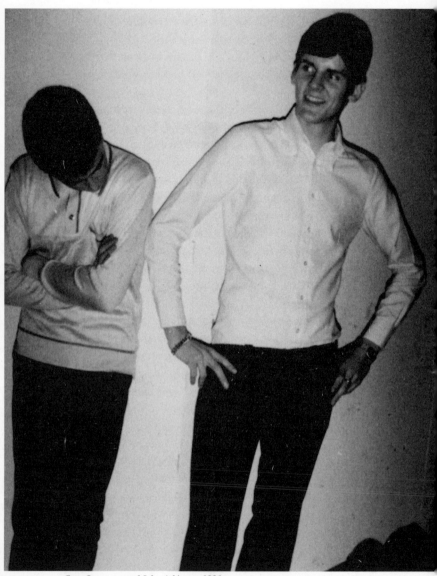

Greg Boraman and John Atkinson, 1986

Paul Hallam: "Because of Cousin Barry I had a massive head start on most of the other kids at school. Although he was not a Mod and was Bowie obsessed, he collected anything and everything. Moving into early 1981 I would take my home-made tapes to school and a hand-held tape recorder and sit in free lessons playing things like 'Tape My Tip' by Bowie and the Kenny Miller version of it, The Yardbirds, along with early Motown tracks that other pupils at Kennington Manor could only dream of owning.

"I still played my Beatles collection at home but became intrigued by the cover versions on the early albums. So, my first point of call with collecting involved finding out about The Shirelles – who the Beatles had covered. Then the Isley Brothers and so on.

"In Chertsey, few miles from where I lived, was possibly the greatest record shop of all time. Mr Waxy's. He had previously had a small room at the back of the Record Scene at Sunbury Cross but had now opened his own shop. I don't think I have ever known a shop like it. There were no records on display and Mr Waxy - whose real name was Mick Scott sat behind a counter drinking lemonade all day with dark glasses on.

"What you had to do was go in and ask for a record and he would go look see if he had it. Or if you were a regular he would dig out a pile for you each visit or do the pre-amazon thing of 'If you like that you will want to own this....'

"I had visited him previously to buy some rare Beatles singles but now I was on a different mission. In the Summer of 1981 Capital Radio, when it was good, ran a radio series called 'Sound of the City' which did two-hour long episodes on the Mod years.

"On one of these shows I heard for the very first time 'Buzz With The Fuzz' by Chris Farlowe. I rang Mr Waxy up and asked if he had a copy. He did – for 20 pounds. That was two weeks money for me – I had a Saturday job working in my dad's motorbike shop that paid £10 a day. I cycled there and back being very careful with the Farlowe single on way back.

"He had recognised me from my Beatles days and was surprised that somebody so young on a push bike was asking for such a rare single. From then on, I would visit him pretty much every week for the next 5-6 years.

"Probably 70 per cent of all my records came from him. He didn't always get it right with the 'If you like this you will love this' sales technique and I remember him trying to sell me Jacques Dutronc 'Et Moi, Et Moi, Et Moi' for months before I finally bought it, and learned to love it.

"Other places that I bought from back then were all the ones in Hanway Street, various ones in Camden, Memory Lane in Morden – run by Mad Mick who had every Motown single (including all the Oriole and Stateside ones etc) up until 1967, Jive Dive in Hanworth and Right Track Records – owned by Terry and Belinda Stokes. In 1984 Terry decided to shut the shop and buy a pub and sold off all his personal collection as well as the stock of the shop. I reckon I must have spent £500 in there that week. At a time when I was lucky to be earning £100 a week through my job in print – though I was probably earning as much as that if not more DJ'ing by this time."

The mid-Eighties would see good Mod clubs in London flourish thanks to great DJ's like Toski, who was DJ'ing at the Phoenix in Cavendish Square on Saturday nights, as well as the likes of Ian Jackson who DJ'd at The Metropolitan on Wednesdays, and a young up-and-coming DJ by the name of Dom Bassett.

Elsewhere in the country, things were happening too. In Liverpool there were events at The Dolphin in Paradise Street, the Sportsman's Arms in Coventry, and in Bournemouth there were events put on by the Inset. Wales, Scotland and Ireland too had thriving scenes.

Probably the most influential in terms of music was the Birmingham scene. The city had a long history of smart, sussed kids who'd danced and posed at venues like Pollyanna's in Newhall Street and the Barrel Organ in Digbeth High Street. By '84 it would be The Outrigger on Moor Street. The jewel in the Birmingham scene's crown was the DJ, Tony Reynolds, who at the time was in his thirties, he'd built up a reputation playing behind the decks of the Barrel Organ but now the Outrigger crowd grooved to his eclectic mic of Soul, R'n'B, Ska, and Jazz.

Paul Hallam and Richard Early meanwhile had given the London of the Eighties it's very own Scene Club.

CHAPTER

TWELVE

SNEAKERS AND THE PATH TO ENLIGHTENMENT

"I started going to Sneakers at The Bush in Shepherds Bush by default. I was 17, it was 1983 and I had my first (road legal) scooter and needed to get out. I was a Mod and many of my school and college mates had moved on to being Scooterists. I felt very isolated and disappointed."

GUY JOSEPH

Paul Hallam: "The summer of 1983 and a new sheet of paper appeared at Tony Class clubs. It had been a one-sided list of clubs he ran called *What's Appening for Mods* but now there was something called *The Phoenix List*. It didn't just have Tony Clubs on it but ALL the clubs around London including ones in exotic places like Chadwell Heath! Me and our scooter club – first The Interceptors then The A-Z decided to check out these far-flung places and travelled to the Regency Suite and The Castle, Tooting amongst many others.

"The Phoenix was an organisation set up to keep the spirit of Mod alive and promote all events – not just Tony Class's. Although I liked a lot of the ideas behind the organisation, I along with many others, dismissed it in public as a dumbing down of the scene. Trying to make it organised like the boy scouts rather than a youth club. The Phoenix Society was around 12-15 strong and If I remember rightly only men - though Tony Class' then wife Jill would go along on occasions.

"Then around the late summer of that year I got an invite to go to a meeting, initially as a guest and then as a member, of this elite club. At the time they met in an upstairs room of the Griffin pub in Shoreditch. I went to print college in Clerkenwell at the time, so Thursday evenings were perfect for me.

"College finished early for some reason that first night, so I was at the pub around 6pm and meetings didn't start til 7.30pm. I wasn't a drinker back then, so I walked around the area for 90 minutes aimlessly.

"Once inside the meeting I kept quiet as some of the older and louder members – Eddie Piller and Mick Mouskos – did most of the talking. At the end, Mark Johnson for some odd reason, commented on what a grand job Tony Class was doing at the Bush on Saturday nights. I at last opened my mouth and said: "Can't we hear some new songs down there? You are playing the same tracks you were playing when I first started going two years ago. How about a bit more R'n'B?"

"Mark Johnson shot me down and Tony didn't even comment.

"Next week I was invited along again and voted in as a member. After proceedings had ended, Tony asked me and Richard 'Shirlee' Early to stay behind – here we go I thought…

"He asked me and Shirlee what we thought he should be playing and why. I blurted out some rubbish about John Lee Hooker having more records than 'Boom Boom' and 'Dimples' and Shirlee talked about the Modern Jazz Quartet. He looked at us and said "If you think you can do better then I'll give you the Bush on Sundays. I'll promote it and pay you and you can play what you like"

"Bloody hell."

"Well what you gonna call it?" he asked.

"I wanted Le Chat Noir or something equally pretentious. But Shirlee said no it should be 'Sneakers' after the Tommy Tucker song.

"Mark Johnson then chipped in that it should be smart dress only and he would do the door to make sure nobody scruffy or in jeans got in. And that was it. Sneakers opened early November 1983."

Sneakers was held at The Bush Hotel, 2, Goldhawk Road, right opposite Shepherd's Bush Green. Just a few feet to the right of it was the BBC Television Studios where Terry Wogan's chat show was recorded at the time.

On the pavement, outside there would be a line of scooters. On entry, the bar would be on the left, with the dancefloor in front of you. At the far end of the room there was a small stage, perched upon it was a table with a set of decks and an amplifier. Stood behind these would be either Paul Hallam or Richard Early AKA Shirlee.

Paul would play more soulful choices but kept away from what is commonly referred to as 'Northern'. We are talking more R'n'B here. Shirlee leaned towards a far more blues and ska-laden set.

The dancefloor was often full. Neat moves, spins, hand gestures.

Big favourites were 'Wade In The Water – Little Sonny, 'Everybody Dance Now' -The Soul City, 'Baby Never Say Goodbye' – The Bo Street Runners and 'Good Lovin' – The Olympics.

Lines of people doing a formation clapping dance to the Hammond organ-drenched 'Bert's Apple Crumble' by The Quik or Maximillian's 'The Snake'.

Peoples feet deftly blocking to old blues tunes such as 'Go To The Mardi Gras' by Professor Longhair, 'Shake Your Hips' by Slim Harpo or 'We're Gonna Get Married' by Bo Diddley.

Guy Joseph: "I started going to Sneakers at The Bush in Shepherds Bush by default. I was 17, it was 1983 and I had my first (road legal) scooter and needed to get out. I was working in a restaurant in Blackheath and my only night off was Sunday. I was a Mod and many of my school and college mates had moved on to being Scooterists or anti-mod. I felt very isolated and disappointed. I was the lone ranger and I had to travel 'all the way' to Shepherd's Bush to find like-minded people. I had so wanted to join my older peers and be welcomed into their life, to ride with them to exotic places – but it was not to be, they had disappeared.

"So, I turned up at The Bush. It was winter, dark and cold. I saw a small group of scooters parked outside. I paid at the door and entered. The room was quite empty. I thought it would be buzzing with loads of hip cats and sexy chicks, it wasn't. I didn't recognise any of the records played, stayed about an hour and tried to leave slightly deflated. There was another scooter parked behind me so I couldn't. I plucked up the courage to speak to the DJ, (Paul Hallam) to ask the owner to move his scoot. We had a little chat, he asked me why I was leaving? I made up some lame excuse of work or something like that and then negotiated my way back to South London. I don't think I returned to Shepherds bush for a while. There was another mixed 'night' of Scooterist and Mods closer to me in Deptford, so I hung out there on my one night off."

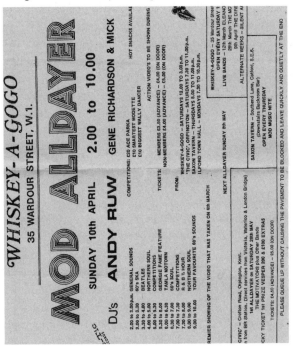

Ann Griffin: "Tony Class was my introduction to the scene, it seemed that every club I went to when I first got into Mod, he ran. To be able to go out every night if the week if you wanted to when you were 15/16 was brilliant. Paul Hallam and Shirlee then started Sneakers which was the complete anthesis to a

Tony Class 'night' – but it was what was needed. The scene started to splinter into Mods and Scooter Boys. Eddie Piller was always a bit of a Face. Then you had The Camden Stylists, who nailed the authentic Suedehead look. Trevor French, Stuart Farnham, Paul Newman, Toski, Nick Aghaudino, just really smart sussed Mods who could all dance. Vicki Hallam, Lucy, Georgia, Ela, Michaela, Minnie were the girls who nailed the authentic Mod look early on. Then there were The Ilford Chaps, Big Bob, The Birmingham lot for their hipsters and dance moves and The Swindon lot for being lary."

Guy Joseph: "Paul Hallam had made an impression on me that first night. He was very smart, and had a beautiful girlfriend, Vicki. His DJ partner Richard 'Shirlee' Early was the best dancer I had ever seen, I used to stare at him and would try do the same moves. He would dance by himself on the empty floor with such confidence and speed. These two Mods were 'top boys'."

"The Camden Stylists were a loose knit group of mates, male and female, who attended Sneakers together from its start till its close," states Alan Handscombe. "The majority of us were from Camden but a few from other parts of London. We never called ourselves that. Who coined that name I still don't know, but it was pretty cool at the time. We had all come from the traditional Skin/ Rude Boy element, so we stood out and were different from the rest of the Mods attending clubs at the time. We never had problems from the Bonehead fraternity in London as at the time we all had the same shit from the Old Bill. We just left each other alone. When I ran The Penny Black reggae nights just down the road, there were the right-wing lot that drank there, but nothing ever happened. As it happened, it was other Mods who we found to be arseholes. A friend of mine went to Ilford Palais Mod night and was jumped by some Mods from East London. He was better dressed than them, in

Roberto Carlo, tailored strides and Bass Weejuns, but he had a
number two crop haircut, so he got a bloody nose."

Ann Griffin:"The Ugly Buglies happened as a reaction really
to a group of lads who thought we were easy targets for mickey
taking. There were a group of us knocking about together
at the time – myself, Anita Phillips, Hannah Marsh, Annabel
Lichfield, Diane Daly and Liz Segal. Diane and Liz were from
East London where there was a big contingent of Mods who
attended Sneakers. For some reason, there were just digs at
each other all the time, mostly done in jest but we weren't
particularly liked as we didn't conform to most teenage males
ideas of a 'Modette' (ie we weren't very pretty!). I found out
from Jim Watson that Andy Orr who was one of the Ilford
Chaps had said "Those girls be very ugly bugly". It has to be
said that Andy Orr was going through a *Clockwork Orange* phase
at the time. We loved it – so we decided that we were going
to have that name for our little group. So, we took that insult
and turned it back round at them! We created the impression
we were gobby and lary and didn't take any shit. So, we played
on that. We were also very sussed, knew how we liked to dress
and gave as good as we got. We adopted the Mod girl look of
63/64, short hair, ski pants and hush puppies. We just made
sure that every weekend we had the best time and just laughed
constantly. To be honest you either loved us or hated us. It's
great to know we were always well thought of, but some people
have said that we intimidated them, and I do feel a bit sad about
that as it wasn't our intention. But then I suppose all these
females looking like extras from *Prisoner Cell Block H* would be
off putting!"

Dave Edwards: "My first real venture out to clubs was things
like Andy Ruw's alldayers in the WAG club on a Saturday
afternoon and The George the Fourth on Brixton Hill, right
next to Brixton Prison where they had a northern soul night

Guy Joseph (in parka)

on Mondays. Then it was Saturday nights at The Bush Hotel with Tony Class and Monday nights there with live bands, The Castle in Tooting and a local pub The Ben Truman had a Sixties DJ on Thursday nights. When Sneakers started up on a Sunday night at The Bush Hotel, it was what I didn't know I'd been looking for. I'd enjoyed Tony Class' Saturday nights, but it was becoming more of a Scooter Boy night rather than a Mod night. Sneakers was tailormade mohair suits, shirts by Katy Stevens, John Lee Hooker, Prince Buster, basically what we'd read about in Richard Barnes' Mods book. There was also a camaraderie there that still exists to this day, many of us were a bit too young to fully appreciate the revival a few years before but had stuck with it and found our own post revival scene and as seriously as we took it all as regards clothes, music and authenticity, we all had a great laugh too."

Guy Joseph: "When I returned to Sneakers it had changed. I wasn't on my own this time. Two brothers, Ian and Chris Parr, old friends from school were with me. I pretended to have some 'insider information' as I had already been. To my delight Paul greeted me kindly. I was 'IN' and I felt like I had been accepted. The place was busier this time and I recognised a few people, even if I still didn't recognise the records.

"Looking back, I realise that the Mod scene was at a low. It had gone from post *Quadrophenia* to small pockets dotted around the country. It wasn't 'Millions like us'! Sneakers was a sanctuary for serious-minded Mods who wanted to enjoy the cool of Mod. The club grew and we felt that we were part of it. I remember being outside once and someone turned up in a silver Messerschmitt bubble car. He cooly climbed out wearing a pork pie and entered the club. This was my most special memory of Sneakers."

Ann Griffin: "The look to us was very important. It was a very boyish Mod look that we were going for. Luckily, Anita was a hairdresser at the time (whose boss was an original Mod) which was why her hair was perfect, and so she cut mine. We were also lucky that in the Eighties you could still get decent clothes from charity shops and markets. Our mums were also pretty good seamstresses, so mine used to alter stuff that I'd find that didn't quite fit. BHS and Littlewoods still did crew neck twin sets, you could pick up decent 3 button tops in 'old men' shops. Anita had a few outfits made by a local tailor, and Diane's mum used to make her some fab clothes. Shoes could be bought new – we really went for granny styles or from markets and charity shops. Diane did get Mary Janes from Anello and Davide which we all thought was really cool. I remember a lot of Sunday mornings trawling Camden Market – you could always find decent stuff, hangovers permitting."

Simon Fane: "Despite from the earliest time being into the Sixties side of Mod music from 1985 onwards I was favouring the jazzier end of things. The Hammond organ sound of Smith and McGriff, the piano-led soul-jazz of Ramsey Lewis/ Young Holt and the gritty instrumental records had featured heavily alongside the funkier Sixties dance-craze records such as Tom & Jerrio and Roy Lee Johnson, heavy Chicago R'n'B from the Chess stable, the big latin-soul explosion of Mongo Santamaria & Ray Barretto and always a love of Jamaican Ska from Island and Blue Beat records. This is what I lived for much more than the Mod groups of the time or the Northern or rare soul sound."

Two Mod groups had, however, emerged throughout 1985 to help spread the live vibe and they would be Makin' Time from the West Midlands and The Untouchables from Los Angeles, who toured over here. Other than that, most new groups were largely ignored by the majority of London Mods and areas like Birmingham and Coventry where original vinyl ruled.

Guy Joseph: "Sneakers had grown. There were Mods coming from all over the country and Europe to enjoy their two and a half hours of Sunday sermon. I made firm friendships with many of them. The music and atmosphere was electric. I was more familiar with the records now. John Lee Hooker, Jimmy McGriff, The Soul Sisters would pack the floor out and Shirley would command it.

"Sweat would drip down from the ceiling, it was really quite uncomfortable but we all tried our best to be on top and look good. I would try and co-ordinate my wardrobe every week and buy new gear so as not to wear the same combination twice. I don't think I ever saw any violence between Mods there. There were some instances between Scooter Boys but there was a strict door policy of 'no jeans' so this kept the standard high. There was a Mod from East London called Stephen and he had a beautiful Triumph Herald, red and white. I remember there had been trouble with scooter boys the week before and there were a few of them hanging about outside. Stephen was wearing a navy blue, chalk stripe suit. He calmly opened the door of his car, hung up his jacket and then attacked 2 blokes with a kung fu move. They were both immediately writhing on the floor."

Paul Hallam: "It ran at the Bush for about 2 years and 4 months. Then the Clarendon in Hammersmith for 6 months – but I never liked that venue. Then the 79 Club in Oxford Street, which history has wrongly remembered as Sneakers plus Mod revival tracks -, in other words, the name of the club confused people. We stayed at the venue for 6 months.

"Then we did a one-off venue that nobody can remember for one night only. Then Portlands until its closure in July 87. By then, it had pretty much become a Latin Boogaloo

The Author, 1988

club. It had its moments after it left the Bush - there were some great nights at the 79 Club and at Portlands but by 1986 a lot of the scene was moving on.

"One thing about Sneakers I am proud of is the way the music progressed. Within 3-4 months all the tracks that were being played were no longer and new ones came in instead – except anniversary and Christmas parties."

The one thing that clubs like Sneakers in London, and The Outrigger in Birmingham did was magnify people's spirit and the need to be different. Whilst all those around the regulars at these clubs were happy to wander about in T-shirts adorned with the words 'Choose Life'. The people who attended these clubs appreciated their fellow club-goer's efforts to get across town to attend, literally taking their lives into their own hands. Inside these venues for the few hours that you were there, the outside world didn't exist. There was no Thatcher's Britain, no Miner's Strike, no Band Aid and certainly no fucking 'Frankie Says…'

The success of Sneakers would also have an effect the following year as the Scooter rally scene of 1985 would change dramatically. Whilst 1984 had provided a breakaway from the National Scooter Rallies as Mods had chosen to go on separate runs organised by The Phoenix Society known as 'Southern Mod Scooter Runs'. Paul Hallam and friends would offer a further alternative.

Paul Hallam: "In 1983 I met a lot of people from East London. One of them was Bob Morris who took an instant dislike to me. This was not helped by my somewhat arrogant interview in *The Face* magazine after Clacton 1984. In fact, at Brighton that year he had intended to give me a good hiding but he had a dodgy leg and I was on my toes.

"Somehow, we became friends. He had been on a self-imposed year or so ban from the Mod scene – preferring to travel away with West Ham on a Saturday than go to clubs and the like. He admitted through gritted teeth that he quite liked what we were doing at Sneakers but wanted to take it further.

Paul Hallam at the tailors

Clive Bushnell, 1989

CHAPTER
THIRTEEN

NO JEANS, NO GREENS
NO CASUALS

*"Me and Piller said why don't we start
an R'n'B club? So, we went into a pub in
Whitechapel and told them we wanted to put on
a jazz night. This little Jewish guy who owned
it said, "I love Jazz!" So we started Friday's
there, and that was the first Crawdaddy R'n'B
club."*

BOB MORRIS

B ob Morris: "The Crawdaddy stuff was in reaction against
the Northern Soul invading our scene. Out of all the 1979-
81 Mods there were very few left by 1982.

"Dick Coombes was running The Greyhound in Chadwell Heath,
Essex, and that was Northern Soul. So, Ray Patriotic and Eddie Piller
started The Regency Suite in Chadwell Heath in direct competition
to that.

"By around 1983 all those 81/82 Mods had all turned Casual or
blown out. So, the few of us that were left carried it on.

"Me and Piller said why don't we start an R'n'B club? So, we went
into a pub in Whitechapel and told them we wanted to put on a jazz
night. This little Jewish guy who owned it said, "I love Jazz!" So we
started Friday's there, and that was the first Crawdaddy R'n'B club."

Paul Hallam: "The Crawdaddy club that people probably
remember most is the Ben Truman – a dark basement in the then
un-fashionable Southwark Bridge Road. Mick Wheeler, another
Crawdaddy member, drank in there in his dinner hour as he worked
nearby.

"Before the Ben Truman I'm sure we did other nights. One in
Whitechapel. One in Leytonstone – where there was a riot.

"We were kind of like The Phoenix I suppose but younger and
angrier. Members were myself, Bob, Andy Drew Orr, Mick Wheeler
and Eddie Piller.

I'm not sure how the pirate rally thing came about, but I had
been DJ'ing on all the Tony Class/Phoenix rallies for some time.
And I guess I thought I'd like to do something a bit more edgy. The
weekend we picked, the Phoenix were doing something far far away
up north, Scarborough to be precise.

"By this time Sneakers and I had gone a bit national. I'd been
DJ'ing at the Outrigger in Birmingham since I was 17. And as people
started to know about Sneakers so I'd get asked to go play around
the country, so myself and Garry Moore, decided to go find a seaside
resort to host our pirate rally.

"While my cool mates at school were going to Marbella for their holidays, me and my family were camping in a little-known rock off the coast of Portsmouth called Hayling Island. That was our first point of call Then we stumbled upon a gem, The Solent club opened by Pete Shepherd. Pete had made his money in London and retired down to Hayling and bought a club – now flats. He seemed to like us and we liked him. The deal was done and the date booked.

"Flyers were handed out around London and the Modernist network. Bob wrote the words on the flyer and Terry Rawlings did the graphics.

"I think it carried a line like – 'A Fuck the Phoenix' Rally - that didn't endear me to Mr Class as you can imagine.

"The first one is probably one of the greatest nights of my promoting career. Everybody had something made especially for it, and to quote Tony Schockman on amphetamines – "its fucking wall to wall mohair, fucking wall to wall mohair."

"We did possibly four events at Hayling – by the time of the last one 1987 – we probably looked more like the Casuals than the local Casuals we were fighting. Ski jackets and Ski jumpers. I'm glad we stopped when we did as there wasn't a bad one in my memory."

Ann Griffin: "By about '86, I sort of grew out of it. A lot of people were drifting off and I started going to 'Casual' pubs that seemed to have sprung up in the mid-Eighties (normally called things like 'Septembers'). I then got into hip hop and by 88/89 was heavily into that and the house scene. However, I still would come out if at some 'normal' club in the west end and then find myself popping into the 100 Club. So, although I was off the scene by the late Eighties I would still frequently go to Mod clubs."

Paul Hallam: "In 1986 me and Ed Piller were thrown out of the Phoenix, I can't remember why. I was dropped from DJ'ing at the Phoenix rallies due to me running events that were in competition to them.

"In the Summer of 86 I'd gone to Paul Murphy's club at Sol Y Sombre behind Oxford Street. It felt illegal. it was hot. It was open late, and it was full of people dancing to the maddest Jazz records ever. Tracks that nobody would have moved to if I had played at Sneakers. I felt that was more me than watching the Purple Hearts come out of the ground on a stage in the Hippodrome.

"I had turned 21 and got engaged. I was saving for my first flat and had been DJ'ing four or five times a week for four long years. I was listening to more and more Latin tracks and less R'n'B.

"I don't think it fell apart. I probably did, not the scene. I think I wanted something different and I found it in of all places: The Beastie Boys and lysergic acid diethylamide.

"I got married and was more interested in taking Mushrooms or Acid and walking in the woods than having trousers hand made.

"I took Acid, I had kids, I started going to Millwall again – 30 games a season home and away – and eventually got into the whole Ecstasy house scene. I was never a fan of the latter but all my mates were doing it so I went along with them."

The Mod scene certainly never fell apart, but it did lose some great characters. Tony Class continued to promote clubs under the banner 'Classic Club International' or C.C.I as everybody called it. Whilst two Mods going by the name of Rob Messer and Andrew 'Mace' Mason offered alternative Pirate rallies under the name 'The Rhythm & Soul Set'.

Bob Morris: "I think a few of us were down Carnaby Street, there were a lot of Mods down there, and there was this geezer dressed up like Paul Weller. Suddenly, all these Arsenal Casuals turned up. All the Mods melted and done a runner. So, our mob battered them.

"I think that day I got home and thought I just can't do this anymore. My mates came around for me, and I told them I wasn't going out.

"That was on a Saturday, and I was back at West Ham the following Saturday, wearing a Smedley, 501's, and desert boots. I just carried on with the same clothes but a different firm.

"People like Gary 'Lager' and Mappy (Tony Matthews) and all the 79'ers were now Casuals. I wasn't a Casual, I bought everything that still looked Mod. We went anti-label, so Smedley were sixty quid. But then I paid £180 for a CP jacket in '86. It was a reversible silk bomber jacket. And it was the best coat I ever bought.

"We started going to rare groove parties, because they were all-nighters, then that's where the Acid House scene came into it. That's why there were so many Mods involved in the Acid House scene, Danny Rampling and all the others were old Mods."

Simon Fane: "In 1988 we'd notice that the older Mods weren't really visible on 'the scene' as much – were they 'blowing out' and becoming 'Trendies" or 'Normals' as people called them? In those days there was always the aspect of people 'blowing out of the scene'. They'd often just go back to mainstream life and in those days it was always a common theme for girls to go out and get their hair permed, and some of the lads too, as a visible sign they'd 'turned their back on the scene'. Some may have taken this route, but actually in hindsight, many were simply moving on, along different paths. Many people we respected were moving on, but still had the Mod attitude of obsession and attention to detail."

BUSH DEAD
SNEAKERS ALIVE !
NOW AT A NICER VENUE WITH A
BIGGER
DANCE FLOOR
THE CLARENDON
GROUND FLOOR SUITE
HAMMERSMITH BROADWAY W.6

STARTING SUNDAY 2nd MARCH
D.J.s
PAUL HALLAM
+
SHIRLEY
SMART DRESS ESSENTIAL
NO EXCEPTIONS
AND THE BEST IN R&B
DOORS OPEN AT 7.30 PM

BE THERE OR BE A
PLEB

CHAPTER

FOURTEEN

ACID JAZZ

"There was a growing jazz-club scene becoming an influence in both music and clothes. The Jazz thing was always an element, but certain DJs were now picking up on the late Sixties funkier sounds or the more Latin influenced stuff."

SIMON FANE

CHAPTER

There was a lot more interest in Jazz on the Mod scene from around 1986 onwards. Records such as 'Take Five' and 'Unsquare Dance' by the Dave Brubeck Quartet had been played since the early to mid 'Eighties along with records such as Jimmy Smith's 'The Cat' and other Hammond organ tunes.

Some of the interest came from Mods going to see bands like The Tommy Chase Quartet, who played in a hard Be Bop style and possessed the most amazing drummer in the form of Tommy Chase. Another dominant factor was the release of the film *Absolute Beginners* that had revived interest as lots of Mods had already read the 1959 Colin MacInnes novel based on London's early Modernist Jazz scene. In truth, the film was abysmal, but it had certainly created a spark of interest. Some would start to listen to Gilles Peterson fill the airwaves of Radio London with his *Mad On Jazz* show. Others would get the word via compilation albums such as Peterson's *Jazz Juice* series or Paul Murphy's *Jazz Club* ones.

The following year the Mod rallies were saturated by the sounds from labels such as Fania, Cotique, Tico, Battle, Uptight and Barry as Latin music became the big sound of 1987. Birmingham DJ, Tony Reynolds, was a big influence on that sound becoming huge. Soon tunes such as 'Soul Drummers' by Ray Barretto, 'Bang Bang' by Joe Cuba. 'Use It Before You Lose It' by Bobby Valentin, 'Subway Joe' by Joe Bataan and pretty much anything by Mongo Santamaria would fill a dancefloor at this time. Tunes like Brian Auger's version of 'Listen Here' and 'Cloud Nine' by Mongo Santamaria meant that a funkier style was creeping in to the Mod club soundtrack.

Simon Fane:"Then there was the growing jazz-club scene becoming an influence in both music and clothes. The Jazz thing was always an element, but certain DJs were now picking up on the late Sixties funkier sounds or the more Latin influenced stuff. I remember the Sunday night London club at Drummonds that summer and the likes of Lou Donaldson's 'Everything I Play is Gonh Be Funky' and Grant Green's "Sookie Sookie" being stand out tracks – obviously influenced by the likes of Gilles Peterson and Paul Murphy etc at the WAG."

Some Mods ventured to the likes of the Electric Ballroom in Camden to see Gilles Peterson spin, Dave Hucker was laying down some mighty fine Afro-Latin stuff at the Sol Y Sombre, and Paul Murphy was playing at the Purple Pit, which was his Friday night club at the Electric Ballroom and ran the Purple Pussycat in the Finchley Road on Saturday nights. Bazz Fe Jazz would play at places such as the Café Loire. You suddenly realised that cool things happened outside the Mod club scene.

One other seismic leap was that scene favourites The Prisoners had split in 1986. But news spread that a new band had emerged that included two former members in the shape of James Taylor, organ player extraordinaire, and thundering bass player Alan Crockford. Their debut release being a funked up version of Herbie Hancock's 'Blow Up'. Released on Eddie Piller's 'Re-Elect The President' label. What more could a Mod ask for? Well, lots it seems, as many considered themselves far too purist to like this whole 'getting funky' trip.

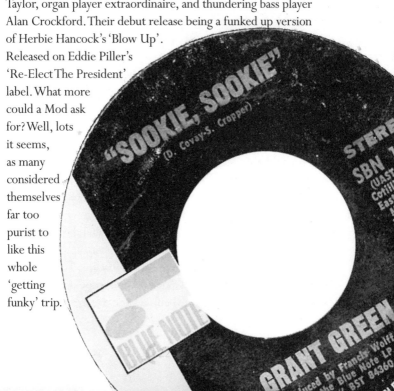

Things would move on through 1988 as DJ Chris Bangs was putting on 'Cock Happy' jazz events with Gilles Peterson, as the Acid House scene exploded in the clubs around the London area and beyond. 'Acid' became a very IN word that summer. So, it was understandable when Gilles Peterson and Eddie Piller set up a record label together and christened it Acid Jazz.

Jonathon Cooke: "My dad had been a Modernist, and he went to The Flamingo. Sadly, he died in 1989. One of the things that he left me was a *Tony Kingsley Live At The Flamingo* album, and that had really got me into the jazz thing, y'know.

"A club we used to go to was Paul Murphy's 'Purple Pit' at the Electric Ballroom on Friday's in '87, and I'd progressed from there.

"So, by the time the late Eighties had arrived it was an exciting time to be in London, because the 'second summer of love' Acid House scene was going on. I've got a brother who's three years younger than me, and he was going to raves, there was so much going on.

"I got swept along by the whole hip hop thing as well, because bands like De La Soul and Gang Starr started replacing jazz, and to me that was like black American underground music, and I thought this is perfect. This really is what Mod is about.

"I was going to Gilles Peterson's thing at Dingwalls on a Sunday. Eddie (Piller) had started Acid Jazz, and as a designer, I came up with the logo for them. Around that time, me and Ed were going to New York and coming home with loads of pairs of Adidas Superstar shelltoe trainers, and then getting Adidas Gazelles. We also started going to Duffer around then. New music, new clothes, real Mod values.

"Me and Paul Newman used to do a club called The Fix over in the Angel and we put The Clique (a band made up of long-standing Mod scene members) on, as I was managing them at the time. I was also working for a promotor called John Curd, who used to put events on at The Clarendon in Hammersmith and other things. He put The James Taylor Quartet on at the old Town & Country Club and I got The Clique supporting them.

"If I went to a club, I wanted to stay out until six in the morning. As for Mod scene clubs, I didn't want to just go to a room above a pub and go home at 12 o'clock, then see my younger brother getting in at six or seven in the morning, having had the time of his life. I'd be there, thinking what the fuck is going on?

"So, from going to Gilles Peterson things, which were great, my brother asked me to go to one of his clubs with him. I did, took ecstasy, and that was it. I was listening to Detroit Techno, Chicago House, taking pills and staying up, dancing all night long in a house or techno club. I was still dressing like a Mod from the Acid Jazz scene, which a lot of people were in those early days, y'know.

"That is when I felt like a Mod, I really did, because I cared about my clothes. I wanted to go into a club, and this is gonna sound egotistical, I suppose it is, but I wanted people to look at me. I felt proud to be associated with it then, and what I felt proud about is that when people would talk to you, that you could tell them that's what you were in to. Some people would have to ask why, because of the way I dressed, and I'd tell them it was because I like black underground dance music, but I'm not going to shift away from my clothes, because to me, they go hand in hand."

Simon Fane: "There was a Mod element that embraced the growing House scene – becoming regulars at The Hacienda to hear Mike Pickering and Dave Haslam in the early days and some of DJ Sasha's first sessions in Stoke and the world of illegal raves around the likes of Blackburn, etc. We were no exception. We just thought that many Mod events were feeling a bit stale, still trying to recreate the 85/86 era, the same records, the same clothes."

Daniel Meaden: "Jazz had always been in the background through Ramsey Lewis, Mose Allison and Georgie Fame to an extent even from the early days, but by the early Nineties it became of more interest to me. I think it's because it sounded fresher. The whole Mod 'umbrella' encompasses so many lovely genres whether it be Jazz, Soul, Ska, Blues, Sixties Beat and revival yet all of these manage to branch out and have their own offshoots. With Jazz you have Bebop, Modern, Latin, Funk, Jazz-Rap, Hip Hop and many more in-between. To dismiss Hip Hop or Funk as not being of a Mods interest in my opinion is being somewhat blinkered, as the music is the same as the style, ever-evolving and adapting to its new surroundings at that moment in time. I can remember hearing The Humble Souls – 'Beads, Things and Flowers' (Acid Jazz) and being blown away, they'd been savvy enough to take a couple of classics in the form of Billy Hawks – 'Oh Baby' and Ramsey Lewis – 'Wade in The Water' and rap over the top. End result was and still is an utterly superb slab of Mod vinyl – They had got it so right."

Neil Barker: "By the mid-Eighties I was totally immersed in Hip Hop and Electro, so as House emerged, I became hooked and felt now, it was truly my generation's time. No one could say "We've done that better before". We had a new music, a new drug and after all the violence of the Seventies and early Eighties, a whole new attitude!

"All throughout my clubbing days, my Mod sensibility remained, my hair style stayed the same (never grew it long or had a pony tail!!) and had a wardrobe full of Duffer of St George and Acid Jazz type styles."

Simon Fane: "I distinctly remember an all-nighter in Hanley in Stoke with a host of DJs from around the country during that summer in 1988. There was a tremendous buzz and people

saying it felt like that same spine tingling sensation they felt
at the first 'proper clubs'. It was a great crowd full of really
smart people in classic Mod dress… and then some mates from
Sheffield turned up in full jazz-club gear such as vintage kipper
ties, hats and looser fitting trousers. They looked the business
and completely hit that vibe that a few of us were already
absorbing from the jazz clubs.

"Onto the look, venturing to Harry's Jazz Bar in Preston and
various jazz flavour nights in Manchester we had spotted 'the
jazz look' of older lads in oversize Baker Boys Caps and heavy
shoes. There were a few articles and images in the likes of *The
Face* and *ID* magazines relating to jazz clubs at WAG and London
in general hinting at the variety of retro styles on the dance
floor. A few of us started getting looser and baggier trousers
made and got some Fifties silk kipper ties from Flip which was
a vintage clothes shop across the road from Afflecks Palace in
Manchester. We got short back and sides haircuts and bought
Brylcream to grease our hair back. We wore wide button-on
braces and got double breasted suits made with wider
lapels than before, It was that jazz dance / Tommy Chase
look. and then we went down to the Hayling Island New
Year Mod weekend organised by the Rhythm & Soul Set at
the end of 1988 with a very different mindset than where
we had begun it."

The big meeting sessions for like-minded people were the
Sunday afternoon sessions at Dingwalls that ran from 12 until
5pm and known as 'Talking Loud And Saying Something'. As
well as a live act, Gilles Peterson and Patrick Forge would play
the most amazing cross the board sounds.

Coming out of the bright sunshine and the hustle and bustle
of Camden Lock Market, you were submerged into a dark
world of jazz. The lighting was perfect and the smell of incense
joss sticks filled the room.

JAZZ WITH ATTITUDE
Sundays 7pm - 12pm (Starts 24/3/91)
At The MILK BAR
The Basement, 12 Sutton Row.(Off Soho Square)
DJ'S PETERSON / FORGE
£3 Before 9pm £4 after

The music though was the knockout punch for that club. The varied selections were unbelievable, taking in so many styles and genres. There was jazz in the form of 'Love For Sale' by Mel Torme, 'Chilli Peppers' by Duke Pearson, and The Art Ensemble Of Chicago's 'Theme De Yo Yo'. Brasilian music from the likes of Tenorio Jr 'Nebulosa' or 'Barumba' by the Tamba Trio. Soulful tunes in 'Our Lives Are Shaped By What We Love' by Odyssey to the Funk of James Brown's 'People Get Up And Drive Your Funky Soul'. Then there was the emerging hip hop records that gave it a whole vibrant feel 'Jazz Thing (Movie Mix)' by Gang Starr, Stetasonic's 'Talkin' All That Jazz' or 'Fight The Power' by Public Enemy. Crowd favourites like 'You've Gotta Have Freedom' by Pharoah Sanders or Airto and Flora Purim's 'Samba De Flora'.

The floor would suddenly empty as some up-tempo Hard Bop monster signalled the arrival of the abundance of great dancers that the club would attract. A circle would form as great dancers such as Jerry Barry would appear.

Jerry was part of the IDJ Dancers, who'd gained a reputation for dancing at Camden's Electric Ballroom, and had honed his craft at old venues such as the Horseshoe in the Tottenham Court Road. It was amazing to watch as they would do drag steps, pirouettes, ball-change-cross, inward turns, fan kicks, they would run up walls and land doing the splits. It was a mish mash of styles from contemporary modern dance moves of house and hip hop through to jazz, Russian folkdance and classical ballet.

The IDJ were not alone in these great moves, as other dance crews would show that the North and Midlands could produce prominent jazz dancers too. Manchester's 'Brothers In Jazz' could set dancefloors ablaze too.

Simon Fane: "I recall walking through Bolton early in 1989 and bumping into an old acquaintance from school who was

a pretty smart 'Casual' at the time – I'd not seen him or
spoke to him since end of term 1986.

"Are you still a Mod?" He asked.

"Yeah sort of – but more into the jazz club stuff now" I
hesitantly replied.

"What like Donald Byrd and that?"

That surprised me.

"Wow - yeah Blue Note records – how do you know his
stuff?"

"My brother's got some jazz funk tapes from some old
Manchester clubs – top stuff"

We parted ways and I've never seen him since – but it
was an early sign that there were 'other people' into 'our
music'. I'd gone for the three or four years in a Mod
bubble thinking we were the only people listening to that
kind of old black music. I'd assumed the soul and jazz funk
clubs were all playing those cheesy Eighties productions
and that seemed a world away from the sound were
absorbing. Up until then my knowledge of rap was only of
the harsh and raw drum machine sound of Run DMC and
those type of guys.

"Another occasion that year, in some clothes shop in
Manchester's King Street, I heard the strains of a jazz
classic from Dizzy Gillespie on the shop's speakers, I
paused to listen to 'Night In Tunisia' and at same time
snippets of a James Brown 45 'Bring It Up' that I had
bought in 1986 from Yanks, it was coming in and out at
same time and then some bloke started rapping. At the
time rap didn't interest me at all compared to the stuff I
was listening too. It was in fact the 'music of our enemy'.
But…. this track, 'Manifest' by Gangstarr, really grabbed
my attention. Around the same time, I'm not sure how,
but I stumbled across the *Buss DJs* show hosted by Stu Allan

on Manchester's Piccadilly Radio on Sunday Evenings. I started to hear more hip-hop tracks with jazzy samples being used. I was really intrigued about Divine Styler using Jr Walker samples, Lord Finesse's downtempo jazzy 'Track The Movement' & Chill Rob G 's funky flute and JB sax led flow of 'Court is Now in Session' which were duly bought from Spin Inn or Eastern Bloc record stores after hearing them on the show. It was another thing that was happening, It was the start of what is now called the 'Golden Age of Hip Hop' with the heavy use of jazz, soul, R'n'B and funk samples with more of a measured spoken word vocal delivery as opposed to the shouty rap that I'd heard before. Another musical avenue to explore at the same time it was evolving. They were utilising samples of stuff I had, or stuff that I then needed to get."

Adrian Jones: "We used to buy our music from Tony's Records in Park Street which was a godsend, with great knowledgeable staff like John Stapleton as well as the great soul, jazz and R'n'B and beat stuff. I would hear him playing the latest tracks by the likes of Public Enemy and NWA and got quite intrigued by the breaks they were using, so I got into hip hop in reverse by getting interested in the breaks first."

Simon Fane: "Expansion Records in Manchester had new staff that year, the manager was now Dean Johnson who had the chat and the salesmanship whilst he sold the latest Street Soul and Swing Beat 12"s to the majority of punters. I'd go into the back half of the shop and flip through the selection of Sixties and Seventies jazz LPs they had in their stock. I'd bought a couple of things before and started to become a regular now I had started work full time in Manchester City Centre. One lunch hour visit I spotted a copy of Joe Bataan's *Subway Joe* LP and took it to the counter and had a quick chat about Latin Soul. Dean talked about the music he "had got away with playing" at the Hacienda at the time during his residency there. The next time I went was on a Saturday, which was the busiest day of the week, with a counter crowded with the Street Soul and contemporary black music buyers checking new releases over the shop's PA. Suddenly the latest New Jack Swing record faded out and Dean shouted out "Hey Simon - check this!" The fluid latin bass line kicked in, and all eyes went to me as I walked up to the counter to find out what was going on, whilst Dean shouted to the other customers "These are real fucking handclaps lads!" just before the vocals to Johnny Colon's 'You Gotta Love Me' on the *Boogaloo '67* LP kicked in. My first LP on the Cotique label was in the bag!"

Adrian Jones: "I bought the *Beat Goes Public*, Acid Jazz compilation when it came out in Tony's Records in Bristol containing all those great Prestige jazz and funk cuts, which probably got attention on the Mod scene due to the inclusion of 'Brother Jack McDuff's 'Hot Barbeque'. Damn, the other stuff was amazing such as Pucho, Charles Earland, Funk Inc, all top-quality tunes!

"The first modern track I can remember hearing was the Galiano track 'Frederick Lies Still', that was a rap over Pucho and the Latin Soul Brothers version of Curtis Mayfield's 'Freddie's Dead' which was pretty interesting, also there was The James Taylor Quartet slowly morphing into the JTQ. I loved the old line up but this was also really interesting stuff with a much bigger line up and guest vocalists. Various friends and I including Matt Ashman from Chippenham went to see the new look 'JTQ' at The Cooker, which was John Stapleton's club on the boat 'The Thekla', formerly known as 'The Old

Profanity Showboat' which was an art space provided by Vivian Stanshall of the Bonzo Dog Doo-dah Band. It was an amazing gig, really interesting to hear the other sounds being played by the deejay's, John and Tin Tin, who's set included 'Theme de Yoyo' by The Art Ensemble of Chicago, 'You Can't Even Walk In The Park' by Johnny Pate', 'Funk Inc' and others. Being exposed to these for the first time was pretty special! Other gigs that followed included early full band gigs by Galliano, I was just blown away by them, so much energy and the lyrics and music were spot on, A rare Bristol appearance from the guvnor Jimmy McGriff with Hank Crawford, who we met, and he said to us: "Hey you guys look like The Beatles!"

Simon Fane: "Another link with Urban Records was the evolution of JTQ. From seeing their first single back in early 1987 they had been getting more into that jazzy soundtrack style with a couple of LPs combining classic Sixties covers and their own swinging Hammond grooves also Eddie Piller's 'Re—Elect the President' label. By the end of 1988 more connections with the jazz club scene became apparent when they brought out their 'Wait A Minute' LP on the Urban Records label. With a move towards that early Seventies funk flavoured originals and cover versions club favourites such as Gene Ammons' 'Jungle Strutt' it highlighted their move towards what had been growing in the 'scene'. But, it was their version of 'Theme from Starsky & Hutch' featuring both Fred Wesley and Pee Wee Ellis from the rare groove legends The JBs, as well as an appearance from upcoming jazz club scene mover and shaker Galliano on the 12" release that cemented the band's reputation as leaders of Acid Jazz. It also gave the green light to Mods everywhere to get loose and feel funky."

Adrian Jones: "After moving to London I started going to 'Talking Loud and Saying Something' which was Gilles Peterson and Patrick Forge's legendary Sunday afternoon club at Dingwalls in Camden. I would meet up with Dave Brown, Paul 'Smiler' Anderson and Matt Ashman. We always made a point of getting there early to watch the jazz dancers, forget Northern Soul, this was some impressive stuff. You've gotta be a good dancer to pull off dancing to a track like, 'Om Mani Padme Hum' by Sahib Shihab. As well as the club there were live sessions by the likes of Johnny Lytle and The Dream Warriors. Just outside Dingwalls, above one of the units was Soul Jazz Records which specialized in rare jazz and funk records. I got some absolute gems in there such as Lyman Woodard Organization 'Saturday Night Special', Oneness of Ju-Ju 'African Rhythms', Johnny Pate 'Outrageous' and Les McCann and Eddie Harris 'Swiss Movement'. Absolutely fantastic times!

"The Brighton Jazz Bop was another highlight on the calendar. I remember seeing Big John Patton and Galliano there, some of the Galliano guys were checking out mine and Dave's Gabbicci's, Galliano's logo of course being a Gabbicci 'G'. White jeans or hipsters were favoured, along with loafers or Adidas Gazelle's. I never went in for the beads favoured by some. 'Duffer of St George' in D'Arblay Street was run by Clifford Bowen, Marco Cairns, Eddie Prendergast and Barrie Sharpe. The latter of which also recorded some great records with Diana Brown. They had some amazing clothes, very influenced by Sixties and Seventies Italian knitwear."

Simon Fane: ""I remember when we first started to go to "other clubs" we actually felt "more Mod" by seeing various types of people around us whilst recognising other "old

Mods" who had that certain take on things. It's very hard to explain, so I'll revert to the classic jazz line that "If you have to ask, you won't understand". But as the Eighties moved into the Nineties there were other places to go and there were a broader range of people, who although not identifying as "Mods" – had that same "Mod attitude" – obsessive and dedicated about "their" particular choice of style and music."

Adrian Jones: "I shared a house with some other Mods in Forest Gate and and distinctly remember their total confusion when I played them the new albums by The Young Disciples and Galliano'... their loss! If I had to name the top clubs around this period it would be 'Talkin' Loud and Saying Something 'at Dingwalls, 'The Cooker' at The Thekla in Bristol, 'Lakota' in Bristol, The Starlight in Paddington, 'Jazz 90' at The Underworld and 'Happiness Stan' at Turnmills in Farringdon."

Jonathon Cooke: "There were also clubs such as Tongue Kung Fu Club at the Gardening Club in Covent Garden. There were all these cool groovy people like Wildcat› Will Blanchard and all those guys. I just loved them. It was all so fresh."

British bands involved around this scene included The Young Disciples, The Brand New Heavies, Galliano, Corduroy, Mother Earth and The Sandals.

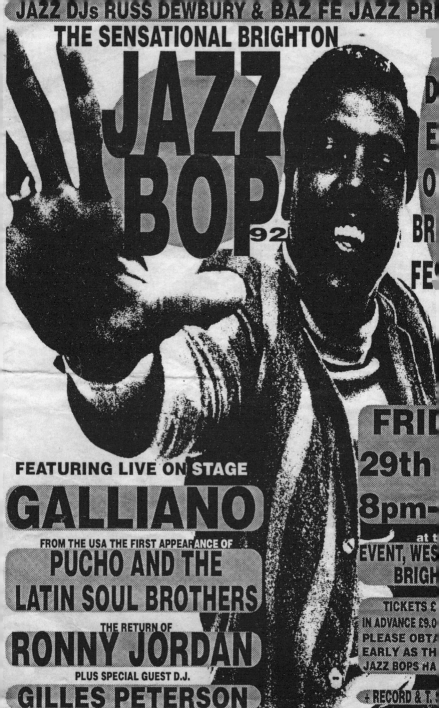

JAZZ DJs RUSS DEWBURY & BAZ FE JAZZ PR...

THE SENSATIONAL BRIGHTON

JAZZ BOP '92

D...
E...
O...
BR...
FES...

FEATURING LIVE ON STAGE

GALLIANO

FROM THE USA THE FIRST APPEARANCE OF

PUCHO AND THE
LATIN SOUL BROTHERS

THE RETURN OF

RONNY JORDAN

PLUS SPECIAL GUEST D.J.

GILLES PETERSON

FRID...
29th
8pm–...
at t...
EVENT, WES...
BRIGH...

TICKETS £...
IN ADVANCE £9.0...
PLEASE OBTA...
EARLY AS TH...
JAZZ BOPS HA...

+ RECORD & T...

TICKETS AVAILABLE FROM THE EVENT BOOKING OFFICE BRIGHTON (027...
ROUNDER RECORDS BRIGHTON (0273) 25440 THE DOME BOX OFFICE BRIGHTON (0273)

TOP 20 ACID JAZZ LABEL SINGLES

(SUPPLIED BY ACID JAZZ HEAD HONCHO EDDIE PILLER)

1	Terry Callier	I Don't Want To See Myself (Without You)
2	Brand New Heavies	Dream Come True
3	Mother Earth	Apple Green
4	James Taylor Quartet feat Alison Limerick	Stepping Into My Life
5	Corduroy	Something In My Eye
6	Night Trains	Love Sick
7	Alice Clark	Don't You Care
8	Goldbug	Whole Lotta Love
9	Graham Dee & Various Artists	The Sound Of Young London (EP)
10	Earthly Powers	A Man Called Adam
11	The Humble Souls	Beads Things and Flowers
12	Leroy Hutson	Positive Forces
13	Snowboy & The Latin Section	Theme from The New Avengers
14	King Truman	Like A Gun
15	Dread Flimstone	From The Ghetto
16	James Taylor Quartet	Blow Up
17	The Third Degree	Mercy
18	Galliano	Frederic Lies Still
19	Matt Berry	Take Your Hand
20	Janice Graham Band	Murder

CHAPTER
FIFTEEN

MARC LESSNER
THE MUSIC MAN

"I guess it was my kind of escapism and reading the sleeves and labels of my parent's records brought a lot of colour into a very grey world. The first memory I have of music was seeing The Beatles on TV on a Sunday night and falling hook, line and sinker."

MARC LESSNER

M arc Lessner would prove to be very important in the emerging days of Acid Jazz. Not least for his passion of records and music in general. It is from him that the scene got to hear massive tunes such as 'Shaft In Africa' by Johnny Pate, 'Don't You Care' by Alice Clark, 'You're Starting Too Fast' by Johnny Pate and 'Melting Pot' by The Boris Gardner Happening.

Marc was born in the East End of London in 1959. His early years were spent in Stepney living off the Mile End Road. There was a cinema five minutes' walk from their front door and a record shop 'Paul For Music' ten minutes' walk away. The seeds were sewn at a very young age. He loved reading, going to the cinema and of course music.

Marc Lessner: "I guess it was my kind of escapism and reading the sleeves and labels of my parent's records brought a lot of colour into a very grey world. The first memory I have of music was seeing The Beatles on TV on a Sunday night and falling hook, line and sinker. The following Sunday morning we went shopping near Brick Lane and they bought me my first ever record which was 'The Twist and Shout EP'. The picture sleeve reminded me of a bomb site just around the corner from where we lived so that record for me was more than just a collection of four songs."

In 1967, he moved to South Hackney which was pretty seismic for him. A new school, new friends and it felt like a lot tougher place to live. However, this was the time that Marc really started caring about the way he dressed and the kind of music he started listening to.

Marc Lessner: "I had a cousin John who was a Mod who went into mourning for a week when Otis Redding died Living in Hackney too meant that we now went shopping on Ridley Road market where there were more than one record stall blasting out mainly the same kind of records that my cousin was into. The one record I so clearly remember was 'Young, Gifted And

Black' which got hammered over the sound system on the Dodgems at the funfair over Victoria Park in 1969. Hummed it all the way home!"

Fast forward to 1974 and attending Dame Alice Owens School at the Angel Islington. A record shop opened up on St John Street a mere stone's throw from Marc's centre of education. It was called 'Pop Inn' and Marc started to spend less time playing football at morning and lunch break and more and more of my time in the shop looking through the racks and chatting to the manageress Liz. She soon picked up on his passion for music and before he knew it she asked Marc if he would like to work in there over the Autumn half term holiday.

By 1976, Marc was working over in Walthamstow. A bloke he worked with asked Marc if he was a 'Soul Boy' simply because of the clothes he was wearing and quite frankly Marc didn't have a clue what he was talking about. The bloke then explained what he meant in terms of the music he was listening to and gave Marc a cassette of Funk, Jazz and Soul. Marc was curious, but not 100 per cent sold on it as he didn't go clubbing and going to see bands was more his thing.

Marc Lessner: "I started listening to Greg Edwards on Capital Radio on a Saturday night and as my school friends also started gravitating towards the Soul Boy scene by 1977 we were clubbing, buying 7" and 12" imports and shopping for clothes down the Kings Road. I left school In 1978 and went out to work with a view of going to University the following year. Although that never happened as I ended working for Our Price Records in 1979. I also had a Saturday job at the time at Lord John and a window dresser, Jeff Innocent, took me under his wing and started turning my kid brother and me onto Augustus Pablo, King Tubby and John Coltrane. A few jazz cigarettes helped at the time to broaden our taste.

"I started clubbing in 1977 as a Soul Boy. Saturday night with school friends meeting up in a pub in Islington before jumping on a 38 bus into the West End and ending up at The Global Village. The DJ was a fella called Norman Scott who at one time we thought was on Capital Radio which of course was Roger Scott. He would play a mixture of Soul, Funk and Jazz because the word disco was never part of our vocabulary although clearly, we were listening to disco in all its guises and styles. Some of our favourite records included Idris Muhammad 'Could Heaven Ever Be like This?' N.C.C.U – 'Washing Machine', Village People 'Fire Island' and Mass Production 'Cosmic Lust'. I can always remember hearing Donna Summer 'I Feel Love' for the first time down there and to be honest even though it was a game changing record it did split opinion amongst my friends at the time.

"In 1978 we also started going to Upstairs at Ronnie Scotts on a Thursday night when a school friend called Russell Jones then suggested that we should check out Crackers on Wardour Street on a Sunday night and I can honestly say it was a real revelation. A lot of the clubbers were from London and mainly Black guys. The DJ was a guy called George Power and I think it's fair to say that the music was a lot harder sounding and definitely had a more Jazz-based playlist. The dancers down there were on another level and the dress code was definitely different too. It felt special because it was a lot smaller venue than The Global Village – and dare I say it more elitist. Some of the big records down there over the Summer included Wilbert Longmire – Black Is The Colour, Rodney Franklin – The Path, Norman Connors – Captain Connors, Willie Bobo – Always There and Gato Barbieri – Poinciana."

In 1979, Marc started working at Our Price Records Charing Cross road. There, by chance, he met the only other Soul Boy on the firm, Paul Murphy, who was working at the Leicester Square branch of Our Price. Marc then ended up working with Paul and that was in itself a real education and a great laugh too. When Murphy left Our Price in 1981 he opened up a record shop called 'Fusions' on Exmouth Street in Islington where Marc became a regular customer.

Marc Lessner: "I wasn't into the New Romantic scene as I thought it was a bit fancy dress and I never really got Electronic music at that time. I also found that I was dressing very much in the Ivy League style, but didn't make any the connection at all with Mods. I knew they were wearing suits, clothes and shoes that were clearly Sixties in style but not like the clothes I was wearing.

"It must have been about 1980 I started attending a Jazz dance night put on by Paul Murphy in the basement of The Green Man pub on Great Portland Street where I met Chris Bangs who little did I know years later would become a lifelong friend. Paul was a fantastic DJ and even though he would be playing really tough Jazz Fusion: Lonnie Smith, Charlie Rouse, Doug Richardson, Jeff Lorber, Manfredo Fest, he would always end up playing Gene Dunlap – 'It's Just The way I Feel' as the last record of the night.

Paul then started being more ambitious with his club nights at The Horseshoe and YMCA Tottenham Court Road and starting bringing over acts from the USA including The Heath Brothers, Jay Hoggard, Alphonse Mouson and Tania Maria.

I can remember our gang going up to a gig in Stoke on a coach Paul had hired where he was playing at a Colin Curtis all dayer and I pretty much went into work when we got back from Stoke the next day.

I found myself going to gigs rather than club nights – sometimes on my Jack Jones as my girlfriend wasn't into Jazz and the older music that I was into. I ended up going to the Capital Jazz Festival at Ally Pally and Knebworth as well as going to the odd gig at Ronnie Scott's and Dingwall to see US acts.

By this point Marc was really was into the whole Jazz thing and then by chance he met Tony Rounce who was working at HMV Lewisham – when Marc by this point was managing the Our Price store in the Riverdale Centre Lewisham.

"Tony was getting a train after work up to somewhere like Peterborough to play at a Northern night, but Tony being Tony was dressed in a very eclectic outfit. We chatted about music until I jumped off at London Bridge and after that when at work I would pop along to see Tony and ask him about Soul and Northern Soul records that he thought I might like. He was like the Encyclopaedia Britannica of Black Music and not a bit patronising or condescending when he started reeling off all the records and labels I should be listening to. A proper gent, friend and someone I have admired for years."

Marc left Our Price in 1984 and went to rep for the distributor Pinnacle Records. He was the West End rep, but also covered most of London too. He went in to all kinds of stores from the chains like HMV, Virgin and Our Price as well as visiting the specialist stores that sold everything from Heavy Metal to Reggae and Rockabilly as well as the Soul, Jazz and Dance.

Marc Lessner: "It was a great learning curve for me because it also meant speaking to record labels direct to let them know how their product was selling and who was buying it. It also was an ideal opportunity to build up contacts who later would help me when I went out on my own and started my own business. There was a guy called Dave Whitehead who introduced me to Pete Macklin at Demon Records who was really a nice bloke and helped me out no end years later. The other big deal was that because I was visiting a lot of shops now as a rep I was able to get access to their stock rooms and basements behind the counter so got crate digging and found lots of old stock that was simply gathering dust at bargain prices."

Marc was then offered a job by one of the shops – Discount Records in Shepherd's Bush which had a wholesale business where he was buying Cut Out albums from the States and then going out on the road to sell them to the same specialist stores that he had been calling on when he had worked at Pinnacle.

Marc Lessner: "In 1985 I then got approached by Record Imports to pretty much do the same thing, but the main incentive for me was that I was sent out to the States to actually buy the product which meant I visited New York, Chicago, Philadelphia and St Louis all in ten days.

"I was visiting warehouses were there would be literally hundreds of thousands of records. I guess it would be fair to say that I had a shopping list with me plus I would do my best to make punts on buying records using some of the knowledge that I had acquired over the years. I was mindful of the fact that I was spending my guvnor's money and so I was as careful and prudent as I could be.

"Records bought then included Jeffree, Johnny Hammond – 'Gears', Jon Lucien- 'Rashida', Weldon Irvine – 'Cosmic Vortex', Headhunters – 'Survival Of The Fittest'. Doug Carn – 'Infant Eyes'. Jerry Bell – 'Winter Love Affair'. Alfonzo Surrett – 'Comin' Out'.

"Over the next couple of years I visited the States at least half a dozen times and built up a great relationship with the companies I had been buying from.

"I was also still on the road and selling new import releases which was a great buzz too. My guvnor, Ron

Boulding, also let me buy product myself to sell on when the Black Music Record fair started at The Clarendon Hammersmith. It was only a matter of time before I went out on my own and by this point I had built up my contacts in the USA and I pretty much knew most of the shops in London that were selling the kind of records I knew I could find in the USA. The Rare Groove scene had kicked off."

There was a definite shift towards a lot more warehouse parties during this period.

Marc Lessner: "I then got introduced to Nicky Holloway by a mate, Mervyn Lyn. This was the start of a long association in the Eighties with The Special Branch, Doo At The Zoo, Mambo Madness and Bournemouth and Rockley Sands weekenders.

"I had, exclusively, a record stall at most of these gigs. Everyone from Pete Tong and Giles Peterson to Chris Bangs, Jeff Young, Bob Jones, Snowboy Simon Dunmore, Bob Masters, Rob Day, Jay Strongman, Chris Brown, Kevin Beadle, Gary Dennis and countless others played a mix of Soul, Jazz, Funk, Hip Hop, Rare Groove, Acid Jazz, Brazilian and House. In fact, I can remember having a conversation with Bangsy and telling him that he wasn't playing jazz, but Mod records and he said "Sure I am, but don't tell anybody!"

"In addition, I was going to a lot of Soul nights in the mid-to-late-eighties put on by people like Simon Dunmore, Ian Clark and Terry Davis. The playlist was mainly Modern and Northern subject to new and Indie soul being played too.

"In 1987, I started up my own business 'Soul Trader'. I was visiting the States a couple of times a year for the next three or four years and some of the records I found included:

SOUL TRADER US IMPORT LIST

(COMPILED BY MARC LESSNER)

O.S.T.	'Shaft In Africa'
Johhny Pate	'Outrageous'
Serenade	'I Like The Little Boy In You' 7"
Staple Singers	'This Time Around'
Smoke	'Risin'
Neal Creque	'The Hands Of Time'
Charles Earland	'Pleasant Afternoon'
The Boris Gardiner Happening	'It's What The Happening'
O.S.T.	'Fritz The Cat'
Rick Holmes	'Remember To Remember' 12"
Faith, Hope and Charity	'To Each His Own'
Alice Clark	'Alice Clark'
Melvin Moore	'All Of A Sudden' 7"
Tyrone Davis	'Is It' 7"
Pigmeat Markham	'Here Comes The Judge' 7"
Aretha Franklin	'Day dreaming' 7"
Lonette Mckee	'Do To Me' 7"
Bobby Jonz	'Win Your Love' 7"
Mary Love Comer	'Come out Of The Sandbox' 7"
The Heavies	'Got To Give' 7"
The Dells	'It's All Up To You' 7"
Kingdom	'Amazing'
Jimmy Cobb	'So Nobody Else Can Hear'
Valerie Simpson	'Silly wasn't I' 7"
Various -Disco Gold. Cold cut	'Say Kids' 12"

"Chicago was always a productive hunting ground and to be honest I do have a soft spot for music from the Windy city anyways. Barneys, Ruby Sales and Bob Shuttleworth plus: Buffalo New York state hit the jackpot Rare Groove 45's. ad LP's Maceo & The Macks, Jackson Sisters, The JB's, Lynn Collins, The Wild Magnolias.

"In St Louis, Great Atlantic: Fantasy albums, Johnny Hammond, Blackbyrds, Funk Inc, Irakere, The 3 Pieces, Side Effect, Sylvester, Pleasure. At Scorpio, New Jersey where I found a hundred copies of the Alice Clark album as well as a shed load of other albums on Mainstream. At One Stop in Albany, New York state where I found Old Skool Hip Hop 12" singles and Jeffrey Collins P.I.R. 45 back catalogue and in New York with Joe Fields at Muse Records.

"I was pretty lucky that I wasn't just looking for Acid Jazz related records, but because of my knowledge and relationship with various DJ's and shops I was picking up indie Soul 45's as well as 2-Step Soul titles too.

"I had a great network too with people like Chris Bangs, Gilles Peterson, Simon Dumore, Terry Davis, Pete Tong, Jeff Young, Eddie Piller , Dean Rudland , Jonathan Moore who as well as buying records from me also tipped me off about records I should be looking for. Especially Bangsy so it was a kind of two-way street where we both benefited from our shared knowledge.

"Danny D who was working at Cooltempo Records came to me with the idea of a scam for a 45 by The Brand New Heavies – 'Got To Give' . We passed it off as an undiscovered rare Groove record that I had found in the USA and I simply distributed it to shops with that story line and hence built up a buzz!

"I would say that I have pretty eclectic taste when it comes to music. Like most people who have gone through various scenes you tend to gravitate at the time to the music that is the soundtrack of that scene. However, because of working in the music business since I was 19 you simply can't have tunnel hearing when it comes to music.

"I've always loved Pop music too, but of late I really don't hear anything that I can imagine wanting to listen to in ten years' time

"After all that I do have a huge part of my heart immersed in Soul, Funk and Jazz. I also love Original scores for movies and am a sucker for most things composed by Ennio Morricone. Over the years I've never stopped listening to The Beatles, Joni Mitchell, Bob Dylan, Bruce Springsteen, Van Morrison, Tom Waits, Captain Beefheart, The Beach Boys, Todd Rundgren, Led Zeppelin, The Rolling Stones and Steely Dan. I love Ryan Adams too and of course Drive By Truckers.

"If I was put on a spot it's all about Curtis Mayfield, Barry White, Bill Evans, Charles Mingus, Little Richard and The Meters."

So, were 'Acid Jazz Mods a reality, or a way of life? *iD* magazine had already run a feature entitled 'Acid Jazz Mods' that had featured Jonathon Cooke amongst others, back in November 1989. After that there were little rumbles and mentions in publications throughout 1990.

Issue 28 of *The Face* magazine (January 1991) certainly caused a few ripples upon release. John Godfrey's two-page article coupled with a two-page spread of photos from Nina Schultz opened a can of worms that would get the traditional underground Mod scene worked up. It didn't help that the article featured Eddie Piller, who'd once been a key member of the classic retro-based Mod scene. Add to that, James Taylor, Hammond organ player extraordinaire from one-time Mod-worshipped band The Prisoners, as well as a few well-known faces including Guy Joseph, Jon Cooke and Nick Agadhuino and you really are asking for trouble. It also didn't help that the feel of the piece was definitely going along the lines of 'these people are dressing up like Mods, but for God's sake don't call them Mods because as we all know, Mods are embarrassing'.

That said though, the basis of the article was true enough. There was indeed an interest in Mod fashions coming from the trendier club scene. The fact that a lot of the House and Rave scenes were full of old Revival Mods was obviously a big factor, but couple that

with shops such as Duffer being choc full of well designed, Sixties influenced knitwear and record shops having some great new music instead of retro stuff, and you have a whole new scene going.... just don't call it a Mod Revival.

Jonathon Cooke: "That thing we did for *The Face* article did cause a few problems. I made up those those top tens of old skool Mod versus New Mod, with Eddie Piller. There were mentions of a lot of hip hop stuff in there. All the things we were referencing all had a connection to Mod.

"A lot of people didn't like it. I remember Guy Joseph telling me he got cornered in a toilet in a Mod club once, and these people were going to beat him up because he was involved in that article. I think they thought we were trying to take it (Mod) away from them, but we weren't. We were just going off on our own kind of adaptation as to what we thought it was about."

Simon Fane: "Our dress sense in early Nineties then was often the classic white Levi's 501's or old stock Big E Cords in Burgundy, Blue or Bottle Green- paired with original Big E Denim jackets or Lacoste golf jackets from Vintage Clothing in Afflecks Palace. I also really liked vintage Izod Lacoste polo shirts that had the John Smedley type collars picked up in a few second-hand Americana shops and stalls. Brand new Smedley jumpers were also popular with trips "down the road" to the factory shop in Derbyshire quite a regular occurrence.

"In winter I remember a few of us getting Fifties heavyweight checked Woolrich coats and collecting Sixties ski jumpers from Paris market stalls. The half-length pop fastened "FBI" anoraks in Burgundy and Blue were a bit of a thing in Manchester during the DJangos days circa 1991. On our feet were deadstock Adidas (Superstar Gazelle Spezials) or Puma Clyde trainers – these were the days when you couldn't buy them new from the high street! Bass loafers were still worn for more formal occasions along with blazers, button down shirts and rep ties.

"In Kendal's in Manchester there was a new franchise area/shop for Polo/Ralph Lauren within the menswear department. This was the only place where you could buy Ralph Lauren clothes in the city at the time. It was expensive, but I got a bottle-green college sweatshirt and some great striped Oxford shirts and some nice club ties from there. I remember one weekend in London going down J-Simons in Covent Garden in the afternoon and then wearing my new madras checked zip-up windcheater jacket with a plain grey Chevignon Togs Tee shirt down to The Fridge in Brixton to the Talkin Loud sessions that night.

"There had been the buzz with Duffers – especially the stripy knitwear and we went to D'Arbly street store a few times when in London. Some of the Duffer gear was stocked at Geese in the Royal Exchange in Manchester at time – along with aforementioned deadstock trainers – so this was a regular haunt at weekends for a period. I liked my bucket/fisherman hats too and often wore them out with vintage wool Baracuta Harringtons in the cold evenings. Old Gabicci collared cardigans were popular and also old Munsingwaer items cropped up – I think this was a few years before the label relaunched. Stussy T Shirts were a regular purchase from the likes of Aspecto's newly opened clothes shop around the corner from my office before I visited the Stussy Store in New York a few years later."

Jonathon Cooke: "I really got into that modern scene. I DJ'd a lot on it, becoming a resident at Fabric (London club playing house and techno) and became their art director for ten years, still keeping up the look. It was important to me to keep that look alive. On that scene was Craig Richards, the DJ, who is a good friend of mine and really in to the vintage look, so he got it, as did Paul Daley from Leftfield."

Surely if Mod was ever to surface again in the Nineties it would come from a dance related form and not a guitar band one? Nobody could imagine what would happen next.

CHAPTER

SIXTEEN

MADCHESTER AND BRITPOP

"Manchester in particular had always had the 'indie' element in clubs, record stores, gigs all through the Eighties with the history of Factory records, etc. By the time the Madchester thing began to get recognised around 1989 the scene as such was much more than one or two bands."

SIMON FANE

CHAPTER

On May 27th, 1990, Manchester band, The Stone Roses had played a giant gig at Spike Island on the Mersey Estuary in Cheshire. No band had ever played there before, and that was the top priority for the band. They had steadily been getting bigger and bigger, and this one-day festival would show just how big they were, when all 29,500 tickets were sold in advance from just one advert in the *NME* A further 3,500 tickets were given out.

It was hardly a proper festival though, as there were only a couple of burger vans and one beer tent to cater the thirty odd thousand fans present. Luckily, the giant drug intake, amongst them supressed their appetites, so nobody really cared.

The fans in the crowd dressed the same as the band, in Reni hats and flares. There was a real feeling of harmony amongst the audience gathered there. The sound was awful, but as a statement it was pretty impressive, and many would agree that the Nineties started right there. At that point in time, The Stone Roses were a connection between the past and the future, between Sixties psychedelia trippy vibes and the burgeoning Acid House scene.

The 'Madchester' sound was not unique to the Stone Roses, bands brought under that name included the Happy Mondays, Inspiral Carpets and 808 State. Most of the bands had formed in the Eighties as guitar bands but had been heavily influenced by the emergence of Acid House, clubs such as The Haciena in Manchester, and the drug Ecstasy.

Simon Fane: "Manchester in particular had always had the "indie" element in clubs, record stores, gigs all through the Eighties with the history of Factory records, etc. By the time the Madchester thing began to get recognised around 1989 the scene as such was much more than one or two bands and all the obvious cliches that appeared in the music and fashion press. Saying that, I really enjoyed the groove that the Happy Mondays and Stone Roses gave to their music – and there was a palpable buzz in the city at the time with this fresh Sixties

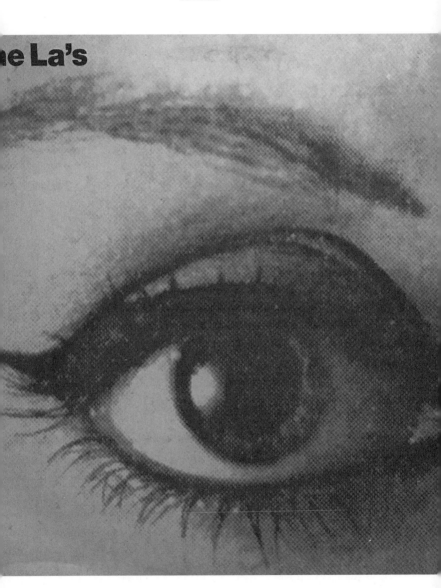

type of influence. Madchester was a breath of fresh air – in the shadows of Smiths or Joy Division fans in long grey coats standing around looking miserable listening to what seemed melancholy jingly depressing guitar music.

"I bought a couple of the 12 inches such as the 'Hallelujah' and 'Fools Gold' in 1990, the same year I bought the first Charlatans 'Indian Rope' 12" after catching a couple of minutes of their stark black and white video on a late-night Granada TV programme. It felt like a bit of recognition that the stuff we were into in mid-Eighties such as the Prisoners or a lot of the Sixties Beat was finally given some credibility by a new generation – as well as being given a new twist with some of the production and remixes from Messrs Oakenfold and Weatherall.

"The 'Madchester' effect lasted a few years after the heights of 1990 and was cited as a big contribution to the demand for students from across the UK and the world to attend University in the city. A number of businesses started off the back of that scene and formed the foundation for the rest of the decade – from clothes shops in Afflecks Palace to records stores and music venues. You couldn't deny it put Manchester back on the map and gave it recognition for its own unique swagger."

Whilst The Stone Roses held the reigns to the future of music in Britain, they took their eye off the ball. They went off to record their second album, but took far too long in the studio, and somebody else stepped into their shoes – a band who were part of the Seattle music scene in America – Nirvana.

Youth in the UK were drawn to the sounds coming from across the Atlantic. US 'Grunge' music, led by the likes of Nirvana, Pearl Jam and Soundgarden began to filter through the airwaves. The apathetic lyrics, joyless and angst-ridden. The image dishevelled and scruffy.

At the same time there was the UK's own 'shoe-gazing'

scene, with bands like Ride, Chapterhouse and Slowdive. The genre's name referring to the way the band members would look down on their effects pedals and the monitors whilst playing. Even lead singers would have their hands by their side and their heads down, to show a lack of ego, as obscured vocals tumbled from their lips. Swirling distorted and flanged guitars reverberating around halls. It seemed as all was lost.

If you knew where to look there were some great British bands around at that time including The La's, Primal Scream, Sun Dial, early Manic Street Preachers, The Revs, The Honey Smugglers, and The Stairs.

Special mention must go to Oxford band, 5.30, who'd started life as a Mod band playing at Mod rallies such as Clacton in '85. In truth, they didn't really progress anywhere. Thankfully, by 1990 they had re-invented themselves, starting off with a baggy look of tie-dye tops, flares and long hair but gradually moving to a better look. Their early singles 'Abstain' (the B-side of which was the immense 'Catcher In The Rye' a re-working of one of their early Mod songs) and 'Air Conditioned Nightmare' blew the heads off most people that heard them, and made it seem that '91 would belong to them. '13th Disciple' and 'Supanova' followed and their sole album, 'Bed', which was released a week before Nirvana's 'Nevermind' in September '91. The Five Thirty's magnificent creation stalled at 57 whilst Nirvana's hit the number five spot.

As for the Mod scene itself, the two main bands were The Clique and the slightly more late-Sixties sounding Aardvarks but they had no chance of getting any kind of media attention. More importantly, was the fact that another organisation calling themselves The Untouchables would be putting on their own events and rallies having split from the CCI events.

Alan Handscombe: "Well I came out in 1991, In the Nineties I still Dj'd at Soul clubs and few of Rob Bailey's nights but I discovered Hard House Techno and Trance so spent a good seven years off my nut on E down at Turnmills in Farringdon. Trade FF Warriors and Melt and Garage at Heaven on a Friday night. Was a fantastic period to go out clubbing brilliant music coming out of Germany: Noom, Harthouse and Patrik Prins Moovin melodies. I didn't blow out and still wore the same clobber. And it was most probably the first time in my life I actually listened to new music which wasn't retro in any shape or form. Of course, some of my mates thought what the fuck, why don't you like vocal house? But it was a reaction because I'd been listening to fantastic vocals on my soul and reggae records, all I wanted was a heavy baseline and some squelchy Roland 303, cue Hardfloor. I did get funny looks turning up at seven in the morning at Trade in my sheepskin and mohair trousers but always got in as I got to know the people running the club. Actually, at Warriors they gave me free membership as I was the best dressed person in the club. Result."

The big talking point of the year would be Steve Marriott, of the Small Faces, death in a house fire on April 20th. A couple of weeks later, Paul Weller appeared on the 'Tonight With Jonathan Ross' show where he performed his new single 'Into Tomorrow' as The Paul Weller Movement, his solo project after the demise of the Style Council a year earlier. Weller was then interviewed and during the chat he happily gave the message "I'm still a Mod, I'll always be a Mod, you can bury me a Mod." After the interview he sang "Tin Soldier" in honour of Marriott.

Weller, himself, had shown lots of interest in the whole Acid Jazz / Neo Mod evolution to the point that he had appeared on a few of the releases. He'd namechecked various people, championing The Young Disciples, Brand New Heavies and American acts like Gang Starr and A Tribe Called Quest.

Rumours of his debut solo album being released on Gilles Peterson's Talkin' Loud label never came to fruition, and he finally secured an album deal with Go! Discs and it was released in September '92. The album was near enough a perfect album which Paul had touted as 'British R'n'B'.

After the rejection by Polydor, in 1990, of his last proposed Style Council album 'Modernism – A New Decade', in which he had taken a house music direction he had gone back to grass roots.

"I really believed that garage house was the new Mod music," he had told an *NME* reporter. But for his solo project he'd reconnected with his old records Stax, R'n'B, The Who and The Small Faces.

The production work on the album by Brendan Lynch and Weller gave a lot of the songs a very modern feel and songs like 'Bitterness Rising' and 'Kosmos' sounded fantastic.

Simon Fane: "A few years later when the first signs of what was to be coined Britpop started appearing, it just seemed like a continuation of what had gone before. In 1992 Paul Weller had made his solo comeback with the Paul Weller Movement and a new LP featuring an influence from the UK jazz and funk scene with connections to Young Disciples – the production feels good all around. I'd got a pirate copy on tape before it had officially come out in UK and it seemed like a real under the radar buzz on it, when you heard he'd been doing some gigs at relatively tiny venues to promote it. His *Wildwood* LP in 1993 gained a lot more exposure with the music press beginning to include the M-word (Mod) and talk of bands like the Small Faces influencing Weller.

"It was that time I remember reading an interview with Weller, where he name-checked Blur as one of the only new bands and he rated with the *Modern Life is Rubbish* LP the same year. Some friends at that time who were more aware of that side of the music scene, knew of further new up and coming bands and also predicting "another Mod revival" with more and more references being made to the Mod culture and Sixties music in general."

On April 8th, 1994, Kurt Cobain, aged 27 and the lead singer of Nirvana, was found dead at his home in Seattle. His death was ruled a suicide from a self-inflicted shotgun wound to the head. Three days later, back in England, a band from Manchester released their debut single 'Supersonic'.

Just a month earlier, Blur had been sat at number five in the UK charts with 'Girls And Boys'. Lead singer, Damian Albarn, had already been quite vocal in interviews regarding his thoughts on what he saw as an American invasion of our charts through bands like Nirvana. "If punk was about getting rid of Hippies, then I'm getting rid of Grunge!" Albarn had told *NME*'s John Harris back in 1993.

In May, *Loaded* magazine appeared on the shelves. There was talk of New Lad culture as the magazine celebrated the tag line 'For men who should know better.'. Editor James Brown announced that "*Loaded* is music, film, relationships, humour, travel, sport, hard news and popular culture. *Loaded* is clubbing, drinking, eating, playing and eating. *Loaded* is for the man who believes he can do anything, if only he wasn't hungover" Of course, Paul Weller was featured in issue one.

There was also a push at this time for what the music papers were referring to as 'The New Wave of New Wave' which included a couple of great bands in S*M*A*S*H FROM Welwyn Garden City who released a great EP in Spring '94 with 'Real Surreal' on it, and These Animal Men from Brighton.

These Animal Men had a great live act that was quite reminiscent of The Jam. Made up of Alexander Boag (vocals, guitar), Julian 'Hooligan' Hewings (backing vocals, guitar), Patrick Murray (bass) and Steve Hussey (drums), they made some fantastic singles including 'Speeed King' and later the very '79 sounding 'This Is The Sound Of Youth'.

NIRVANA STAR'S SHOTGUN SUICIDE

MELODY·MAKER

IN MEMORIAM

APRIL 16, 1994 75p

KURT

1967 - 1994

Eight-page special on the bloody end to a troubled life

The music papers had noted that after Kurt Cobain's demise, interest in American music was dwindling as a notable number of British bands started to break through.

Simon Fane; "I never got 'really into' the Britpop and Indie scene as such, although it was one element of many things going on through Eighties and Nineties that we experienced. The Nineties period had so many other things going on with innovative new music and more rediscovering of amazing 'old' music from the previous decades, that the general Britpop movement of guitar-based bands simply didn't cut it with me. I also don't really buy into that definition of 'Britpop' – that was invented by the press. To me it was many things colliding together over a long period that created the overall atmosphere of the times – rather than a handful of bands in one part of the decade."

In August 1994, 'Live Forever' became Oasis' first top ten hit, reaching number ten on the British singles charts. That same month, the Oasis debut album *Definitely Maybe* was released and went straight to number one in the UK Albums Chart and became the fastest-selling debut album in the UK at the time.

Simon Fane: "In 1994, sat at my desk at work, the office typist came up to me for a chat. She was a middle-aged lady, born and bred in South Manchester and wanted to know about records shops – as she was fully aware of my lunchtime record shopping habits....

"Eh, Simon – you know about record shops, don't you? My old friend Peggy told me her boys have got a record out soon – where do you think I might be able to buy it?"

"I told her I'd help them out and pick up a copy. I think I probably suggested Piccadilly Records and had a bit of small talk of the band to humour her – I remember them having the same name as the underground clothes and record market just of Market Street – which I thought was a bit of an odd choice.

"The same night I was on the phone to a mate who mentioned he'd heard a record on the radio from a new band – it was called "Supersonic" by Oasis and it had sounded so Sixties. I think a few weeks later they had been booked for a free concert at a public park up in Preston. The attendance was bit more than the council had expected in the relatively small tent on the site.

"Around the same at Oasis hitting the scene in 1994 – the Brighton Beach nights started in Leeds. It was a big main room catering for the indie and classic Mod bands sounds from the Sixties – some live appearances by some new up and coming bands such as Shed Seven and Supergrass whilst the "Kaiser Chiefs to-be" hung out in the background. Another old mate from the Eighties was holding down the fort in the small room with the biggest buzz – Mark Ellis – playing all the classic Mod club range of tunes to a mixed audience of teenagers and "old Mods from the Eighties scene", still in their 20s in those days. The venue was always full to the capacity of 1,000 every week, something that the Mod scene of just a few years previously would have thought impossible to be happening! Later on in the decade Brighton Beach also started a monthly night in Sheffield at The City Halls with a similar large attendance and with two rooms –– playing a cross section of classic indie, Brit Pop and Mod club sounds.

Adrian Jones: "I felt the Mod scene in London in the early Nineties was kind of repeating itself, it felt like it had hit a bit of a brick wall, the other thing that was happening was that psych was replacing Beat, which wasn't really my thing. Swirlies were on the rise and this split clubs squarely into Soul or Psych / Garage / Beat camps…. very little jazz and R'n'B was getting played!

In September 1994, *Select* magazine offered a natty little four-page feature on 'the New Mods', entitled 'Parkalife' that featured an expose' of the extra-youthful Ace Faces at Camden Town's Blow Up club. The article was based around a night in July that year. There was a small interview with Paul Tunkin who ran Blow Up and a Q&A with Blur guitarist, Graham Coxon.

The piece soon showed how far the new pretenders had strayed from the original Modernist Blueprint, when, during an interview with Christopher Gentry, the guitarist of, then un-signed, band Menswear, afforded the readers the advice that "When you're a Mod, it's really important to have a good-looking girl on your arm." He had completely missed the whole, self-obsessive nature that had laid the foundations of Mod in the first place.

A couple of months later, and 'Touched by the hand of Mod' declared the headline on an eight-page special feature in a November issue of *Melody Maker*. This report on what was happening on the streets turned out to be pretty much nothing more than a few lists of best 'Mod' films, books, icons and classic records. There were features on two of the lesser-known new bands, Oxford's Thurman, and Mantaray hailing from Essex.

The centrespread featured the, by now, most over-hyped new band on the scene, Menswear, daring to walk up the hallowed street of Savile Row W1 in a collection of ill-fitting shabby suits paired with some of the most heinous crimes in the shoe department that the world had ever seen.

There was one redeeming feature in the whole sorry affair, however: *Melody Maker* did Britpop the greatest service by employing the services of writer, Kevin Pearce. You see, Pearce had just written a nifty little 50-page book entitled *Something Beginning With O*. He is one of the few that actually gets it, and luckily, he was on hand to educate some of these fad-following oiks a thing or two.

The bad news was that it isn't exactly what they wanted to hear, but he dropped the best paragraph of the whole Britpop period when he started the piece with these words of enlightened wisdom:

'Mod was, is now, and ever shall be, about moving and learning. That's why, in the Mod scheme of things, a young Blur Boy in his three-button hand me down and scuffed Doc Martens stands no chance next to the Mo' Waxnik in his Burberrys, button down and perfect Patrick Cox loafers, but everybody has to start somewhere.'

BOOM! That was it. The whole notion of what 'Mod' was actually about in the Nineties.

David Edwards: "The scene had changed drastically in the late Eighties, people dropped out, went raving and come the early Nineties it needed a kick up the arse. There were a few

bands still around such as The Clique and The Aardvarks plus a few revival-styled groups, the best of which were The Revs from Twickenham who, despite not looking particularly Mod, had the sound down to a tee. Club night Blow Up started in Camden and kind of reinvigorated the Sixties club scene with its mix of Sixties soul, pop, soundtracks and easy listening. It attracted a younger crowd, got a lot of press and made a lot of Mod clubs take notice leading to nights like Night Train, Brighton Beach and myself and Paul Hallam's Popcorn night. Some clubs became more geared to late Sixties rock and psychedelia while the Acid Jazz scene thrived using an original Mod template of obscure black dance music and sharp threads."

Paul Hallam: "Myself Dave Edwards and Danny De Courtelle started the 'Vault of Vibe' band nights at the 100 Club in Oxford Street, which included putting on The Chords first gig back in mid-Nineties, and still holds a record bar take I believe, for the club. We also put on the Buzzcocks/ATV/ Subway Sect with the legend Mark Perry in a 20-year homage to the original punk festival of 1976. OK, we did it in 1997 so we were a bit out. Then, the owners of the 100 Club thought the jazz nights had become a bit stale and wanted to replace them. So, myself, Dave, Danny and Kev Roche, my brother in law, started 'Club Popcorn; a kind of alternative to the Blow-Up Club.

"Brit pop gave me a second teenage life. I went to probably as many clubs and gigs then as I had at any time since mid-Eighties. OK, I was 30 now but this didn't seem to matter. I think one of best nights I was involved with at 100 Club was when the unknown band Cast played. It was an amazing night full of scousers who thought I was plain clothes copper."

Adrian Jones: "I was there pre-Britpop, in particular at the Indie club –The Gas Club – in Piccadilly, with my old friend

Erol Alkan who deejayed there. This was followed by other
midweek clubs, Going Underground and the legendary club
Trash. Around 1992 the *NME* were banding around the lazy
acronym NWoNW [New Wave of New Wave] and attempting
to create a scene. However, despite this desperate journalistic
practice some of the bands that got cobbled together under
that dubious label were actually pretty damn exciting,
S*M*A*S*H, These Animal Men and Elastica specifically. You
could feel something was in the air when Blur released 'Pop
Scene' as a single and the album *Modern Life is Rubbish* was
further confirmation. I heard about a little club called Blow
Up at the Laurel Tree pub in Camden, which had a very Mod
influence – every week people started turning up looking
more and more like Mods. I used to meet in the Good Mixer
pub beforehand and it was quite a sight, the young kids were
more sussed than the people I left behind on the official
Mod scene, though they shied away from actually calling
themselves Mods... which was understandable at the time.

"Blow Up used to attract quite a few well-known faces in the
early days. It wasn't uncommon to bump into Graham Coxon
of Blur and his then girlfriend Jo from Huggy Bear in
there. Andy Lewis the deeay at Blow Up was a mine of
information musically and a very nice chap. There was
an annoying bunch of chancers that got signed up from
the Blow Up/Good Mixer crowd, but I'm not going
to name them because their 15 minutes of fame has
definitely expired!"

Simon Fane: "It was around the early Nineties that we
had started to visit friends in Southend on a regular basis.
There was a very rich music scene – especially with the
Mod sstuff – and more relevantly at the time for me, the
Jazz and Funk club scene. SAKS night-club had a number
of different club nights in monthly rotation in those days

and the Sunrooms had newly opened featuring DJs too.

"One weekend we might be able to check out Snowboy's Jazz-Dance sessions on one night and a Funk 45 based night such as 'Porno On Acid' on another. Or another weekend could be a jazz funk session in Sunrooms with a Rare Groove and Hip Hop night at Saks from the likes of Gary Dennis.

"On one of our visits, my mates were talking of a new night at Saks called The Periphery and its links to a new club up in Camden run by the same crowd called Blow Up. A couple of them had gone up and DJ'd and told how busy it was across several floors of a small pub called the Laurel Tree. There was a range of music with a new twist on the Sixties Mod sound. A lot of of the newly discovered KPM library music was being given exposure by the organiser Paul Tunkin alongside the current trend of Easy listening/Exotic club sounds from the DJs known as The Karminsky Experience and Andy Lewis.

"I remember Martin Morgan was regularly involved, doing and playing many of the old favourites that we'd enjoyed in the Eighties Mod clubs such as The Quik's 'Berts Apple Crumble' , Mongo Santamaria's 'Cloud Nine' and Jacque Dutronc's 'L'Responsible'. There was the talk of the guys from Blur being regular attendees and some young lads went up to Martin to ask him "What clothes do Mods wear?" They had just formed a band called Menswear apparently."

By the time 1995 had arrived, if Britpop had given us anything, it felt that it had at least delivered the country a feel-good buzz. It seemed history was repeating itself, just as people had grown tired of the nihilistic promises of punk and the Mod Revival had offered a more positive mood, Britpop had slain the beast that was Grunge.

In April 1995, Chris Evans had taken over the Radio One Breakfast Show, not everybody's cup of tea for sure but Evans put on 600,000 new listeners over the previous presenter, Steve Wright. He also played lots of the British bands and later championed the Acid Jazz release, 'Whole Lotta Love' by Goldbug which got to number three in the charts.

On the verge of Paul Weller's third solo album, *Stanley Road,* he spoke in *New Musical Express* about his album and the resurgence of supposedly Mod-related groups: "Yeah it's pretty much gone full circle in those terms. For me Mod will never go out of fashion, and I think there will always be people who understand that and get what they want from it. I hate the way that it's getting used at the moment. I don't want to talk about bands individually, but they aren't Mod bands, are they? How can they be? It pisses me off a bit, it's like none of them are making Mod records, no matter how Mod they might look. If you want to hear a Mod record, stick on a good James Brown album. That's Mod."

Neil Lee: "I've been a Mod since 1995. Before then, I didn't really know what I was. I loved my clothes, football and music but I wasn't a Mod. Then at the age of 16 I got into it. Music wise, I was into Britpop and indie, bands like Blur, Pulp, Ocean Colour Scene, Menswear, Elastica etc.

"Around this time Paul Weller was constantly being name-dropped by most of the 'cool' bands of that era and as a result was going through quite a resurgence. Thru this I discovered a band called The Jam, and they had a song called 'A Town Called Malice'. I first heard/ saw it on a programme called *MTV Greatest Hits* in 1995. The song, the video, literally the entire look, the sound of the music, it has a kind of Motown sound it to it, just blew me away. As soon as I saw it, that's what I wanted to be. I was a Mod from that day forward. Although for a few years I was on my own, didn't know any other Mods or the existence of a Mod scene. This was pre or very early internet days."

The culmination of the whole Britpop saga would take place over a contrived 'battle' of the two leading bands Oasis and Blur by releasing the first singles off their new albums on the same day. The British public seemed to love it, and they were made to be reminded of the Sixties in a kind of Beatles versus the Stones clash on various television news features. It was sold to them as North versus South, working class versus middle class, the proper lads versus a bunch of ponces.

Neither song chosen by the bands to represent themselves were particularly good. Oasis chose 'Roll With It' whilst Blur went with 'Country House'.

Blur would scupper Oasis by 270,000 sales to 220,000.

Simon Fane: "By the time the whole Blur vs Oasis thing came about in the summer of 1995, the whole 'BritPop' tag felt contrived and stale. On one hand it seemed like a cynical attempt by the established music press and industry to bring back so called *proper* bands to the fore. I think the late Eighties and early Nineties had seen the massive move to club-based music had really worried the industry – with the true indie scene now consisting of bedroom producers and DJs making a record one day and then playing it on a white label to thousands the next night at a club or rave – as opposed to a marketable band to sell LPs or fill stadiums. But the industry certainly got its way… yet on the other hand it brought a whole new generation into the wider world of Modernism – the music, fashion and culture in a broad way. Many from this Nineties generation, would soon be involved with other clubs and bands in the years that followed."

In 1995 Supergrass, Blur, Oasis and the Boo Radleys all scored No.1 albums, whilst both Blur and Oasis each had a number one single. At least the British music industry did well out of it.

For some perplexing reason the whole Britpop fad had managed to wash away the stigma of being a Mod in its brief lifespan. It was as world had been fed some giant ecstasy tablet. Everybody who had hated Mods beforehand, suddenly felt the love, and wanted to know about it. They had laughed, pointed and fought all the way, but suddenly they wanted to embrace it.

New bands continued to namecheck musical influences on their sound, but no longer content with just the obvious Jam/ Who/Kinks nods they'd progressed to bands like The Prisoners and The Eyes.

Riding a scooter had been a life choice that could have got you killed a few years earlier, as Casuals attempted to knock you off in their Ford Capri's or Boneheads would appear en masse as you sat at traffic lights. Now the good old *Sun* newspaper's 'Bizarre' page would run articles such as 'Scooting Stars' featuring celebs on their two wheeled steeds and giving you the chance to win a Velocifero scooter just like Chris Evans or Noel's.

The aftermath of Britpop meant that club nights such as 'Brighton Beach' could be held in cities and towns with big student populations, such as Leeds, Sheffield, Leicester, Newcastle and Middlesbrough. These type of club nights would often involve at least one person on the DJ team who had come from the actual Mod scene and would have a working knowledge of the rarer tunes as much as the pop side of things.

In the case of Blow Up they had Ian Jackson, whilst Brighton Beach was musically richer for having the likes of Mark Ellis behind the decks.

It would be unfair to assume though that the people who got involved via this period were just bandwagon jumpers. On the contrary, that period had given the actual Mod scene fresh impetus and a whole host of emerging kids dedicated to the cause.

Neil Lee: "Uptight- that word will always be synonymous with my first experience of Mod clubs. By that I don't mean the Stevie Wonder's track, but a long-standing Mod/ Sixties style club in Liverpool. The first time I visited Uptight it was 1998 and I was a nervous 19-year-old who had a few years earlier discovered the Mod lifestyle via Britpop. It had taken me two long years of research and clothes buying and I was about to experience my first amphetamine fuelled night of bespoke clothes, dancing, and Soul. I entered the club as a naïve and nervous 19-year-old who didn't know where this journey would take him.

"I can't remember much about the night, but it gave me a hunger. For the next two years I religiously visited "Uptight" nearly every weekend. During this apprenticeship I met like-minded souls who introduced me to other clubs not only in Liverpool but further afield in Manchester, Leeds and Sheffield. The clubs were amazing, but it was in Manchester that I found my Mecca; the Hideaway Club. The Hideaway came about during the late Nineties when the Mod scene was going through a strange period. Most of the major clubs had given up on the black American roots of Mod music and adopted a later Sixties psychedelic policy. Not the Hideaway though, I remember going there for the first time in 1999 and not knowing a single track that was played that night. It was like a revolution. Although it's fair to say the chap that greeted me on the door that night almost put me off going in, he's still a friend to this day.

"Overnight my entire outlook on Mod changed. I had discovered the true essence of Mod music, R&B."

The Hideaway club had started life at The Mitre Hotel in Manchester in 1999, before moving to The Waldorf within the first year. The resident DJ's Neil Henderson, Paul Welsby & Mike Warburton would dedicate the entire evening to vintage R&B with a sprinkling of early Ska for good measure. It would become a dominant force in the discovery of unheard vintage records that got bigger as the internet age began to open up.

At the time, The Untouchables Organisation that had continued to put up clubs and rallies had folded, and original Untouchable member Rob Bailey would continue to promote under the name The New Untouchables. The organisation would often be criticised for taking the 'Mod' scene into a much later Sixties period style that would be considered more 'psychedelic meets Hippy' with its use of visuals and an accompanying soundtrack of psychedelic, Sixties European, and beat music.

Simon Fane: "During the Nineties whilst the eyes were on Britpop, I thought there was far more musical innovation in so many genres, across the world in the mid-Nineties. There were brand new labels being created on what seemed like a weekly basis every time I went to the record shop to check the latest arrivals. From the legendary Mo' Wax Records and Ninja Tunes onto the likes of dozens of UK labels such as Wall of Sound, Skint Records, Ultimate Dilemma, Nuphonic and Clean Up Records alongside Yellow Productions from France, Ubiquity from USA, Compost from Germany, Right Tempo from Italy and Bellisima from Japan.

"There was also some real innovation in British music onto the Bristol connections with down-tempo beat stuff from Massive Attack through Portishead and Tricky. Although, I hated the term Trip Hop, and then onto was termed Big Beat from the likes Chemical Brothers or Monkey Mafia and onto whole new genres being created and refined with Roni Size and LTJ Bukem Drum and Bass excursions in the second half of the decade. These culminating in amazing live shows where studio technology fused with live musicianship in something genuinely new.

"One thing I always found annoying at the time was that many of these guitar bands of mid-Nineties were effectively doing nothing new compared to the days of Fifties Beat Groups –but were given so much praise as being this next big thing or saviours of live music. Whilst other acts rooted in the Soul or

Jazz traditions, who were technically better musicians and also more experimental in productions and range of influences, were classed as revivals of old music or just labelled club music in a derogatory manner. I suppose that is where I have an issue with Brit Pop being a made-up movement – that was just a reflection of one aspect of all the various movements that were happening in those times.

"I remember the crowd at the Indie Clubs I went to in Manchester would fill the floor to 'Block Rockin' Beats' by Chemical Brothers or 'SureShot' by Beastie Boys or other club tracks – just as much as 'There's No Other Way' by Blur or 'Roll With It' by Oasis. Yet nowadays most Nineties nostalgia-based TV programmes will have you think everyone was listening exclusively to guitar bands and being coked-up in Camden, hanging around with Damien Hurst and Keith Allen whilst fawning over Toby Young's *Vanity Fair* Cool Britannia cover story which was three years too late at the time!"

The actual Mod scene of the Nineties was a strange beast. Whilst the media had courted the Mod wannabes during the heady days of the Britpop tag. The long-running underground scene would be split between those clinging to original Sixties ideals of a soundtrack of R&B, Soul, Jazz, and Ska, coupled with tailormade clobber and short smart haircuts, and an organisation like The New Untouchables that needed to keep attendances on rallies and in clubs high, to provide better-quality live acts or decent venues.

The New Untouchables could be accused of diluting the scene somewhat by broadening the appeal to the more psychedelic side of things. Whilst true, in their defence, they were quite visionary in connecting globally and helping to organise events across the world – especially the European scenes. So, whilst you were as likely to meet someone from say France at a Modstock Alldayer or a Mousetrap Allnighter in London, there was a chance that you might catch up with them next at a Euro Yeh Yeh bash in Gijon, Spain.

It was because the New Untouchables has broadened the dress code policies that they could hold bigger music festivals and attract bigger and better live acts. One major coup being that they got the complete original line up of The Action to reform.

Once again, these events were all taking place away from any kind of mass media, but as the Nineties faded and a new millennium beckoned, the internet would provide ample opportunity to spread the word. Now there would be no need for cut and paste fanzines or barely-readable photocopied newsletters.

As the age of technology moved on, flyers became colourful,

newsletters became very professional-looking before disappearing altogether as everything was read online.

A very important part of the early internet days were the Mod forums where people could connect, reunite, discuss, show off and usually argue! A special mention and a medal has to go to Dave Walker, who to this day, still runs the Modculture forum that was such an important communication point, before the social media sites came, and still is.

Thanks to the forums, it was like having an instant fanzine to advertise events and bands. The world had literally become a smaller place. The Mod scene used this to its own advantage, and cheap flights meant that floors across the world would shake to the sounds of Hammond organ and fuzz guitar. All Saints Mod Holiday's in Lavarone, Italy; Purple Weekend's in Leon, Spain; Mod weekends in Gothenburg, Sweden or La Rochelle in France. Most notable were The Italian Job events held in Rimini, Italy, which was the longest running overseas Mod rally ever.

The choices were certainly there.

Back in Blighty, you could bust your moves at clubs such as Crossfire at The Venue, The Capitol Soul Club at The Dome, The Shotgun Allnighter at Belushi's or The Mousetrap Allnighter at Orleans – all held in London, or maybe you could shing-a-ling at Friday Street in Glasgow.

Neil Lee: "From early 2000 till 2003 I attended every Hideaway. I was a convert to the music they played. Each visit never let me down – a new track would be heard or a new friend made. From 1998 to 2005 it wasn't just the Hideaway and Uptight I was visiting but clubs up and down the country. Once a month there would be Brighton Beach in Leeds, then the religious visit to Hideaway in Manchester. You also had clubs virtually every month in Birmingham, Brighton Beach in Sheffield, Heavenly Blocked in Bristol, the odd visit to a club in Nottingham and, when flush, Shotgun in London. Add to this the New Untouchables and

Underground rallies and it was a full calendar of Mod events. A heady mix of purist, psyche and indie friendly clubs to cater for all Modernist tastes. The early Noughties was a good time to be a Mod.

"In 2001 I moved to Leeds which at the time had one of the most bustling and electric Mod scenes in the country. From 2001-2009 I was obsessed, and it was one of the few points in my life where football took a backseat. Mod had taken over my life. Leeds back then was amazing, it seemed like everybody on the scene lived there. Well, all my mates did. I was still working in Liverpool from 2001-2003 and I would be there Tuesday – Friday morning. I would leave Liverpool about noon on Friday, home to Leeds, drop off my work bags, quick change and out into Leeds City Centre for 1:30. Have a mooch in Positively 13 O'Clock, haircut by Sean at Modern Hairdressing, quick look round Hip Clothing see what Duffer stuff was in and then I could guarantee somebody would be out drinking, probably in Baby Jupiter. Normally Tetley or Lee Miller would be propping up the bar.

"Most of the weekends would be spent out clubbing or drinking. Even if a Mod club or rally wasn't on then somebody would be having a party – or we would be out in Leeds. At the time Jonathon Marsden had moved in with Tetley just around the corner from Steve Brazil. I was living with Nick Brady about half a mile away. We lived virtually in each other pockets."

Back in London, you could pick up clobber from Mendoza in Brick Lane, What The Butler Wore, in Waterloo or maybe if you wanted bespoke you'd go to George Dyer in the Walworth Road or maybe George in Harringay.

In truth though, the internet meant that clothing could be purchased from all over the world – you just had to know where to look.

Neil Lee: "The number one place to shop was Manchester's seminal male boutique 'Oi Polloi'. It opened its doors in 2002 and quickly established itself with people in the know that wanted to look sharp. It wasn't a Mod shop covered in target wallpaper – thank god! And ok, they may of stocked the odd strange item, but for every Kway Mac there was rare Clarks Desert Boots in cola – hard to find back then, or Saint James striped sweaters. When you visited the original shop the first thing you noticed was its relaxed feel with friendly staff that were knowledgeable about the stock they sold. It always made me imagine this was what a shop on Carnaby Street in the early Sixties would have been like.

"The ever-changing stock always included Mod staples like Fred Perry, Clarks, Beams Plus, Ralph Lauren, Gitman Vintage, Burlington, Pantherella, Levis Vintage, Lee 101, John Smedley, Sebago, Saint James, Baracuta and Bass. Plus, there were always bargains to be had in their sales. The real Modernists shopped at places like Oi Polloi. I still shop there now, my tastes in clothing may have evolved over the years but Oi Polloi always seems to stay bang on the money for the style I want."

the Modfather Clothing Company

the CHRISTMAS PARTY → 2016

FRIDAY DECEMBER 23RD AT DINGWALLS CAMDEN 7PM-2A

the faces experience

SMALL FAKERS

PLUS VERY SPECIAL GUESTS AND THE ORIGINAL SMALL FACES BACK LINE

VINYL SETS FROM
PAUL SMILER ANDERSON
AGENT BADLAM
LES PETITS FEET
PLUS
THE MEYER DANCERS

£15 EARLY BIRD TICKETS AND £20 THEREAFTER

PRICE INCLUDES A DONATION TO PROSTATE CANCER UK

TICKETS FROM MODFATHER ON 020 7267 2672 & MODFATHERCLOTHING.C

CHAPTER SEVENTEEN

'INTO THE MILLENIUM AND THE YOUNG FACES'

"As far as the style and clothing go, it's becoming far more difficult to obtain anything decent with the demise of markets and decent charity shop gear. The way to do it nowadays is to become an OCE – Obsessive Compulsive eBayer, as the clothes I want aren't accessible in shops anymore."

SCARLETT BAYLISS

CHAPTER

In June 2013 the *NME* ran a feature on 'Mod in 2013' with articles on The Who touring their *Quadrophenia* album live again and shining a spotlight on new music artists such as Miles Kane and Kasabian. Sadly, Tom Meighan, lead vocalist of Kasabian, ruins any sort of rebellious, rock 'n' roll credibility when he is asked 'How should you be a Mod in the modern age?' with an answer of "Well I believe I'm a Mod! I wanted a scooter when I was 18, but my mum my mum wouldn't let me have one in case I killed myself, which is fair enough".

Hope I die before I…er…don't bother Tom!

Thankfully the Millennium brought some hope for the Mod world in the form of sussed youngsters who were prepared to sacrifice the norm and take an alternate route through life. Without the help of it being fashionable as it was by the mid-Sixties, late Seventies or mid Nineties. Young people getting the look spot on. Amongst the new breed are Zack Stoneham, Ryan Brown, Scarlett Bayliss, Lucas Gomersall, Charles Whitehouse, Scott Fraser Simpson, Katie Town and Leah McIntosh who all seem to be making their own indent on the scene.

Scarlett Bayliss is nineteen and from Canterbury, Kent: "I grew up in a village not far from Canterbury all my life and have only recently moved to a somewhat more cultured city. Such influences into the clothes, the music and the people first came about when I was twelve years old however my Dad dropped subtle hints throughout my life. With him growing up with a bunch of Scooter boys and my mum knocking about with likeminded 'Sixties throwbacks', I guess it was inevitable that I was going to stumble into it somehow. From that age onwards, I took it upon myself to read every book I could get hold of. Living so remote that even the buses didn't bother turning up half the time meant I was left to my own devices for the best part of three years. I'd have constant frustration over images of youths in the Sixties and Eighties in their masses, all

having a laugh. And there I was at a dismal all-girls school with an androgynous haircut and an iPod playlist that was completely foreign to those I had classes with. What a way to become an outcast. Somehow though, the concept of 'Mod' and the style just blew me away despite being an outsider in the eyes of 'the boring'."

Charles Whitehouse is 23 and also lives in Canterbury, Kent. "When it comes to buying clothes I often find myself not actually knowing what I want exactly. I will either see something in a shop that will just grab me, or I look back at photos and try to keep an eye out for similar styles. I always want to be one ahead with pieces I've not seen anybody wear, because let's face it, people look at you like you're the muts nuts! Whilst I do not copy outfits entirely, I most definitely am influenced by photos from the early Sixties. No matter where I am I will always stick my head into a vintage/charity shop and see what's to be had, hoping there will be the lucky find. I believe in 'less is more', so try to keep away from bold patterns and colours, opting for pale coloured strides and pastel shirts. When wearing a suit, I'll often wear different trousers to my jacket, giving it more of an eye-catching appearance in my opinion. I do my best to collect Italian/American vintage knits also. It isn't all vintage though, I am a huge fan of DNA Groove shirts and some of the independent small brands producing one-off pieces are often great. It's the shoes that a huge struggle for me, with original size 8s just being so few and far between."

Scarlett Bayliss: "As far as the style and clothing go, it's becoming far more difficult to obtain anything decent with the demise of markets and decent charity shop gear. The way to do it nowadays is to become an OCE – Obsessive Compulsive eBayer, as the clothes I want aren't accessible in shops anymore. After thorough online 'digging' however I find much luck finding jackets and shoes from America. Two items I severely collect. I have learnt that there is a definite basis and staple look for someone who's into the Mod aesthetic. However, I have also developed a personal conclusion that every single person has their own interpretation of this particular style; and also, these differences should be respected and not slated. Mod to me can be defined by having the utmost appreciation for clothing, looking smart, trying to be different in a crowd full of followers and most importantly, to enjoy, laugh and make the most out of every weekend. Excuse the in-depth tangent."

Katie Town is 19 and from Maidstone in Kent: "I got drawn into Mod when I was around 14. I appreciated generic styles and music from the Sixties beforehand and found Mod after being obsessed with the period. I am completely inspired by early Mod girl fashion and gained most of it from old photographs of Mod girls. 90 per cent of my clothes are all either from vintage shops or eBay. People say Mod is expensive but it's not when you know what to look for!"

Scarlett Bayliss: "As far as styling is concerned, one of my favourite looks is simple and casual. Jeans or straight legged trousers, a tight crew neck top (stripes are always preferred- I just love them!) and a pair of plimsoles or leather lace ups paired with a lightweight jacket and a duffel bag. To me, it's a popular yet timeless and comfortable look for either male or female. It never fails to look the business."

Charles Whitehouse: "Mod for me was a form of progression. At the age of 16 I was hanging around with a group of Casuals and although I found parts of their clobber stylish and exciting, it was apparent I was the odd one out; hungry for something else. The music we were into at that time was mainly British Indie bands, The Libertines, The Courteeners, early Arctic Monkeys, that sort of thing. Alone, I found myself looking into what influenced them; where did they get their sounds from?

"I had a brief period in around 2011 of being really into the 2tone sounds, as well as bands like The Clash, The Undertones and The Jam. This finally landed me back to Sixties legends such as The Animals, The Rolling Stones, The Yardbirds and The Who."

Scarlett Bayliss: "Moving onto music. I have travelled through the genres as if I actually experienced every decade and I can confidently say I have quite an eclectic music taste. When I first got into the Sixties Mod scene there was one do in my area that I could legally go to and it was in Deal. Self-explanatory really. It was Northern Soul and had the potential to be very successful. However, after a couple years of trying as hard as possible to get out and about I grew tired of northern soul and I ventured into a Rhythm and Blues coma. I find it's got grit, edge and attitude. Lightnin' Slim, John Lee Hooker, Howlin' Wolf and BB King; they had me and that was it. My favourite music style forever. As far as new music is concerned – I have very little interest. No originality and generally just a load of mass-produced forgettable tracks. It doesn't take a lot for someone to cut a record anymore which makes making music these days lack feeling and hard work. I have always felt distant to today's youth and their music and my wavelength has always been far from theirs."

Katie Town: "My favourite genre of music is R&B, when I'm at clubs it's my favourite thing to dance to because its quick and energetic. I'm not sure what I would say my definition of Mod is, because everyone has their own interpretation and take on it. I guess my definition would be someone who a snappy dresser is, enjoys going out dancing and having a laugh with their mates. Being obsessed with clothes is a bit part of it for me, it's always about what is next and changing things up to keep your look fresh."

Charles Whitehouse: "As time has gone by I have met various people nationwide who have introduced me to new sounds. The current state of my love for music has landed me deep in a pit of rhythm and blues. Subconsciously, I find myself nodding or tapping whenever I hear the blues. You almost feel it going through you! I love my R&B also, with deep sax, and husky vocals being my favourite kind of sounds. With Blues, R&B, Jazz and a good selection of Latin music all being some of my favourite sounds, I have developed a certain soft spot for instrumental only records. With regards to new music, I can appreciate the talent of some of these artists yet feel no connection to the sounds at all. It's all a bit artificial for my liking!"

Katie Town: "My favourite clubs are definitely Fast Way Of Living (biased probably as it's run by Lucas Gomersall), Sidewinder and Modesty in Brighton (which is run by Ian Bryden). There is always a sharp crowd full of young people and really good music which is the main priority for me. Fast Way Of Living in particular is my favourite – there's nothing better than a Saturday night out in a basement club in the West End dancing to good music with an amazing crowd. Dreamsville is my favourite weekender as the people who run it are fantastic and the music is so broad. Recently I went to Flamingo Club in Turin which was such a good experience, seeing how other countries interpret Mod is so interesting and the people were fantastic!"

The highly talented Emma-Rosa Dias has produced a trilogy of documentaries on Mod subculture, including *Faces In The Crowd*, *For The Love of Mod: London* and *For The Love Of Mod: Tokyo*. The series has been viewed and downloaded in over 100 countries and has gained international acclaim with reviews praising the authentic portrayals of the Mod scene.

FOR THE LOVE OF
MOD
L O N D O N

In 2016 she made a film short that can be viewed online that captures the new young Mod scene perfectly. *Devil* covers a look into a timeless British scene as real Mods from the Sixties, Eighties and the 21st century come together for a night out. It features Mickey Modern (an original Mod) and a lot of the younger breed of Mods including Ryan Brown, Lucas Gomersall, Zack Stoneham, Katie Town and Scarlett Bayliss.

The music is provided by Big Boss Man and Mother Earth It's written by Mark Baxter and narrated by Paul Weller and offers a glimpse of what to aspire to if you are interested in being involved.

Paul Weller and Steve Cradock, 2017

CHAPTER EIGHTEEN

WHERE ARE WE NOW

"I see very little real Modernism on the Mod scene of today, it's like a glass case in a museum, which given its original concept of taking influence from modern black music is quite depressing. My personal view on Modernism is to take influences from the past and the present."

ADRIAN JONES

M od may have started as a youth culture back in the Fifties and Sixties. It was pretty much a youth cult back in the Revival period of the Seventies and early Eighties too. Personally, these days I believe it is more of a lifestyle choice. A conscious decision to opt out of conventional ways of living.

The internet has busted everything wide open, and these days it is easy to track down rare clothing, records or scooters as you have a whole world to choose from instead of a local *Exchange & Mart* magazine, record list or jumble sale. All you need is a means of getting online, a credit card or bank account and away you go. Sadly, this also means that part of the mystery is gone.

The positive aspect though is that knowledge is endless. There is no limit to the Mod-related sites, webpages, downloads and shows available all over the net. Whether they be Facebook sites such as the excellent *Original Modernists – 1959 to 1966* that holds a never-ending stream of snippets and information on the original Mod days to various music shows on Mixcloud, Soundcloud and Spotify. YouTube is a treasure trove for music, films and long-gone television programmes.

That is why it is so hard to understand the rise in recent years of the Comedy Mod. As we have seen, throughout this books pages there has always been an element of the un-sussed, the un-hip and the generally ignorant of the expected Mod standards. They have gone by such names in the Sixties as 'Tickets', 'States' and 'Feds' (Portsmouth area) amongst others. In the Eighties they were known as 'Moddy Boys'. The one factor that all these shared though was youth. To be too young to afford good clothing or nice scooters was excusable. To not have knowledge on music or styles was understandable, there was time for them to learn.

What is strange about many of todays Comedy Mods, or Jurassic Parkas as they are sometimes called, is their age. Many are in their late forties and continue up to their seventies.

Stranger still is the fact that many have only just been attracted to the culture. Why had they not chosen the path in their youth? Was it that they were married, settled down and secretly longed to be whizzing about on a Vespa? Is it the fact that only in the last 20 years has the Mod image not been one of ridicule and a case for violent intervention by the public?

The other bone of contention aimed at them is why in a world that has so much information available than ever before do they continue to get it so wrong?

Meanwhile, in the other corner, are the Mod purists who sneer at the thought of ever being compared with these creatures, and yet often fail in the actual concept of 'Modernism' by being retro obsessive idealists who don't want to step out of their blinkered Sixties-based nirvana. They are, in a way, completely missing the whole ethos of Mod, and are not dissimilar to the Teds that the original breed of Modernists replaced back in the Fifties. Dinosaurs of a bygone age.

The saddest part of recent times has been the rise of far-right supporters who have been attracted to the Union Jack and target symbols often associated with Mod culture. The whole British red, white and blue imagery appeals to their senses, and yet they cannot perceive the irony of dancing to predominately black music such as ska, reggae or soul and riding around on Italian modes of transport. It certainly seems a smack in the face to the proud heritage of a culture based on their love of European styling and embracing black culture from the very start.

From my own point of view, Mod will always be about moving forward, adopting, adapting, creating. Taking the best and most sussed things from the past and mixing them with the best things that modern life can offer. Racism, sexism and homophobia have no place in society, let alone Mod culture.

So, what is on offer?

Well it depends on what you want really. There are literally hundreds of clubs and events. Since the internet came, everybody is a DJ. But that just means you have to sort out the good stuff from the bad stuff, depending on what you want, and how wide your musical tastes are.

In my opinion, it is best to avoid any type of *Quadrophenia*-styled event. This is not knocking the actual film-related events with film cast members and so on, but the bandwagon jumpers who think they can draw people in by using a few targets, a screen to show the film and records off of a laptop.

At the time of writing this, if you are into real vintage sounds that at least have proper crate-digging DJ's who make an effort and will give you value for money. Look out for events put on by or including these people: Greg Belson, Dave Edwards, Bill Kealy, Alan Handscombe, Mik Parry, Mark Ellis, Neil Barker, Dean Thatcher, Rachelle Piper, Andrew 'Mace' Nason, Ian Jackson, Jo Wallace, Wendy May, Andrea Mattioni, Mark Thomas, Neil Lee, Guy Joseph, Eddie Piller, Lee Miller, Chris Dale, Pid, Gav Arno, Callum Simpson, Fonsoul, Mick Farrer, Marc Lessner, Daniel Watkins, Paul Molloy, Mark Watkins, Mark Sherlock, Adrian Jae, Gilo, Ian Bryden, Mike Warburton, Daniel Jamaica, Lucas Gomersall, Andy Lewis, Dean Chalkley, Jim Watson, Ian Hurford and Vinny Baker. The list is endless, and I'm bound to have missed gems, but this will give you an idea.

Events to look out for include Sidewinder (London), Looking Back (Stoke), Dreamsville (a weekender once a year in Lowestoft), the Glasgow Mod Weekender, Pow Wow (Sheffield), Fast Way Of Living (London). Modesty (Brighton), Hip City (London), For Dancers Only (Ireland), Studio 45 (London), Hip City (London), Chez 66 (London), The Hideaway (Manchester), Crawdaddy (London).

GRITS AND GROOVE 45 RPM

SAT 18TH JULY

BRIGHTON

EDDIE PILLER ACID JAZZ

DAVE EDWARDS

(SIDEWINDER)

WITH RESIDENTS

COL & IAN

(MODESTY)

SERVING UP A SLICE OF R n B SOUL, ROCKIN BLUES & SKA...

BRIGHTON

FRIDAY 28TH AUGUST
BANK HOLIDAY SPECIAL

PAUL SMILER ANDERSON

STACIE STEWART

BIG BOB MORRIS

BASEMENT OF AL DUOMO

9.00PM - 2.00AM

7 Pavilion Buildings, Brighton, BN1 1EE
ENTRY £6 ADV. MOTD
Tickets: Loot Clothing & wegottickets.com

Most of those are vintage R&B/Soul clubs. A special mention must go to The Modcast events, ran by Eddie Piller and Sarah Bolshi. Here, the playlist is eclectic, so you can expect to hear anything from Sixties Soul, vintage R&B, Funk, Hip Hop, Rare Groove, Jazz, Brazilian, Seventies Soul, '79 Revival, Ska, Reggae and new releases. There are a range of venues from boats on the Thames to inland events. They always sell out fast, so look out for details online.

Bands at the time of writing, and covering a wide range of styles: Paul Weller The James Hunter Six, Proper, The Fallen Leaves, The Scene, King Mojo, Stone Foundation, Len Price 3, French Boutik, Nine Below Zero, The Dualers, Gene Drayton Unit, Dr Bird, James Taylor Quartet, The Spitfires, Corduroy, Eight Rounds Rapid, Magnus Carlson and The Fay Hallam Group. If it's a covers band you are after, The Small Fakers, covering The Small Faces material are about as authentic sounding as it is possible. Also look out for any band that includes Graham Day (Ex- Prisoners) usually The Gaolers or The Forefathers, any band that features Nick Corbin (ex-New Street Adventure) and events put on by Albert at The Bird In Hand, Brixton.

At the time of writing (July 2018), there are countless Facebook sites to check out Mod on.

Here are some of the better ones I'd recommend:

1. International Modernism (closed group)
2. The UK Mod Scene
3. Original Modernists 1959 -1966
4. Mod to Boot Boy
5. Modernistas

There are millions of shows to check out on SoundCloud, Mixcloud or Spotify.

There are so many different opinions of how Mod is going, I thought it only fair to hand it over to a cross-section of some of the interviewees in this book.

Adrian Jones: "I see very little real Modernism on the Mod scene of today, it's like a glass case in a museum, which given its original concept of taking influence from modern black music is quite depressing. My personal view on Modernism is to take influences from the past AND the present. The only club with the balls to adhere to this concept is Eddie Piller's Modcast events, the only place I can think of where you are likely to hear Hip Hop rubbing shoulders with Jazz, R'n'B and Soul."

Alan Handscombe: "As for the Mod Scene in 2018, well, in the last few years its exploded with many people returning to it from all the decades it's been in existence which is a great thing. I know it will still be there in one form or another for many years to come. What's not to like? Fantastic music of so many different genres, great clobber, everyone getting together and having fun. If I had my time again I wouldn't change a thing but maybe buy more Arnold Palmers and Harry Fenton's for me to wear in my Fifties and of course buy even more one pound 45s!"

Ann Griffin: "It's great that it's still going strong and that there's such an interest in it. Sometimes there seems to be a bit too much choice and it seems a bit splintered. The youngsters coming through now need to be encouraged and supported in their efforts or else they'll lose interest too."

Simon Fane: "Clothes-wise it has also been a journey of discovery. I suppose my general style now is of the Ivy League off-the-peg persuasion rather than the classic Mod tailor-made wardrobe. Over the last ten years I've probably learnt more about the history and the range of styles than I had known for the previous 20+ years since first being familiar with the concept of Ivy, to be honest.

"The internet has been part of spreading the word amongst like-minded aficionados – but I've been soaking up the information from many sources – vintage clothes dealers, specific books on the subject such as *Ivy in Hollywood* and *Ivy Handbook*, DVDs of certain films from *Jazz On A Summers Day* to *Rosemary's Baby* – all this coming on top of the opening of J-Simon's new shop and a period of regular shopping trips to New York a few years back.

"Just as Mods had done in Sixties with their magpie attitude to "having some of that" I'm always open to find out more about 'stuff' that fits into my remit and suits my stage in life. The broad notion of Ivy League clothing to me is to do with having the right clothes for different requirements and situations – there's formal ivy, outdoor ivy, casual ivy, beach ivy, etc – all linking back to the heritage of different brands and particular styles. It's a paired down approach and reflects the Modernist design ethic of no need for superfluous details.

"This leads onto my view that the concept of Modernism is far more than just a club-based music scene or a certain fashion. There was always the art and design element in all aspects of life.

"On researching the roots of the Modernism movement in art and design from the early 20th Century I've made the connections of various movements, each influencing each other whilst creating new ideas. From the ideas of Charles Rennie McIntosh and Le Corbusier influencing European Modernists in art and architecture creating Bauhaus and Art Deco movements directly influencing the product designers behind the Gaggia coffee machine or the Vespa GS – these people were already "thinking modern" before the Mod generation were even born. I'm finding books and online articles about mid-century modern graphic designers such as Alvin Lustig and Paul Rand – or making the connections between some of the works of

Matisse with Saul Bass graphics — and then seeing the link to Reid Miles and the Blue Note record covers.

"There are great example of Modernist product design today. The sleek lines and functional design of the latest Apple products have their roots in chief designer Jony Ive's appreciation of Dieter Rams — who designed modern space age-looking products for Braun in the Fiftie through to the Seventies and who was deemed as a successor to the Bauhaus movement. His motto was 'Less, but better' and came up with the 10 Good Design Principles that can equally be applied to many aspects of an overall lifestyle. Knowing what I know now, I would class the archetypal young Sixties Mod as a chapter in this whole Modernism arc. Not the be all and end all.

"They were a natural by-product of the overall aesthetics and attitude of the Modernist movement, which was both directly and indirectly shaping the first post-war generation of teenagers in the late Fifties. They were experiencing the rise in consumerism combined with the opportunities of rebuilding and a new start to life across many communities. They were open-minded in accepting influences from many cultures as a result of the changing demographics and arrival of immigrants in various UK cities – whilst embracing the new ideas of the art and design – both consciously and sub-consciously.

"John Simons summed this up brilliantly by saying it was like being a piece of blotting paper – soaking it all up without even knowing it – almost like osmosis. The true Mods would evolve through the times – in various directions."

Neil Lee: "In 2013 I started going out again as I had the money and the time to attend again. Now at 40, I don't do as much as I used to and my style has changed considerably, much more Ivy League now, but still 100 per cent Mod. I still have the Mod arrogance and outlook. I only wear a suit that's bespoke, my belt has to match my watch strap, shoes and wallet. If I have a white shirt then my silk pocket square has to match. There are certain items of clothes I would never wear now such as hipsters – but the Mod style never leaves you it just evolves. I still put 100 per cent thought into any outfit. If I'm at the football its red & white Adidas Japan with vintage bootcut Levis with a Seventies Liverpool top and Saville Rogue cashmere red & white scarf. If I'm at a wedding it's a bespoke midnight blue Dormeuil Tonik 2000 three-piece suit. Three button single breasted jacket, silk knitted tie, tailored shirt and Claps cuff links.

"When I was out and about every week on the Mod scene I was obsessed, like most Mods, with my wardrobe. It wasn't just the tailored side that I wanted to get right but also the casual. Too many Mods think a two-piece mohair in midnight blue is the be all and end all of the Modernist wardrobe. Of course, it's not! It's easy to find a good tailor and get a suit made; for me the real test of the smart Mod was perfecting that casual wardrobe! And with all that was available back

then there was no excuse for slackness in the casual stakes. You had Hip In Leeds, Wade Smith in Liverpool, Samuel Walker & J. Simmons in Covent Garden — the list was endless.

Jonathon Cooke: "These days I'm still really clothes-obsessed. Usually vintage clothes, and I'm on eBay literally every single day looking at American clothes. I'm really into the Ivy look, and I do it as best as I can because I research and read about it all the time. I love those clothes, and I'm a bit obsessed with it. In my wardrobe I've got a good section of Ivy stuff that I really cherish.

"It's the detail thing I love. It's like back in 1987 when I heard about something like big E Levi's. From then on, it had to be big E Levi's, so it became about tracking them down. There was a shop called 'The Emperor of Wyoming', right at the top of the Kings Road (by American Classics) that used to get them in — but they didn't really realise what they were. Then gradually, that whole big Levi E thing became massive. Levi's then cottoned on to it and started bringing out their vintage range. I was definitely one of the originators of that look on the Mod scene.

"So, the reason I got into Ivy is that every single jacket has to have a hook centre vent, a sack cut, natural shoulders and two buttons on the cuff. I love all that. I guess that's the thing with being an artist and a designer.

"I don't wanna be called a Mod, even though I still love Mod. But, because of its association with the whole 'Comedy Mod' thing I can't be deemed to be part of that. Some people look at me and think that I'm a Mod, but it's much more of an American mid-century Modernist Ivy thing that I'm big on now.

"These days, nearly all my friends are people who DJ or are involved in bands from the House and Techno scenes, and I'm the only one who looks like this, but then again, that's what I love. I go to a club with those guys, somewhere like DC10 in Ibiza, and I'm wearing a beret and dressing like this."

Pete Downs: "I think a Mod is a person who thinks for themselves and doesn't blindly follow the crowd. It is an inner feeling first and foremost and not necessarily about wearing certain clothes or liking a particular type of music. Like most things in life there is a constant need to evolve and progress to keep things fresh and being a Mod is no different. With around 60 years of history there is plenty to refer back to for inspiration – but there will always be change.

"Of course, the reason a lot of people adopt the Mod lifestyle is because of the traditional suits, scooters and Sixties music but it doesn't have to be the be-all and end-all of the scene."

Marc Lessner: "As long as I can remember I loved clothes too, especially shoes. As a kid I would place a new pair of shoes at the end of my bed and stare at them in awe until eventually falling asleep. I couldn't wait for my dad to teach me how to tie shoe laces and polishing my shoes for school on a Sunday night was never a heavy burden.

"It's kinda weird, but my style isn't that much different from when I was about ten or eleven years old. Very much smart, but casual and a a nod to American workwear. It's all about the Ivy League look for me. I can remember going to see the film *Animal House* in 1979 and that just reminded me of how much I still loved that American collegiate style. I still wear big E Levis, Florsheim Imperials and button-down shirts. I have never stopped wearing Buck shoes, Paraboot shoes, Converse All Star, Redwing Boots, Bass Weejun loafers. chinos and a Baracuta Harrington, Westaway knitwear, La Coste Polo shirts as well as Pendleton shirts and Burlington Argyle socks.

"I haven't followed fashion trends that much since I was 30 years old and year-in, year-out buy pretty much the same things. Occasionally, I might discover something new to me for example Velva Sheen t-shirts, Sunspel boxer shorts, Sanders Chukka Boots or Bates hats, but that's as much as I have strayed from the aesthetic over the years.

"I've also learnt that its cheaper and better to have something made like a coat, jacket or a pair of trousers, than to buy something off-the-peg with an expensive label and therefore expensive price tag. If you get something made it will fit better, be more unique and of course make you feel better. Yes, it's conservative in a way and has a Sixties vibe but pretty timeless which has meant that every so often it comes back in fashion.

"My love of movies, crime fiction, pop art, photography, architecture and design is a combination of Modernism and Post-Modernism and seems to fit in to a large degree with the kind of music and clothing I especially love and have stood by over the decades. I know it's a cliché, but Steve McQueen, Lee Marvin, James Coburn, Sidney Poiter, Bill Cosby and Paul Newman always looked pretty cool to me on a big screen or on the telly when I was a kid!

Marc Lessner and the author, 2016

"My dad always way said that it worth spending a few extra bob on a classic piece of clothing and of course it's all in the detail. He swore by clothes and shoes made in Britain and I have to some degree embraced his wisdom. He explained that fashion was for season and clothes were for life!"

Dave Edwards: "I think it's fairly healthy now, not so much of a scene but more of a collection of like-minded individuals. It's great seeing some really smart youngsters around like Zack, Lucas, Leah, Niamh, Scarlett and Charles, they've all managed to get the look bang-on and have begun to stamp their mark on the scene, putting on their own dos and making it their own — which is how it should be. I love events like Modcast where the crowd is a little bit older, not necessarily any wiser but just loving a great range of music and wearing smart threads."

Charles Whitehouse: "Today, Mod to me is about having fun and appreciating the styles and sounds that brought us all together in the scene. Too many people see competition and try to better one another and that leads to the fun being drawn away. If you heard new sounds or see a new style, introduce it to people! There are many fantastic events and clubs all over the country and I often try my best to attend them regardless of location. I think people should always support their local do's and favourite DJs! I don't have a particular favourite club but recently I have been to Looking Back which I thought was brilliant. I certainly don't think everything has to be 100 per cent perfect all of the time, as proved by my kind of scruffy 1961 Vespa Sportique. As fantastic as the clubs are, where everybody looks great, I equally love going to a scooter rally to sit in a fold up chair drinking beer in a pair of Jeans. But, saying all of that, Mod is definitely how you perceive it personally. I will always choose fun over being pretentious, but who am I to tell you someone else's idea is wrong!"

CHAPTER

Marc Lessner: "The world we live in has changed drastically over the last twenty years or so due to the internet. Therefore, the traditional music business model has had to change and adapt too. Unfortunately, that has meant that I get sent very little new music by the record companies and seldom get invited to new artist showcases. Therefore, I listen to a lot more radio shows, read a lot more album reviews and take heed of what my mentors and friends post up on Facebook and the like. However, I do believe that there is an abundance of talent out there and they have to find different ways of finding revenue streams to keep their head above water and earn a living.

"I'm still the same old eclectic me and will listen to everyone from Janelle Monae to New Street Adventure and Max Richter. I have to say that I think Nick Corbin is a very talented songwriter and it's only a matter of time before he writes a massive hit. I try my best even as an old git to keep in touch with the hip and happening even though it may be outside my comfort zone. There is clearly a Jazz revival/scene going on, be it in Peckham, Los Angeles or in the back room of a boozer in mid-Sussex. Please don't get me wrong if someone goes out and buys the new Kamasi Washington album which in turn means they buy into John Coltrane that can only be a good thing. However, I do read a lot of rubbish in the music press and listen to presenters on the BBC reading off a hymn sheet when clearly know very little about Jazz and are simply jumping on the next bandwagon. It would be nice to think that people stick with it as it is such a broad genre and there is so much wonderful music to draw from. Sadly, I can't say the same for my beloved soul music, but by the same token I have never seen so much material available – be it on a reissue 45 or a sumptuous deluxe CD box set. Even I hear things that I haven't heard before, so you can truly say that you can teach an old dog new tricks.

The Modcast events have been my club choice over the last few years. I love the music, the people and the vibe. It reminds me a bit of the great times I had when the Acid Jazz scene first kicked off. I'm sure a lot of people looking-in would think that it is purely a Mod thing, but clearly that is not the case. Yes, of course there is a Mod sensibility to it, and you are bound to hear an old 45 on UK Sue or Blue Beat or a Weller-related song but you are just as likely to bump into a Rockabilly sporting a Hawaiian shirt dancing to a Hip Hop record as you are a someone in an original Mary Quant dress dancing to a Chicago House record or even my daughters going crazy to hearing their favourite Gladys Knight record. I've heard new records played at the gigs too by artists like Nick Waterhouse, Eli Paperboy Reed and Stone Foundation so that is just important to me too. That is why I love the events and of course it gives me an opportunity due to the kindness of Eddie and Sarah to let me spin a few tunes too."

Alan Handscombe: "As for record collecting, well I used to be a mad record collector and the Eighties and Nineties were perfect as you could still pick up stuff relatively cheap. Come the Noughties that all started to change. I generally now just buy stuff I'd like to play in my DJ sets and you can still pick up great music for less than 50 quid if you bother to hunt it out. I tend to sell all the big records nowadays and work with what I've got which makes it much more fun – but if you're a good DJ you'll get 'em dancing."

Dave Edwards: "Mod to me will always be the eternal quest to be cool, be it in the eye for detail, an ear for a tune. It flows through everything you do, your appreciation of a building design, furniture, a nod to the past and a look to the future. If it doesn't look right, then it isn't."

Martin Gainsford:"The whole Mod thing has been integral to my life since the late Seventies. In terms of clothing I think I will always favour a button-down shirt, Levis, three button jackets, a Harrington, loafers or brogues and anything with that sort of Sixties flavour. Over the last ten years or so I have perhaps erred more toward what some refer to as 'Ivy Style' simply because it is better-suited to a bloke my age than boating blazers, bowling shoes or yards of swirling Paisley. Similarly, my music taste is quite varied – but the core to what I listen to and play is and will always be similar to stuff I was listening too as a teenager. I don't necessarily expect to hear The Chords or The Purple Hearts at an event played by a DJ but often still listen to them at home and have great fondness for that 'pop-punk' type of music they played back then.

"Being a bloke who has never had kids I have always been able to go to gigs and events when others may have had to ease off a little due to family commitment. Fortunately, my partner Max, although never a Mod herself, has always enjoyed live music and nights out with dancing so to this day we enjoy a variety

Dave Edwards, 1990

of events in London and around the South-East. The Modcast Boat Parties are always 'must do' events for us as well as things like Dreamsville, as they enable us to combine what many can simply consider as 'a nice day out' along with the chance to meet old pals and hear music we love. Obviously, with people involved in the 'scene' for the greater part now being middle-aged things are more relaxed than they were when I was a teenager. Rarely, if ever, do I see aggression or conflict. Conversation is easy with folk from anywhere in the United Kingdom and even as far afield as Japan, Europe or the US as most of us have had a similar journey to get to where we are today.

"Over the years there have been splits and divisions within the movement as a whole with some concentrating on scooters, others drifting toward the 'Psych' scene, some looking back even further than the early Sixties into the Fifties. However, all seem happy to fall under the same banner with events catering for them either individually or all encompassing. There are many younger faces to be seen – many of whom are some of the best dressed I have ever seen at events. This is of course something to be welcomed but how long they stay a part of things remains to be seen. I hope for all their lives.

"There is a fear that older Mods or those with an interest in it all are looked upon by the public, or even within the scene itself, as slightly comedic or part of a re-enactment group but for me if no one means any harm and they enjoy themselves good luck to them. Over the years there have been people I have immediately connected with and formed strong friendships with – some of which have lasted twenty-five years or more. However, there are others I avoid like the plague – but that doesn't make them bad folk or any less worthy of being or feeling they are part of the scene any more than myself or anyone else."

Welcome to
Dreamsville
Lowestoft

Katie Town: "I see the Mod scene today as a community. You meet so many interesting, funny people who become friends for life. I feel like it is a lot more varied now, but in a sense, I like that because it brings people from all over the place together for a dance. It is still about getting that chance to dress up, see your friends and dance your socks off, which is all you need."

Neil Lee: "My opinion of the current Mod scene is not high. Too many mid-40s to early-50s men who claim to have been Mods in the Eighties, but nobody has heard of. You get the feeling that owning one Jam record in 1981 qualifies you as a Mod these days. With the advent of the internet everybody can become an expert by clicking a few buttons and create a fake history. Everybody seems to be a DJ and music knowledge now comes from YouTube and not attending club's week in week out. In the late Nineties and early Noughties you would be excited wondering what a certain person would be wearing or what 45s might be played at a rally. Now every Monday, before a big event, you will see numerous posts and photos online of Mods saying they are getting their clothes ready or play boxes sorted for an afternoon slot. You know though they will be wearing the same old shit or playing the same 20 records they played last year. It's also too easy now to be a Mod, with facsimile Mods propping every bar and dancing badly at every Mod event."

Pete Downs: "I like the new Jazz that is being made by artists such as Kamasi Washington and Chip Wickham although I appreciate that these new artists are heavily influenced by the likes of John Coltrane, Pharaoh Sanders and other greats. Nothing wrong with that though if they continue to make great music.

"The Mod scene these days is in a great place as far I am concerned. There are so many events to attend either at home or abroad that you are spoilt for choice.

"One thing I do like is the age span at events. It is great to see people enjoying the same things whether you are seventeen or seventy. The youngsters getting into the scene will ensure that it carries on long after the originals and the latecomers like myself have hung up their loafers.

"It is also great to hear some DJ's at events being adventurous these days as well. Not just playing the Mod classics from the sixties but adding some House, Roots/Dub Reggae, Rock and Hip Hop to the mix. Of course, you will always get the dissenters to anything new, but Mod is about moving forward and not standing still."

Scarlett Bayliss: "Favourite clubs; that is something I struggle with. Obviously with me mentally still in 1963 or 1984 it's difficult when going out to come to terms with the fact that it's the 21st century and there are not groups and groups of similar ages into the same thing. My friends come from all across the country so going out isn't like it was. After coming to terms with that depressing conclusion I would have to say the best nights I have been to recently would be the return of the 'Lookin' Back' night which is now in Stoke. I can't compliment Stoke much however it's all forgotten once you're there and having not gone for the first-time round I was loving its atmosphere! Besides from that, I have gone to a few up North and down South and although they all excel with tunes and the DJ's to play them, I feel a sense that somethings missing – a smile. As silly as it sounds that pretty much concludes how I perceive the Mod scene today.

"I have met some of the best people I could ever meet and experienced things I never knew I would. From a younger person's point of view however I believe there are a select few who have been there and done it that seek to portray way too much of a pretentious attitude. And as a nineteen-year-old it's not cool as, after all, it's all about looking sharp and making memories. Well it always has been for me. Never shall I ever detract away from its ability to timelessly epitomise cool as it's just simply brilliant."

Paul Hallam: "To quote the legend that is Buddy Ascott, "I've got 5,000 friends on Facebook and if it wasn't for Mod I'd have 50". and he is right. Mod has been a HUGE part of my life. Cut me open and I'll bleed Mod. The best man and all the ushers at my wedding were Mods. My wife was a Mod. Both my brother in laws Jens and Kevin were Mods. Even the man who fixes my radiators is Ronnie the Mod plumber Diamond – who got on that bus to Cheeky Pete's with me back in 1981.

"I think the new breed that have come through in last few years are brilliant and probably smarter and more clued-up than we ever were. Look at Lucas, Zack, Katie, Scarlett. Brilliant, Brilliant, Brilliant. Head and shoulders above us back in the day with far less people to bounce ideas off.

"Since my book came out a few years ago I've had more publicity than I ever did in the previous 30-plus years. I've been invited to talk at a number of TV/radio stations. I even did several talks at photographic events with real photographers. This is a bloke who took a few photos on an Olympus Trip nearly four decades ago. I even spoke (a lot) at an event for Chivers Regal Whiskey and made my own 'Hallam' mixed blend which went into their hall of fame cabinet. The podcast of that went to No.1 in the iTunes spoken word charts. No, honest.

"I've been quoted in enough books to fill a shelf – I have the shelf to prove it, and oddly enough none of them want to talk about my life in print or my short-lived political career. I'm not a Mod at 52 – but it never leaves you. I wake up on a Sunday morning and go out for coffee. There are very few people on the streets of Cobham but I still make sure I take off my bed clothes, put on a clean T-shirt, comb my hair (maybe I made that up) and make sure I'm tidy and colour co-ordinated just in case anybody sees me. That's what being a 52-year-old Mod is all about."

Katie Town: "I see the Mod scene today as a community. You meet so many interesting, funny people who become friends for life. I feel like it is a lot more varied now, but in a sense, I like that because it brings people from all over the place together for a dance. It is still about getting that chance to dress up, see your friends and dance your socks off which is all you need."

Simon Fane: "To me now, in 2018, there is no single national Mod club scene in the way it got close to it in the Eighties. Partly that's because after around 1989 I went to a wider range of clubs and events, of which "exclusively Mod" clubs were a smaller and smaller aspect, but it was also about the continuing evolution of the people that effectively "stayed on the scene".

"It appeared that, from the late Eighties onwards, it splintered off into various pathways and clubs appeared to be more and more compartmentalised – with either separate rooms for genres or completely different nights. By the Nineties you would have hardcore Psych/Rock type nights for one crowd wearing a late sixties swinging style with big hair flares and an abundance of man-made fibres. Or you'd have an R'n'B night playing stuff from late Fifties-early Sixties with far less hair on display and with a crowd dressed in tailored mohair. Another night may have been more Sixties soul-based with a casual Mod/Skinhead feel to the crowd.

"The scene I knew in the Eighties was a picture of all these "Mod sub-tribes" and DJs playing a range of music that would cater for all of them. Just one DJ would have played a set which covered classic Sixties soul or R'n'B, some club Jazz or Latin boogaloo, a slice of British Beat and some Ska – all in a 40-minute set. That was ideal for me as I loved stuff from all the genres. Yet even as much as I like one particular genre, if it was that same genre all night, it would feel diluted and lose its impact after a period of similar sounding stuff for hours on end."

Neil Barker: "I got to Weller's Heliocentric tour of 2000 when I got the privilege to DJ for Paul at five of the gigs at Guildford Civic, The

Albert Hall and Brixton Academy.

"My involvement in the scene nowadays evolves around Modcast events and club nights like Studio 45, which are always fantastic parties, so for me the beat truly goes on, with a vibrant exciting scene and I am still discovering new music!"

Jonathon Cooke: "When I think about clothes, especially with the Ivy thing, it is your take on it. It's not a uniform. The main thing when you wear vintage clothes like that is you've just got to look natural in them. You can't look like you're some mannequin out of a museum, it's got to be like a second skin.

"It's just your take on it really. That's the trouble with the Mod scene, if you deviate from it, they think that you don't get it, maybe because you aren't wearing a certain item or whatever. I just don't think that it's as rigid and claustrophobic as they think it is. It's a personal thing and you wear it how you want to wear it. Basically, it comes down to you –you either get it or you don't."

Simon Fane: "With the advent of the internet and social media post-millennium, there appears to be a wide range of clubs and events catering for many aspects of Modernism across the world. For me events like the Pow Wow club in Sheffield set out to precisely bring back the wider range of musical genres in one night – yet still bringing in new sounds alongside a few forgotten old favourites.

"At the same time there appear to be some nights and weekends that people go to, just so they can relive the Eighties scene and want to hear the same records that were played at the rallies in 1986. Each to their own. I don't mind a bit of that once in a while – it's all great music. It's just there's so much other great music I want to explore – old and new.

"And on the really negative side is the sight of 50-year olds going down to Brighton every August dressed like really bad 13-year-old kids from the Mod revival period – they couldn't be further from the concept of modernism if they tried.

"In many ways I find the idea of a Mod club is a bit strange in this day and age. Looking back to the Eighties I can entirely see why they existed – as there was no real choice anywhere else and it was such a self-contained scene along with the added danger of conflict from external sources. It had to go through that period to come to the other side.

"In the Sixties there weren't Mod clubs – just clubs that Mods went to, but were frequented by a range of people – some of which influenced the Mods in a kind of cross-fertilisation.

"In conclusion, Modernism today for me is a combination of recognising classics whilst still being open minded by the new – whether it's music, clothes or art and product design. The important thing is knowing more about the past, in order to have an informative opinion on the present. It's continuously topping up on knowledge and having an attention to detail for things to be just right. It's being mature by recognising that quite often the more you know on a subject, the more that you need to know."

Steve Dench "For me, what Mod did was make me appreciate clothes, something that continues to this day. I didn't really ever acknowledge anyone unless they were smart. I was just rolling along then. I never went out and had a bad time. Wherever I went, I saw new clothes, heard new music, met new girls. If you had a money, you had a great time.

"Whatever era was in, I would try and keep up with it. I hung to the Mod look until the late Sixties – 1969 really. I have never grown out of it. I didn't want to let go. Never let it go."

So, there you have it. Mod is wearing a parka, but only on a scooter, wearing tailormade threads, or casual modern wear, with shoes only, apart from certain trainers, whilst listening to rare R&B only, well apart from House, Hip Hop, Jazz, Northern Soul, Ska, Detroit, Techno, Funk, Drum & Bass, Jungle, Mod Revival, Crossover Soul, and Rocksteady.

Just don't ask me what a Mod is.

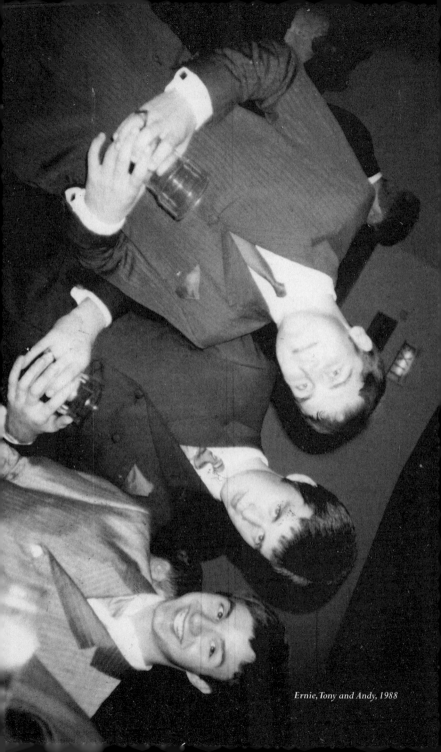

Ernie, Tony and Andy, 1988